A Lifetime of Fiction

A Lifetime of Fiction

The 500 Most Recommended Reads for Ages 2 to 102

WILLIAM PATRICK MARTIN

ROWMAN & LITTLEFIELD
Lanham • Boulder • New York • Toronto • Plymouth, UK

Published by Rowman & Littlefield
4501 Forbes Boulevard, Suite 200, Lanham, Maryland 20706
www.rowman.com

10 Thornbury Road, Plymouth PL6 7PP, United Kingdom

British Library Cataloguing in Publication Information Available

Library of Congress Cataloging-in-Publication Data

Martin, William P. (William Patrick)
  A lifetime of fiction : the 500 most recommended reads for ages 2 to 102 / William Patrick Martin.
    pages cm
  Includes bibliographical references.
  ISBN 978-1-4422-2939-6 (cloth) — ISBN 978-1-4422-2941-9 (ebook)
  1. Fiction—20th century—Bibliography. 2. Fiction—21st century—Bibliography. 3. Best books—United States. 4. Picture books for children—Bibliography. 5. Children's stories, American—Bibliography. 6. Children's stories—Bibliography. 7. Young adult fiction, American—Bibliography. 8. Young adult fiction—Bibliography. 9. American fiction—20th century—Bibliography. 10. American fiction—21st century—Bibliography. I. Title.
  Z5916.M37 2014
  [PN3503]
  015.73—dc23   2013040163

Printed in the United States of America

For Zack and Abby

Contents

Acknowledgments   ix

Introduction   xi

1   Preschoolers (Ages 2–5)   1
2   Early Readers (Ages 4–8)   27
3   Middle Readers (Ages 9–12)   51
4   Young Adults (Ages 13–17)   77
5   Adults (Ages 18+)   101
6   Special Interests   125
7   27 Writers You Should Know   161

Appendix 1: Preschool Booklist   181

Appendix 2: Early-Reader Booklist   185

Appendix 3: Middle-Reader Booklist   189

Appendix 4: Young-Adult Booklist   193

Appendix 5: Adult Booklist   197

Bibliography   201

Acknowledgments

I am grateful to the librarians, educators, journalists, and literary critics who generated the extraordinary booklists I used in this project. I want to acknowledge Fallon Stoeffler and Joyce Brander for their excellent proofreading and writing assistance, and thank Robert Hayunga and Charles Harmon from Rowman & Littlefield for their support and editorial guidance. I am especially thankful to my wife, Marianne, for helping me collect and evaluate the books and for assisting me with virtually every aspect of the manuscript preparation. Her encouragement and knowledge of children's literature added immeasurably to the project.

Introduction

A Lifetime of Fiction: The 500 Most Recommended Reads for Ages 2 to 102 is the most authoritative best-book guide in America. How can I make such a bold claim?

A Lifetime of Fiction is a composite of the most noteworthy English-language book award lists, best book publications, and recommended reading lists from leading libraries, schools, magazines, and parenting organizations. Organized into five age-group lists of 100 books each—preschoolers (ages 2–5), early readers (ages 4–8), middle readers (ages 9–12), young adults (ages 13–17), and adults (ages 18+)—the book reflects the thinking of a diverse and formidable group of literary experts. It has no real competitors it has not assimilated.

Who are these experts? *A Lifetime of Fiction* amalgamates the knowledge of 139 booklists, a veritable who's who list of literate and popular culture. Here is a sample:

- Boston Public Library's 100 Most Influential Books of the Century
- American Library Association Notable Books
- Caldecott Medals
- Coretta Scott King Awards
- Harvard Bookstore Favorite Books
- Horn Book Children's Classics
- Kirkus Reviews Best Fiction
- Los Angeles Times Book Prizes
- Man Booker Awards
- Modern Library's 100 Best Novels
- National Book Awards
- National Education Association's Top Books for Children
- New York Times Notable Books

- New York Public Library's 100 Favorite Children's Books
- Newbery Medals
- National Public Radio Top Teen Books
- PEN/Faulkner Awards
- Publishers Weekly Best Adult and Children's Fiction
- Pulitzer Prize for Fiction
- Pura Belpré Awards
- School Library Journal Best Books Lists
- Stonewall Book Awards
- Time Magazine's 100 Best English-Language Novels
- USA Today's 100 Greatest Books for Kids
- Women's Prize for Fiction

To generate the five reading lists, I entered over 23,000 books from the many sources into a database, classifying each book by age group. When I completed the inputting, there was no need for formulas or algorithms, just sorting and math. For every age cohort, I tabulated the "votes" for the most often recommended books, ranking them in ascending order. The books that made it to the lists were the ones upon which most experts agree. By bringing together different booklists, mostly from the United States, with a few from Canada and Great Britain, *A Lifetime of Fiction* stakes out first-of-its-kind common ground. The result is an appealing and sometimes surprising mix of classic and current titles.

I created *A Lifetime of Fiction* because as a parent, grandparent, and professor of education, I could not find a book guide that really satisfied me, personally or professionally. The problem was that the existing award lists and best-book guides were too idiosyncratic, reflecting the quirks and biases of their creators. Moreover, they often did not explain the basis for their book recommendations, yet expected readers to trust their judgments. I wanted to create something better, a best book guide that would be more objective and authoritative, with annotated reading lists identifying the essential fiction appropriate for different stages of life. I sought to produce a new resource for teachers, parents, and grandparents who are looking to make reliable fiction reading choices for themselves, their friends, and their children.

Some books turned out to be incredibly popular. *The Very Hungry Caterpillar* and *Madeline* easily outpaced the competition to emerge as the top preschooler and early-reader books, respectively. The top middle-reader spot went to the Harry Potter series, the most recommended young-adult book was *The Giver*, and the top adult honor went to John Updike's Rabbit book series.[1]

New titles are well represented. For example, the preschool list includes *Oh, No!* and *Nighttime Ninja*, the early-reader list includes *Sleep Like a Tiger* and *This Is Not My Hat*, the middle-reader list has *Splendors and Glooms* and *Wonder*, the young-adult list has *Code Name Verity* and *The Fault in Our Stars*, and the adult list contains *Bring Up the Bodies* and *This Is How You Lose Her*.

In addition to the rank-order lists, *A Lifetime of Fiction* also sorts the books by special interest and age group. Chapter 6 categorizes the titles by alphabet books; adventures; animals; bedtime; classics; dystopias; fairy tales, fables, and myths; families; fantasy; friendship; historical fiction; humor; literary fiction; love; multicultural; mystery; perseverance; picture books; read-aloud books; recent fiction; rhyme and verse; school life; science fiction; survival; and war. One technical note: while library classification systems categorize fairy tales, fables, myths, and legends as nonfiction, *A Lifetime of Fiction* follows the inclination of readers to treat them as fiction.

When I created the reading lists, I felt that the multiple contributors deserved special recognition. I decided to write sketches of the 27 authors and illustrators who had contributed three or more books to the reading lists, capturing something distinctive about their lives and accomplishments. Many of the most interesting facts came from their childhoods. Margaret Atwood, for example, spent much of her early life in the forest of northern Quebec with her father, who was an entomologist. Audrey Wood's earliest memories are of living among circus performers and being bounced on the knee of the world's tallest man. Roald Dahl began writing by keeping a secret diary that he hid at the top of a tree in his family's garden. Walter Dean Myers suffered from a speech impediment, Avi struggled with a writing disability, and William Steig supported his family during the Depression by selling cartoons to the *New Yorker* magazine. A snake and a baboon spider once bit J. R. R. Tolkien, and Dr. Seuss's father was the curator of a small zoo.

The annotated bibliography documents the award organizations, best-book guides, websites, magazines, and school and community reading lists that are the foundation of the lists. They are the most well-known and recognized literary resources in the English-speaking world. This chapter also recognizes the contributions of schools and libraries: small and large, rich and poor, urban and rural, secular and religious, progressive and traditional, famous and obscure, representing almost every region of the United States.

When *Time* magazine senior writer Richard Lacayo introduced his magazine's list of the 100 best English-language novels, he observed, "Lists like this one have two purposes. One is to instruct. The other of course is to enrage."[2] I know how he feels. Nothing has the potential to stir up literary controversy like a recommended reading list. Book lovers hate to see masterpieces overlooked or substandard writing overrated. Trusting in the common wisdom of a diverse body of experts, I believe I have avoided this risk, but no methodology is infallible. Some readers will be happy to see their favorite books included on the lists, and others will be displeased if a beloved title is missing. This is to be expected.

My hope is not that readers will agree with every title in *A Lifetime of Fiction*, but that they will see the book as a stimulating resource and unique barometer of our collective literary tastes.

Notes

1. Following the lead of the booklist creators, four out of the 500 books in *A Lifetime in Fiction* are actually book series. They are Rowling's Harry Potter heptalogy, Tolkien's The Lord of the Rings trilogy, Collins's The Hunger Games trilogy, and Updike's Rabbit tetralogy.

2. Lacayo, Richard, "How We Picked the List," *Time*, January 6, 2010, http://entertainment.time.com/2005/10/16/all-time-100-novels/.

CHAPTER 1

Preschoolers (Ages 2–5)

Children are made readers on the laps of their parents.

—Emilie Buchwald

1. *The Very Hungry Caterpillar.* Written and illustrated by Eric Carle. (World Publishing, 1969.) A caterpillar goes from egg to chrysalis to beautiful butterfly, devouring many different foods along the way. This bright picture book introduces the concepts of days of the week, counting to five, and the life cycle of a butterfly. Children will enjoy poking their fingers through cutout holes in the pages.

2. *City Dog, Country Frog.* Written by Mo Willems. Illustrated by Jon J. Muth. (Hyperion Books for Children, 2010.) This picture book features two improbable friends who teach each other new games against the backdrop of changing seasons. During his spring visit to the country, City Dog finds Country Frog sitting on a rock and asks him, "What are you doing?" Country Frog responds, "Waiting for a friend . . . but you'll do." The new friends first play frog games that involve time in the water. When they meet again in the summer, they do dog activities such as sniffing and fetching. In the winter, the little frog is naturally absent, and his canine companion misses him.

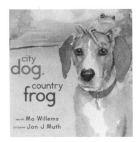

3. *Goodnight Moon*. Written by Margaret Wise Brown. Illustrated by Clement Hurd. (Harper & Row, 1947.) A small bunny gets ready for bed in his green bedroom filled with familiar objects such as a red balloon, a dollhouse, and the moon outside his window. Before he goes to sleep, he says goodnight one by one to everything he can see.

4. *Where the Wild Things Are*. Written and illustrated by Maurice Sendak. (Harper & Row, 1963.) A boy named Max is angry with his mother because he was sent to bed without supper. Dressed in a wolf suit, he dreams of sailing to an island inhabited by strange beasts. After a wild romp, he becomes homesick and returns to find his hot supper waiting for him.

5. *The Snowy Day*. Written and illustrated by Ezra Jack Keats. (Viking Press, 1962.) This book captures a little boy's wonder and curiosity about freshly fallen snow. Dressed in a red snowsuit, Peter navigates his city neighborhood and wanders about, making snow angels and footprints. Keats was a pioneer in his use of brightly colored collage and his depiction of an African American child as the chief protagonist in a picture book.

6. *The Quiet Book*. Written by Deborah Underwood. Illustrated by Renata Liwska. (Houghton Mifflin Books for Children, 2010.) This bedtime picture book explores many ways of expressing silence and being silent. A variety of animal characters, including bears, rabbits, fish, birds, owls, and iguanas, flesh out an impressive taxonomy of quiet moments. These include being the first one awake in the morning, taking a first glance at your new haircut, dropping your jelly sandwich, holding your breath at the apex of a roller coaster ride, going to bed, waiting for a concert, listening to a story, and falling asleep.

7. *Brown Bear, Brown Bear, What Do You See?* Written by Bill Martin Jr. Illustrated by Eric Carle. (Holt, Rinehart & Winston, 1967.) Martin designed this book to help preschoolers link colors and meanings to common animals. He asks different animals, such as a brown bear, red bird, yellow duck, and blue horse, what they see. Each one replies that it sees another animal. The book is known for its rhyming, repetitive text, and Eric Carle's tissue-paper collages.

8. *The Lion and the Mouse.* Adapted and illustrated by Jerry Pinkney. (Little, Brown Books for Young Readers, 2009.) In this wordless retelling of one of Aesop's classic fables, a lion spares a mouse from death when the mouse lands in his grasp after escaping an owl. The lion is rewarded for his kindheartedness when the mouse returns the favor by freeing him from a hunter's snare. The mouse and lion learn that acts of kindness are rarely wasted.

9. *Chicka Chicka Boom Boom.* Written by Bill Martin Jr. and John Archambault. Illustrated by Lois Ehlert. (Simon & Schuster, 1989.) The letters of the alphabet race to the top of a coconut tree and then fall down in a heap. The rhyming text is great for reading aloud. Bold and chunky illustrations make it the perfect introduction to upper- and lowercase letters.

10. *The Tale of Peter Rabbit.* Written by Beatrix Potter. (Frederick Warne, 1901.) Unlike his sisters Flopsy, Mopsy, and Cottontail, mischievous Peter goes against his mother's warning and sneaks into Mr. McGregor's garden. He eats Mr. McGregor's vegetables and is chased about until he finally escapes. Peter's dramatic misadventures are illustrated in watercolors.

11. *Corduroy.* Written and illustrated by Don Freeman. (Viking Press, 1968.) A small, lovable teddy bear in overalls lives in a department store. During the night he comes alive, climbs down from his shelf, and looks for his missing button. Corduroy eventually finds a home with a little girl who has purchased him with her piggy bank money. She sews a button on his overalls.

12. *Curious George.* Written and illustrated by H. A. and Margret Rey. (Houghton Mifflin, 1941.) *Curious George* is the first in a long series of books about a well-intentioned monkey whose curiosity gets him into trouble everywhere he goes. He comes to the big city after being captured in Africa by a man wearing a yellow hat.

13. *If You Give a Mouse a Cookie.* Written by Laura Joffe Numeroff. Illustrated by Felicia Bond. (HarperCollins, 1985.) A boy sees a mouse and gives him a cookie. After eating the cookie, the mouse wants a glass of milk, then a straw, then a mirror to see if he has a milk mustache, then scissors to trim his hair, then a broom to sweep it up. Then he wants to nap, listen to a story, draw a picture, and hang the picture on the refrigerator. After looking at the picture, the mouse becomes thirsty and asks for a glass of milk and a cookie to go with it!

14. *Millions of Cats.* Written and illustrated by Wanda Gág. (Coward McCann, 1928.) An elderly couple needs company, and the wife decides she would like a cat. The husband travels far from home and returns with far too many cats. The wife suggests that they keep only the prettiest feline, so they ask the cats to decide which one will stay. This suggestion produces an enormous fight that results in the cats eating each other, but one not-so-attractive kitten survives. The couple cares for the kitten, and it grows into the perfect cat.

15. *Freight Train.* Written and illustrated by Donald Crews. (Greenwillow Books, 1978.) A traditional freight train hurtles through tunnels, over trestles, past cities, and through the countryside, always picking up speed. Illustrated in bold shapes and colors, this book creates the excitement of movement as the colorful cars blur together.

16. *The Story of Ferdinand.* Written by Munro Leaf. Illustrated by Robert Lawson. (Viking Press, 1936.) Ferdinand is a Spanish bull who would rather sit under an old cork tree and smell flowers than fight. When a bee stings him one day, men mistakenly take his puffing and snorting for aggression and send him to the bullfighting ring. Despite the matador's goading, he sits in the middle of the bullring, a model of peace and contentment.

17. *Swimmy.* Written and illustrated by Leo Lionni. (Pantheon, 1963.) This book celebrates the value of teamwork and being different. Swimmy is a tiny black fish, alone in the world after a tuna swallowed his school of fish. To protect against predators, he gets the idea to cooperate with a school of red fish. With little Swimmy as the eye, together they form a camouflage pattern that makes them appear to be a single large fish.

18. *Harold and the Purple Crayon.* Written and illustrated by Crockett Johnson. (Harper & Brothers, 1955.) Harold is an imaginative 4-year-old boy. One night he creates a world simply by drawing it with his oversized purple crayon. Harold draws himself a walk in the moonlight and has a magical journey. Finally, he draws his own home and bed and goes to sleep.

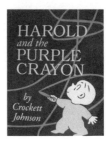

Jules Feiffer

19. *Bark, George.* Written and illustrated by Jules Feiffer. (HarperCollins, 1999.) George is a puppy who can't say "arf." His mother repeatedly asks him to bark, but instead he meows, quacks, oinks, and moos. Out of frustration, she takes him to a veterinarian, who looks inside the little dog. Lo and behold, the vet pulls out a cat, a duck, a pig, and finally a cow. When they return home, George's mother again asks him to bark. He replies, "Hello."

20. *Guess How Much I Love You.* Written by Sam McBratney. Illustrated by Anita Jeram. (Walker Books, 1994.) This is a tender bedtime tale of love between a father and son. Little Nutbrown Hare and Big Nutbrown Hare come up with one expression of love after another, trying to one-up each other. Nearly asleep, Little Nutbrown Hare finally declares, "I love you right up to the moon."

21. *The Story of Babar.* Written and illustrated by Jean de Brunhoff. (Random House, 1933.) After a hunter shoots Babar's mother, the young elephant flees his jungle home. He visits the big city, becomes educated, and returns to bring civilization to the elephants. After the current king eats a poisonous mushroom and dies, Babar is crowned king of the elephants.

22. *Blueberries for Sal.* Written and illustrated by Robert McCloskey. (Viking Press, 1948.) A little girl named Sal and a baby bear are gathering blueberries for their mothers. Each mother-daughter pair is hunting berries to prepare for winter. Both Sal and the little bear lose track of time and end up following the wrong mother. The mothers discover the mistake, the right pairs reunite, and they return home.

23. *Oh, No!* Written by Candace Fleming. Illustrated by Eric Rohmann. (Random House Children's Books, 2012.) Set in a bamboo forest, one animal after another falls into a big hole in this amusing read-aloud picture book that gives children the perfect chance to shout "Oh, no!" after each fall. A heroic elephant finally arrives on the scene and uses its trunk to save the restrained animals. He does not retrieve the hungry tiger first shown on the cover of the book. When the tiger asks for help, the other animals all cry, "Oh, no!"

24. *Doctor De Soto.* Written and illustrated by William Steig. (Farrar, Straus & Giroux, 1982.) A mouse dentist has an office in the city, where he and his wife treat large patients by getting hoisted into their mouths. Dr. De Soto works on cows and donkeys, but not on animals that will eat him. He makes an exception to this rule when a fox with a toothache arrives in his office. After pulling the tooth, he outsmarts the fox, which intended to eat him, gluing the fox's teeth together.

25. *Kitten's First Full Moon.* Written and illustrated by Kevin Henkes. (Greenwillow Books, 2004.) A kitten sees a full moon in the sky and thinks it's a bowl of milk. She licks and leaps at the moon, falling down the stairs in a comedy of mistakes. Illustrated in black and white, this beautiful picture book captures the frustration of the kitten's many attempts to get to her elusive goal.

26. *No, David!* Written and illustrated by David Shannon. (Blue Sky Press, 1998.) *No, David!* is a semiautobiographical catalog of misbehavior and of a parent's desperate and ineffective attempts to correct her son. David is anything but endearing as he flits from one sour deed to another, picking his nose, writing on the wall, and breaking things. The nonstop scolding ends with David's mother holding him in her arms and saying, "Yes, David, I love you."

27. *Where's Spot?* Written and illustrated by Eric Hill. (Putnam, 1980.) This lift-the-flap book is the ideal format for telling the story of Sally, a girl who has lost her puppy Spot. As she looks for Spot, who has not yet eaten his supper, the reader finds something funny behind each flap. There are surprises under the bed, under the stairs, and in the clock.

28. *Don't Let the Pigeon Drive the Bus.* Written and illustrated by Mo Willems. (Hyperion Press, 2003.) A little bug-eyed pigeon tries every persuasive tactic to get behind the wheel of a bus in this portrait of tenacity. The pigeon tries straightforward requests such as, "Hey, can I drive the bus?"; "How 'bout I give you five bucks"; and "I have dreams you know!" Some of his requests are silly: "I tell you what: I'll just steer." Eventually, his demands escalate into a full-blown temper tantrum, but he never succeeds in overturning common sense.

29. *Harry the Dirty Dog.* Written by Gene Zion. Illustrated by Margaret Bloy Graham. (Harper & Row, 1956.) Harry detests baths, and he gets so filthy his family no longer recognizes him. Once a white dog with black spots, he has become a black dog with white spots. Harry plays in coal chutes and in the railroad yard and avoids having a bath by hiding his scrubbing brush. He finally gives in and gets a bath, but hides the brush again.

30. *How Do Dinosaurs Say Good Night?* Written by Jane Yolen. Illustrated by Mark Teague. (Scholastic, 2000.) This funny read-aloud book is written in rhyme and shows human parents putting different dinosaurs to bed. It playfully explores the premise that dinosaurs can be a lot like people, illustrating some of the strategies kids and dinosaurs employ when it is time to say "good night."

31. *The Runaway Bunny.* Written by Margaret Wise Brown. Illustrated by Clement Hurd. (Harper, 1942.) A little bunny is comforted by the realization that his mother will always be able to find him wherever he goes. In a game of hide-and-seek, the bunny imaginatively takes on forms such as a fish, bird, flower, and rock, but his mother always manages to find him.

32. *The Snowman.* Illustrated by Raymond Briggs. (Random House, 1978.) This is a wordless adventure story of a boy who builds a snowman that comes to life. The boy invites the snowman into his house; they play together and go on a magical flight. At the end the snowman melts away.

33. *Go Away, Big Green Monster.* Written and illustrated by Ed Emberley. (Little, Brown & Company, 1992.) This book allows children to cope with fear through the page-by-page process of assembling and then disassembling a monster. Bold, bright die-cut pictures show the monster's big yellow eyes, purple hair, and scraggly green face.

34. *Happy Birthday, Moon.* Written and illustrated by Frank Asch. (Prentice-Hall, 1982.) A bear goes on a journey and climbs a mountain to get closer to the moon, intending to give the moon a birthday gift. Hearing the echo of his own voice, the bear thinks the moon is talking back to him. The bear returns home, buys the moon a hat, and places it in a tree. During the night, the wind blows the hat down to the bear's doorstep. The bear happily concludes that the moon has gotten him a hat for a present, too!

35. *The Kissing Hand.* Written by Audrey Penn. Illustrated by Nancy M. Leak. (Child and Family Press, 1993.) "I know a wonderful secret that will make your nights at school seem as warm and cozy as your days at home," says Mrs. Raccoon to her son, who just wants to stay home. She shows him the secret by taking his hand and kissing the center of his palm. If

he ever feels lonely, she says, he can press his palm to his check and feel her love. Touchingly, the raccoon boy reciprocates, giving her a kissing hand, too.

36. *Mouse Paint.* Written and illustrated by Ellen Stoll Walsh. (Harcourt Children's Books, 1989.) With simple illustrations, *Mouse Paint* creatively explores color and color mixtures. Three white mice encounter three jars of paint: red, yellow, and blue. They climb in and begin to paint and combine the paints to make new colors. The mice clean up by washing themselves in the cat's water bowl.

37. *Sheep in a Jeep.* Written by Nancy Shaw. Illustrated by Margot Apple. (Houghton Mifflin, 1986.) This book is short, at only 83 words, but it is long on humor as it describes five silly sheep setting out for a Jeep road trip. "Jeep goes splash! Jeep goes thud! Jeep goes deep in gooey mud!" are the type of goofy rhymes preschoolers will love.

38. *Not a Box.* Written and illustrated by Antoinette Portis. (HarperCollins, 2006.) A small rabbit shows that with imagination even a plain box can be almost anything. In a question-and-answer format, the rabbit reveals that he thinks of the box as a race car, a mountain, a burning building, and a robot. The covers of the book are brown paper just like an actual cardboard box.

39. *Seven Blind Mice.* Written by Ed Young. (Philomel, 1995.) The old Indian tale of the blind men and the elephant is reworked in this classic picture book. Over successive days, individual blind mice report that they have found a spear, a snake, and a pillar, which ultimately turn out to be a tusk, trunk, and foot. Using their sense of touch, the mice finally figure out that their object of study is an elephant. They learn that the whole is greater than the sum of its parts.

40. *Pocketful of Posies: A Treasury of Nursery Rhymes.*
Compiled and illustrated by Salley Mavor. (Houghton Mifflin Harcourt, 2010.) Mavor chose dozens of classic rhymes for this collection, made fresh through illustrations of intricately embroidered pieces of fabric. A good sampling of old favorites such as "Baa Baa Black Sheep" and "Mary Had a Little Lamb" is combined with some lesser-known verses. The fabric pictures, full of natural objects such as stones, shells, and acorns and human artifacts such as buttons, beads, and bells, seem to lift off the page.

41. *The Story about Ping.* Written by Marjorie Flack. Illustrated by Kurt Wiese. (Viking Press, 1933.) Ping lives with his family of ducks on a riverboat in the Yangtze River. They spend their days foraging for food and know that it is bad to come home late because the last duck back onboard gets a spanking. To avoid this fate, Ping wanders off, is captured, and is then released. Ping returns to his family and doesn't mind the penalty.

42. *Ten, Nine, Eight.* Written and illustrated by Molly Bang. (Greenwillow, 1983.) The book is filled with lush images of a father and his little girl as they make a game of counting down from 10 to one to get her ready for bed.

43. *Tikki Tikki Tembo.* Written by Arlene Mosel. Illustrated by Blair Lent. (Holt, 1968.) Set in ancient China, this is a story about why the country's children supposedly have short names. When a child with a short name falls into a well, his name is easily shouted out and he is quickly rescued. But when the same thing happens to his older brother, who by tradition has a much longer name, the rescue is delayed, putting the older boy at risk.

44. *We're Going on a Bear Hunt.* Written by Michael Rosen. Illustrated by Helen Oxenbury. (Margaret K. McElderry Books, 1989.) A family of brave hunters noisily encounters many obstacles—tall grass, a river, mud, a blizzard, and finally a cave—in search of a bear. When they find him in the cave, their bravery disappears, and they zoom past the same obstacles as the bear chases them back home.

45. *"More More More" Said the Baby.* Written and illustrated by Vera B. Williams. (Greenwillow Books, 1990.) Watercolor drawings depict three separate love stories between babies and their grown-ups. A mother, a father, and a grandmother hug, chase, and tickle their chubby toddlers until they beg for more, more, more. The vignettes are multiracial and multigenerational.

46. *Bedtime for Frances.* Written by Russell Hoban. Illustrated by Garth Williams. (Harper, 1960.) Frances, a little badger girl with a lot of energy and imagination, specializes in delaying bedtime. She uses many strategies to avoid going to bed, such as requesting milk and more kisses. Frances says she is afraid because there are spiders, tigers, and even giants in her room.

47. *Good Night, Gorilla.* Written and illustrated by Peggy Rathmann. (Putnam Juvenile, 1994.) As a tired zookeeper makes his nightly rounds, the gorilla slyly steals his keys. Matching the color of the keys to the locks on the cages, the gorilla quietly frees the animals. The gorilla, lion, giraffe, and others follow the zookeeper home and sneak into his bedroom. Preschoolers will appreciate this almost wordless tale and will love the expression on the face of the zookeeper's wife when she discovers the animals in her bedroom.

48. *Is Your Mama a Llama?* Written by Deborah Guarino. Illustrated by Steven Kellogg. (Scholastic, 1989.) Lloyd the Llama approaches all his friends by asking, "Is your mama a llama?" Each friend answers no, but they give enough details to help readers figure out through guessing-game rhymes that their mothers are other types of animals.

49. *Shark vs. Train.* Written by Chris Barton. Illustrated by Tom Lichtenheld. (Little, Brown Books for Young Readers, 2010.) Two boys conduct a series of bizarre contests with their shark and train toys, including high diving, burping, basketball, ping pong, trick-or-treating, roasting marshmallows, bowling, and hot-air ballooning. In each competition, either animal or machine has a distinct advantage that produces a clear winner. The rival toys egg each other on, showing disappointment and glee at the outcome of each face-off.

50. *King Bidgood's in the Bathtub.* Written by Audrey Wood. Illustrated by Don Wood. (Harcourt Children's Books, 1985.) This beautifully illustrated book captures the absurdity of King Bidgood's bathtub adventures. Various members of the king's court try to help him out of the tub, but instead end up in the water with him. They have a great time fishing, dancing, eating, and doing battle with toy ships, until someone pulls the plug.

51. *Mama, Do You Love Me?* Written by Barbara M. Joosse. Illustrated by Barbara Lavallee. (Chronicle Books, 1991.) In a remote Arctic setting, an Inuit mother and daughter show that love is universal and unconditional. The daughter learns that no matter how much mischief she makes, her mother will always love her. Readers will like the window into another culture.

52. *The Rainbow Fish.* Written and illustrated by Marcus Pfister. (North-South Books, 1992.) A vain fish loves its beautiful, iridescent scales and refuses to give any of them away. After meeting a wise octopus, he learns to overcome his selfishness. The fish learns that the way to be happy is to share the beauty of his scales. The distinctive feature of this book is its glimmering, holographic special effects.

53. *Rosie's Walk.* Written and illustrated by Pat Hutchins. (MacMillan, 1968.) When Rosie the hen decides to leave the chicken coop for a stroll, a hapless fox keeps messing up his opportunities to catch her. Oblivious to the fox, Rosie leads him into one failure after another.

54. *Come Along, Daisy!* Written and illustrated by Jane Simmons. (Little, Brown Books for Young Readers, 1998.) Interesting things in the swamp constantly distract Daisy the little duck, while Mama duck keeps urging her to "Come along." She doesn't listen to her mother, instead becoming preoccupied with bugs, frogs, and lily pads, and gets lost. Daisy is afraid when she thinks that she is alone, but Mama suddenly appears, teaching Daisy a lesson.

55. *Ella Sarah Gets Dressed.* Written and illustrated by Margaret Chodos-Irvine. (Harcourt Children's Books, 2003.) Ella Sarah is a flamboyant toddler with her own distinctive sense of fashion who resists her family's attempts to tone down her clothing. When her friends arrive for a dress-up tea party, they are equally bright and bold. Independent Ella Sarah feels vindicated.

56. *Dear Zoo: A Lift-the-Flap Book.* Written and illustrated by Rod Campbell. (Four Winds Press, 1983.) A little boy writes to the zoo looking for a pet. He receives animals that are too big, too fierce, and too jumpy. After several pets don't work out, he gets one that is just right: a puppy.

57. *Five Little Monkeys Jumping on the Bed*. Written and illustrated by Eileen Christelow. (Perfection Learning, 1989.) Five little monkeys say good night to their mother, but instead of settling down to sleep they create mayhem. They each jump on the bed with abandon, until they fall off one by one.

58. *Froggy Gets Dressed*. Written by Jonathan London. Illustrated by Frank Remkiewicz. (Viking Juvenile, 1992.) Froggy wants to play in the snow instead of hibernating for the winter. In this read-aloud favorite, the frog is constantly returning to his house to get properly dressed for the cold. All the bundling up wears Froggy out and makes him ready to sleep.

59. *Jamberry*. Written and illustrated by Bruce Degen. (Perfection Learning, 1982.) A boy and a bear romp through an exciting world of berries. "One berry, Two berry, Pick me a blueberry" and "Raspberry, Jazzberry, Razzmatazzberry" are some of the silly verses that the reader will encounter in this excellently illustrated adventure.

60. *Koala Lou*. Written by Mem Fox. Illustrated by Pamela Lofts. (Ian Drakeford, 1988.) Koala Lou, the oldest of her brothers and sisters, is told often, "Koala Lou, I DO love you!" But she becomes insecure when her mother becomes busy with her siblings. She enters the gum tree–climbing event in the Bush Olympics, thinking she needs to win to gain her mother's love and attention.

61. *The Little Mouse, the Red Ripe Strawberry, and the Big Hungry Bear*. Written by Audrey Wood. Illustrated by Don Wood. (Child's Play International, 1984.) Throughout the book, the narrator tells the Little Mouse that the Big Hungry Bear wants to eat strawberries. The Little Mouse will do everything he can to save his delicious strawberry from being eaten, even if it means sharing it with the reader.

62. *Knuffle Bunny: A Cautionary Tale.* Written and illustrated by Mo Willems. (Hyperion, 2004.) A baby named Trixie and her father visit the laundromat, where a crisis ensues when they leave her favorite stuffed animal, Knuffle Bunny, behind. The baby is too young to explain her dilemma, but when they get home her mother realizes that Knuffle Bunny is missing. The three run back and rescue Trixie's bunny from the wet laundry. Trixie is so happy she speaks her first words: "Knuffle Bunny!"

63. *Miss Bindergarten Gets Ready for Kindergarten.* Written by Joseph Slate. Illustrated by Ashley Wolff. (Dutton Juvenile, 1996.) As the kindergarten teacher prepares her classroom, 26 different small animals get ready for their first day of school. From Adam the alligator to Zach the zebra, every student has a name that begins with a different letter of the alphabet.

64. *The Relatives Came.* Written by Cynthia Rylant. Illustrated by Stephen Gammell. (Bradbury, 1985.) A bunch of relatives from Virginia come for an extended family visit and crowd the house. They stay for several weeks and must sleep in cramped quarters, but all ends well in this family reunion book full of warmth and chaos.

65. *Timothy Goes to School.* Written and illustrated by Rosemary Wells. (Dial, 1981.) Timothy's story is about the impact our success-oriented society has on children. On the first day of school, Timothy meets opinionated Claude, who hurts Timothy's feelings, but gets praise for everything he does and says. When Timothy meets Violet, who is also feeling down, they become friends. The book comforts children who are nervous about the start of school with the message that they do not need to be perfect.

66. *When Sophie Gets Angry—Really, Really Angry* . . . Written and illustrated by Molly Bang. (Scholastic, 1999.) Sophie is playing with her favorite stuffed animal when her sister takes it away. Sophie stomps and hollers and runs off to be by herself and returns to the family when she regains her composure. Sophie's powerful emotions are reflected in blazing color text and illustrations.

67. *Time for Bed.* Written by Mem Fox. Illustrated by Jane Dyer. (Harcourt Children's Books, 1993.) Gentle rhymes show a variety of animal parents getting their offspring ready for bed. The book begins with, "It's time for bed, little mouse, little mouse, Darkness is falling all over the house," and ends with a human mother tucking in her toddler.

68. *Where's Walrus?* Written and illustrated by Stephen Savage. (Scholastic, 2011.) A mischievous walrus breaks out of the zoo pool while the zookeeper is sleeping. In this wordless adventure, the blubbery creature evades capture over and over by hiding in plain sight. He dances onstage in a line of showgirls, he assumes the pose of a mermaid in the city fountain, he poses with mannequins in a store window, and he even joins a team of swimmers and executes a high dive. On the cover of the book, the walrus wears a hat and sits with a group of men having coffee at a diner counter.

69. *Duck on a Bike.* Written and illustrated by David Shannon. (Blue Sky Press, 2002.) Duck sees a boy's bike and decides to ride it. He pedals by all the other farm animals, who at first think he is being too silly. But when a group of boys leave their bikes unattended, the barnyard animals change their minds and hop on!

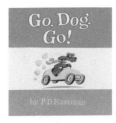

70. *Go, Dog. Go!* Written and illustrated by P. D. Eastman. (Random House, 1961.) This classic first reader has the look of a Dr. Seuss book. It depicts dogs doing many unusual things, such as driving cars and going to parties. The book also shows the growing relationship between a boy dog and girl dog and his reactions to her increasingly elaborate hats.

71. *Have You Seen My Duckling?* Written and illustrated by Nancy Tafuri. (Greenwillow Books, 1984.) A mother looks for her duckling, who she believes is lost. Though none of the pond animals know where he is, the reader can find him safe and sound on different pages. The book has great pictures, very little text, and a happy ending.

72. *Abuela.* Written by Arthur Dorros. Illustrated by Elisa Kleven. (Dutton, 1991.) Rosalba and her grandmother, her abuela, go to the park to feed the birds. The little girl wonders what it would be like to fly like a bird. Rosalba imagines soaring above New York City with her abuela in tow, flying over the ocean, and circling the Statue of Liberty. They make imaginary visits to different locations in the city—the pier, convenience store, and an office building—where Rosalba's relatives work. The book mixes Spanish and English words.

73. *I Must Have Bobo!* Written and Illustrated by Eileen Rosenthal. (Atheneum Books for Young Readers, 2011.) Earl, the family house cat, keeps on stealing little Willy's beloved sock monkey. The toddler relies on the stuffed animal for everything and is in a constant tug of war with the sneaky feline. The three end up happily snuggling on the couch until Earl runs off with Bobo again.

74. *I Stink!* Written by Kate McMullan. Illustrated by Jim McMullan. (HarperCollins, 2002.) *I Stink!* is a book about a swaggering New York City garbage truck. It features an "alphabetical soup" of the things the truck gobbles up along its route. Most preschoolers, generally fascinated by all things disgusting, are sure to like the trucks and will love the references to "dirty diapers" and "puppy poo."

75. *The Paper Bag Princess.* Written by Robert N. Munsch. Illustrated by Michael Martchenko. (Deco Media, 1980.) Princess Elizabeth is about to marry Prince Ronald when a dragon crashes the party, burns her clothes, and kidnaps Ronald. Wearing only a large paper bag, she finds the dragon and rescues the prince. Instead of being grateful, Ronald criticizes her appearance. Princess Elizabeth decides she is better off without him, and they do *not* live happily ever after.

76. *Snow.* Written and illustrated by Uri Shulevitz. (Farrar Strauss, 1998.) Snowfall transforms a dreary city into an exciting winter landscape. Grown-ups insist that the snow won't amount to anything even as it starts to fall. But a boy and his dog have faith that more flakes will come, and when the town is transformed by snow, the boy and his pet are joyful.

77. *Angelina Ballerina.* Written by Katharine Holabird. Illustrated by Helen Craig. (ABC/The All Children's Co., 1988.) Angelina is a beautiful little white mouse who loves to dance. She wants to become a ballerina. The problem is that she does not want to do any of her household chores. After her parents send her to ballet school, she becomes more responsible and willing to do work she doesn't enjoy. After many years of work, Angelina becomes a great ballerina.

78. *Chicken Soup with Rice: A Book of Months.* Written and illustrated by Maurice Sendak. (Harper, 1962.) This excellent read-aloud book has witty rhymes and images for every month of the year. Though the seasons vary, Sendak believes there is one food that is good all year round: "Each month is gay, each season nice, when eating chicken soup with rice."

79. *Pirates Don't Take Baths.* Written and illustrated by John Segal. (Philomel, 2011.) A piglet tries to argue his way out of taking a bath by citing an impressive list of characters—Eskimos, cowboys, knights, and pirates—who seem to do quite well without bathing. "Pirates . . . plunder, they pillage, they sail the seas in search of treasure, but they DON'T TAKE BATHS!" he tells Mama pig, who counters every example with reasons why he would not want to be an Eskimo, cowboy, pirate, or anything else.

80. *Color Zoo.* Written and illustrated by Lois Ehlert. (HarperCollins, 1989.) Ehlert combines simple geometric shapes and vivid colors to make a variety of animal faces. "Shapes and colors in your zoo, lots of things you can do," she writes. "Heads and ears, beaks and snouts, that's what animals are all about."

81. *Farmer Duck.* Written by Martin Waddell. Illustrated by Helen Oxenbury (Candlewick Press, 1991.) A poor hardworking duck does all the work! While he chops the wood, weeds the gardens, cleans the dishes, irons the clothes, and does almost everything on the farm, the lazy owner of the farm does nothing. He nearly collapses from all the work. The other animals decide to band together and chase the owner away.

82. *In the Rain with Baby Duck.* Written by Amy Hest. Illustrated by Jill Barton. (Candlewick Press, 1995.) The baby duck does not want to walk in the rain to Grandpa's house. Her mother says she's never heard of a duck that hates the rain. When they arrive, Grandpa sympathizes with the little duck and digs up her mother's old boots and umbrella. He gives them to the baby duck, and she gleefully goes outside to play.

83. *Goldilocks and the Three Bears.* Retold and illustrated by James Marshall. (Dial Books for Young Readers, 1988.) This is the famous fairy tale of three bears that come home to find a strange little girl sleeping in one of their beds. This version of the story has all the familiar features, but the author gives it new life by making Goldilocks decidedly more headstrong and rude.

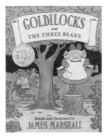

84. *Horton Hears a Who!* Written and illustrated by Dr. Seuss. (Random House, 1954.) An elephant named Horton finds a clover inhabited by microscopically small creatures known as the Whos. When the kindly elephant hears a cry of help from an inhabitant of this miniature world, he does everything he can to protect the tiny creatures.

85. *In the Night Kitchen.* Written and illustrated by Maurice Sendak. (Harper & Row, 1970.) A boy named Mickey is sleeping and wakes when he hears a noise. He loses his clothes and floats into a magic kitchen where he falls into a large mixing pot. Three bakers mix the batter with Mickey in it and are about to put it in the oven. He emerges covered in batter, helps the bakers find milk to finish their work, and finally returns to bed.

86. *Jesse Bear, What Will You Wear?* Written by Nancy White Carlstrom. Illustrated by Bruce Degen. (MacMillan, 1986.) Carlstrom and Degen collaborate in a cheery depiction of the everyday activities and clothing changes of a little bear. From sunup to sundown, the bear's day includes playing in the sandbox, chasing insects, and listening to his mother. After playing all day, Jesse is tired and ready for bed.

87. *Ten Little Caterpillars.* Written by Bill Martin Jr. Illustrated by Lois Ehlert. (Beach Lane Books, 2011.) This counting book shows the life and hazards of 10 distinctly different caterpillars. Creeping and crawling through flora and fauna, one bug ends up being held in a jar, one is carried off to school, one climbs a cabbage head, and another becomes a butterfly. Some of the caterpillars encounter hungry birds or fall into the water. The book, originally published in 1967, has a set of bold new images.

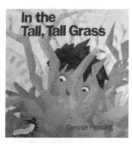

88. *In the Tall, Tall Grass.* Written and illustrated by Denise Fleming. (Henry Holt, 1991.) A toddler gets down in the grass and follows the progress of a furry caterpillar inching his way along. Each page has an animal or insect that can be found in the grass. From the caterpillar's perspective, the toddler experiences the world of fireflies, moles, bees, ants, beetles, and hummingbirds. Rhyming words describe what everyone is doing.

89. *Nighttime Ninja.* Written by Barbara DaCosta. Illustrated by Ed Young. (Little, Brown, 2012.) While his family is asleep, a little boy crawls slowly through the dark house in search of a snack. His mother interrupts this covert activity when she turns on the light and finds him with a spoon stuck in chocolate ice cream. She suggests that the make-believe ninja abort his sugary mission and return to bed.

90. *Knuffle Bunny Too: A Case of Mistaken Identity.* Written and illustrated by Mo Willems. (Hyperion Books for Children, 2007.) As in the first *Knuffle Bunny* book, Trixie again finds herself in a panic over the loss of her beloved stuffed animal. She brings her special Knuffle Bunny to school and finds that another girl has one just like it! The girls accidentally bring home the wrong animals from school and realize that a terrible mistake has been made. Their fathers fix the problem by arranging for a midnight bunny swap.

91. *Llama Llama Red Pajama.* Written and illustrated by Anna Dewdney. (Viking, 2005.) Told in short rhyming stanzas, this is a story of a little llama who has trouble getting ready for bed. When Mother leaves the bedroom, the little guy worries that she will not come back. After he makes a loud fuss, she returns and says, "Please stop all this llama drama and be patient for your mama."

92. *Off to School, Baby Duck!* Written by Amy Hest. Illustrated by Jill Barton. (Candlewick Press, 1999.) The baby duck is nervous on her first day of kindergarten, but her grandfather convinces her to enjoy it. When she meets her teacher and makes a new friend, her worries disappear. This a good book to read to children on their first day of school.

93. *The Lorax.* Written and illustrated by Dr. Seuss. (Random House, 1971.) This cautionary tale begins with a boy asking a recluse named Once-ler why everything is so run down. The strange man explains that the area once had plenty of plant life, but that he needed to chop down all the trees for raw material for his factory. The Lorax, a spokesman for the trees, warned Once-ler about the harmful effects of his actions, but the man didn't listen.

94. *Pat the Bunny*. Written and illustrated by Dorothy Kunhardt. (Golden Books/Western, 1940.) This book is perhaps the original toddler's touch-and-feel book. There are many interactive features such as patting a bunny's fur, touching Daddy's scratchy beard, smelling flowers, and looking in a mirror.

95. *My Friend Rabbit*. Written and illustrated by Eric Rohmann. (Roaring Brook Press, 2002.) "My friend Rabbit means well. But whatever he does, wherever he goes, trouble follows," says the mouse about his best friend at the beginning of the book. The rabbit gets the mouse's new toy airplane stuck in a tree and convinces some animals to stand on each other's shoulders to help retrieve it.

96. *One Fine Day*. Written and illustrated by Nonny Hogrogian. (MacMillan, 1971.) In this Armenian folktale, a sly fox steals milk from an elderly lady who then cuts off the fox's tail. In order for the fox to get it back, he must get milk for her, which turns out to be difficult. He must find others to help him, but they all expect something in return.

97. *Owl Babies*. Written and illustrated by Martin Waddell. (Toronto Scholastic, 1975.) When their mother disappears, three young owls are left in a scary forest. But Mother is only on a night flight. Upon her return, they rejoice by jumping up and down. Great illustrations capture the worry on the little owls' faces.

98. *Press Here*. Written and illustrated by Hervé Tullet. (Chronicle Books, 2011.) Children follow basic directions involving colorful dots that are the book's only illustrations. Simple instructions guide the reader to press, shake, rub, or tilt the book and to see what happens. As the pages are turned the dots proliferate, change direction, or increase in size. The last page of the book ends with a yellow dot and the question, "Want to do it all over again?"

99. *Fiesta Babies.* Written by Carmen Tafolla. Illustrated by Amy Córdova. (Random House Children's Books, 2010.) Happy adorable toddlers and babies wear sombreros and flower coronas as they joyfully participate in a neighborhood fiesta. This book celebrates many aspects of Latino families and culture. Children of different races in vibrant costumes march in a parade, sing mariachi songs, eat salsa, and frolic in the grass. The simple rhymes are written mainly in English, while Spanish words are explained in a glossary.

100. *Pie in the Sky.* Written and illustrated by Lois Ehlert. (Harcourt, 2004.) The story begins, "This tree was here when we moved in. Dad says it's a pie tree." In their backyard, a father and child follow the life cycle of a cherry tree, waiting for the cherries to ripen. The book includes a pie recipe.

CHAPTER 2

Early Readers (Ages 4–8)

Children want the same things we want: to laugh, to be challenged, to be entertained and delighted.

—Theodor Geisel, also known as Dr. Seuss

1. *Madeline.* Written and illustrated by Ludwig Bemelmans. (Simon & Schuster, 1939.) In the 1930s, Madeline is a spunky redheaded child who attends a Paris school run by Miss Clavel. The youngest and bravest child at the 12-girl school, Madeline is always disrupting Miss Clavel's orderly operation. In this first book in a popular series, Madeline wakes up and is rushed to the hospital to have her appendix removed.

2. *Sleep Like a Tiger.* Written by Mary Logue. Illustrated by Pamela Zagarenski. (Houghton Mifflin Books for Children, 2012.) This bedtime narrative deals with the perennial problem of a child not wanting to go to sleep at night. A little princess and her royal parents go through the familiar rituals of getting washed up and getting dressed in her pajamas. Telling her that she can stay awake as long as she wants, the parents go on to talk about how different animals need sleep, including their dog and cat, bats and whales, snails and bears, and a tiger. The little girl dozes off and recognizes that even the great tiger requires sleep to stay strong.

27

3. *Make Way for Ducklings.* Written and illustrated by Robert McCloskey. (Viking Press, 1941.) Mrs. Mallard and her eight ducklings waddle along busy streets to get to an island safe haven located in a pond in Boston Public Garden. Along the way, they stop traffic and are helped across the street by a kindly policeman.

4. *Caps for Sale.* Written and illustrated by Esphyr Slobodkina. (Harper, 1947.) A peddler sleeps with his merchandise, his caps, piled high on his head. A band of monkeys steal them. The naughty monkeys mimic the peddler, refusing to give the caps back. When he finally throws down his own cap in frustration, the monkeys follow suit, and he is back in business.

5. *A Chair for My Mother.* Written and illustrated by Vera B. Williams. (Greenwillow Books, 1982.) Rosa, her mother, and her grandmother lose all of their furniture in a fire. They all save coins in a jar to buy a comfortable chair for Mother, who is a waitress. By working together, this resilient single-parent family is able to buy a lush pink chair covered with roses.

6. *The Napping House.* Written by Audrey Wood. Illustrated by Don Wood. (Harcourt Brace, 1984.) The story opens with a granny snoring in a cozy bed on a sleepy afternoon. Eventually a sleepy child, dog, cat, mouse, and flea all come into the bed and pile on top of the plump old woman. The flea bites the mouse, triggering a chain of events that results in the pile falling and the bed breaking.

7. *The Polar Express.* Written and illustrated by Chris Van Allsburg. (Houghton Mifflin, 1985.) A young boy in pajamas hears a whistle and finds a train and conductor outside his home. He boards the train and takes a thrilling ride to the North Pole on Christmas Eve. He meets Santa Claus, who gives him a silver bell that rings only for those who believe in Christmas.

8. *Over and Under the Snow.* Written by Kate Messner. Illustrated by Christopher Silas Neal. (Chronicle Books, 2011.) While they are out in the woods skiing together, a father tells his daughter a story about how different animals spend the winter in a "secret kingdom under the snow." Across the landscape, many different animals such as foxes, deer, and mice hibernate, forage for food, and look for prey. The girl learns to read the signs of forest animals, returns home to a meal cooked over an open fire, and finally goes to bed.

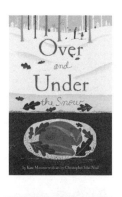

9. *Alexander and the Terrible, Horrible, No Good, Very Bad Day.* Written by Judith Viorst. Illustrated by Ray Cruz. (Atheneum, 1972.) Alexander wakes up with gum stuck in his hair, and the day only gets worse. He trips on his skateboard getting out of bed, has a bad day at school, and back at home is forced to have hated lima beans for dinner. He even gets soap in his eyes during his bath. His mother assures him that there will always be bumps in the road and that everyone has bad days.

10. *The Little Engine That Could.* Written by Watty Piper. Illustrated by George and Doris Hauman. (Platt & Munk, 1930.) A little blue train helps a broken-down train get to the other side of a high mountain. The broken train is loaded with animated toy animals, dolls, food, and candy for good boys and girls. Bigger trains declined to help the stranded train, but the little blue engine does not want to disappoint the children or toys. The little engine accomplishes the job with his well-known refrain, "I think I can, I think I can."

11. *Mike Mulligan and His Steam Shovel.* Written and illustrated by Virginia Lee Burton. (Houghton Mifflin, 1939.) The theme of this book is how old gives way to new. Mike and his trusty steam shovel Mary Anne have accomplished great things together, but they are replaced by more modern machinery. They find useful work and a safe home in a small town.

12. *Frog and Toad Are Friends.* Written and illustrated by Arnold Lobel. (Harper & Row, 1970.) The everyday rewards of true friendship are displayed in this calm and cheerful book. Five adventure stories show children the value of kindness and affection. Frog and Toad seem to complement each other in every way.

13. *Owl Moon.* Written by Jane Yolen. Illustrated by John Schoenherr. (Philomel Books, 1987.) A father and daughter go into the still forest to see a great horned owl. Animals watch them as they trudge through the snow. Under a full moon in the silent winter night, they hear the whoo of the owl and see his icy stare. In the final picture, the father carries his child out of the woods toward home.

14. *Strega Nona.* Retold and illustrated by Tomie dePaola. (Prentice Hall, 1975.) Strega Nona is a witch who hires a helper named Big Anthony to do her chores. When she is away visiting a friend, he takes her magic pasta pot into town to feed people, but things get out of control. When the pot makes so much pasta it nearly buries the little Italian town Strega, Nona must save the day. *Strega Nona* is the first book in a series.

15. *Sylvester and the Magic Pebble.* Written and illustrated by William Steig. (Windmill Books, 1969.) Sylvester the donkey collects small stones and comes across one that grants wishes. When a lion frightens him, he impulsively asks the magic pebble to turn him (Sylvester) into a rock. However, he then lacks the means to hold the pebble and turn back into a donkey.

16. *George and Martha.* Written and illustrated by James Marshall. (Houghton Mifflin, 1997.) In this collection of stories, George and Martha are lovable hippo best friends who play jokes on one another, have fun at the beach, and go to the movies. George must find a way to diplomatically tell Martha he does not like her split pea soup, and Martha comforts George when his hot air balloon does not fly.

17. *Jumanji.* Written and illustrated by Chris Van Allsburg. (Houghton Mifflin, 1981.) A mysterious board game found in the park creates danger and excitement for Peter and Judy. When Peter rolls on a lion, a real lion appears, and the beast traps them in their mother's bedroom. Many wild jungle animals invade their home, including monkeys in the kitchen and a rhino crashing through their living room. Excellent black-and-white pencil drawings add to the suspense.

18. *This Is Not My Hat.* Written and illustrated by Jon Klassen. (Candlewick, 2012.) In this funny tale, a little fish steals a blue bowler hat from a big sleeping fish that is determined to get it back. "This hat is not mine; I just stole it," says the plucky little thief, who adds, "And even if he does notice that it's gone, he probably won't know it was me who took it." When the two fish disappear into the seaweed, the big fish returns with the tiny hat back on his head, and the reader is left to decide what happened.

19. *Miss Nelson Is Missing!* Written by Harry Allard. Illustrated by James Marshall. (Houghton Mifflin, 1977.) Meek and easygoing Miss Nelson is replaced by a dreadful disciplinarian, Miss Viola Swamp. The catch is that the iron-fisted substitute teacher is actually the kindhearted Miss Nelson in disguise. The students regret their misbehavior and rejoice when Miss Nelson returns.

20. *Olivia.* Written and illustrated by Ian Falconer. (Atheneum Books for Young Readers, 2000.) Olivia, an energetic little piglet with an oversized personality, does everything with gusto and wears everyone out. Readers will be taken with Olivia's spunk and imagination and admire her mother's patience. This book is the first in a series.

21. *The Mitten.* Written and illustrated by Jan Brett. (Putnam, 1989.) A Ukrainian boy's grandmother, Baba, knits Nicki a pair of white mittens, and he loses one in the snow. Though she warned him that white mittens would be easy to lose, he didn't listen. The lost mitten is stretched to capacity when several animals—including a mole, rabbit, hedgehog, and owl—somehow occupy it.

22. *The Cat in the Hat.* Written and illustrated by Dr. Seuss. (Random House, 1957.) When Mother is away, the Cat in the Hat pays a visit to entertain two young children. Outrageous silliness ensues. The cat soon straightens things up, but the children can't decide whether to tell their mother what happened.

23. *Lilly's Purple Plastic Purse.* Written and illustrated by Kevin Henkes. (Greenwillow Books, 1996.) When Lilly brings her purple plastic purse to school, her teacher, Mr. Slinger, confiscates it for the day. Lilly gets angry and seeks revenge by placing an ugly picture of Mr. Slinger in his book bag. He responds with a kind note.

24. *Click, Clack, Moo: Cows That Type.* Written by Doreen Cronin. Illustrated by Betsy Lewin. (Simon & Schuster Books for Young Readers, 2000.) Farmer Brown hears typing sounds coming from the barn. The cows have started writing him letters. The cows, who complain the barn is cold and demand electric blankets, go on strike when they don't get what they want.

25. *The Little House.* Written and illustrated by Virginia Lee Burton. (Houghton Mifflin, 1942.) Over time a small country house is surrounded and threatened by an ever-encroaching city. Skyscrapers and subways replace apple orchards and fields of flowers. The little house feels neglected and lonely and misses nature's simple pleasures. Finally, the house is rescued from the urban sprawl and returned to pastoral bliss.

26. *Mufaro's Beautiful Daughters: An African Tale.* Written and illustrated by John Steptoe. (Lothrop, Lee & Shepard, 1987.) Mufaro has two beautiful daughters: Nyasha, who is sweet and unselfish, and Manyara, who is spoiled and ill-mannered. They are among the beauties from which the young king will choose a wife. Manyara rushes to see the king first in hopes of being selected, while Nyasha stops along the way to do good deeds.

27. *The True Story of the Three Little Pigs.* Written by Jon Scieszka. Illustrated by Lane Smith. (Viking Kestrel, 1989.) The wolf recalls his side of the story from a prison cell in this parody of the famous tale. He claims he was framed: he only visited the pigs to borrow sugar for a cake he was baking for Grandma. As for the huffing and puffing, it was a sneeze brought on by a cold.

28. *Amelia Bedelia.* Written by Peggy Parish. Illustrated by Fritz Seibel. (Harper & Row, 1963.) Amelia is a lovable but literal-minded housekeeper who works for the Rogers family. Be careful what you ask for, because she will do exactly as you say, including "dressing" chickens in real clothes! *Amelia Bedelia* is the first in a series of books.

29. *The Carrot Seed.* Written by Ruth Krauss. Illustrated by Crockett Johnson. (Harper & Brothers, 1945.) A little boy plants a carrot seed and waits and waits for it to grow. Though he doesn't receive encouragement from his family, he still perseveres. His enduring faith, as well as plenty of weeding and watering, pays off when a carrot sprouts.

30. *Are You My Mother?* Written and illustrated by P. D. Eastman. (Random House, 1960.) Mother bird is out finding food, thinking her egg is secure in its nest. Having hatched while his mother is away, the baby bird falls from the nest. When he doesn't see his mother on the scene, he goes in search of her.

Asking everyone and everything he sees, "Are you my mother?" the sweet little bird goes from hen, to dog, to boat, to plane and eventually finds her.

31. *How to Heal a Broken Wing.* Written and illustrated by Bob Graham. (Candlewick Press, 2008.) A young boy sees a pigeon fall out of the sky onto the city sidewalk. He and his mother wrap the injured bird and take it home. With his mother and father's help, he gently heals the broken wing and nurses the creature back to health. This tale of tender loving care, a supportive family, and steady recovery ends well when the bird is able to fly away.

32. *Cloudy with a Chance of Meatballs.* Written by Judi Barrett. Illustrated by Ronald Barrett. (Atheneum, 1978.) Three times a day, food and beverages fall from the sky onto the tiny town of Chewandswallow. Having burgers, mashed potatoes, and soup rain down is not such a bad deal, that is, until the portions get bigger, the weather spins out of control, and people start to fear for their lives.

33. *Little Bear.* Written by Else Holmelund Minarik. Illustrated by Maurice Sendak. (Harper & Row, 1957.) The book of four simple stories emphasizes the emotional bond between mother and child. In the first, the little bear wants to go outside in the snow, but feels he needs protection from the cold. His mother makes him a hat, coat, and pants, reminding him that he already has a fur coat. In another story, the little bear imagines he is on the moon. Upon his return, his mother has a hot lunch ready.

34. *Officer Buckle and Gloria.* Written and illustrated by Peggy Rathmann. (Putnam, 1995.) Officer Buckle speaks to groups of students about safety, but he is quite boring. When his dog Gloria joins him on stage, she dramatically acts out his safety tips behind his back while he is talking and without his knowledge. When, for example, he reads, "Never sit on a thumbtack," the dog jumps into the air, holding her bottom like a thumbtack has just poked her. At first, Officer Buckle is disheartened, but then he realizes that there is nothing wrong with needing a partner.

35. *Stone Soup.* Retold and illustrated by Marcia Brown. (Scribners, 1947.) In this old folk story, three hungry soldiers persuade local people in a French town to give them food. At first, no one in the town offers hospitality to the men, but then their stone soup sparks the villagers' interest. The townsfolk add soup ingredients to the stones simmering at the bottom of a big pot of water. Many villagers stop by, each adding another ingredient, and together they produce a hearty meal big enough to feed the whole town.

36. *Chrysanthemum.* Written and illustrated by Kevin Henkes. (Greenwillow Books, 1991.) A little mouse named Chrysanthemum loves her unusual name until she starts school and children make fun of it. When Mrs. Twinkle, a teacher, reveals that she also was named after a flower, Delphinium, the children all want flower names.

37. *Miss Rumphius.* Written and illustrated by Barbara Cooney. (Viking Press, 1982.) Many years ago Alice promised her grandfather that when she grew up she would go to faraway places, live by the sea, and do something to make the world beautiful. Alice grew up to become Miss Rumphius, an adventuresome librarian, and kept her promises. In her old age, she scatters lupine seeds, which grow into beautiful wildflowers, along the coast of Maine.

38. *Leo the Late Bloomer.* Written by Robert Kraus. Illustrated by Jose Aruego. (Windmill Books, 1971.) Mother was patient, but Father was worried that their son Leo couldn't read, write, or draw. But he was just late getting started. He blooms in his own good time. At the end, Leo is able to happily proclaim, "I made it!"

39. *Martha Speaks.* Written and illustrated by Susan Meddaugh. (Houghton Mifflin, 1992.) After eating alphabet soup, Martha, the family dog, begins to speak. The problem is that Martha talks way too much and isn't the least bit discreet. To one visitor she says, "Mom said that fruitcake you sent wasn't fit for a dog. But I thought it was delicious." Her feelings get hurt when she's asked to pipe down.

40. *Owen.* Written and illustrated by Kevin Henkes. (Greenwillow Books, 1993.) A little mouse named Owen has a beloved yellow baby blanket named Fuzzy. With kindergarten fast approaching, his parents and a meddling neighbor, Mrs. Tweezers, think it is time for him to give it up. Owen resists all attempts to separate him from Fuzzy until his mother comes up with a solution. She transforms his blanket into a bunch of handkerchiefs that Owen can take with him anywhere.

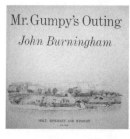

41. *Mr. Gumpy's Outing.* Written and illustrated by John Burningham. (Holt, Rinehart & Winston, 1971.) When Mr. Gumpy decides to go on a boat trip, an assortment of children and animals—a dog, sheep, pig, cat, rabbit, and others—want to come along. He agrees to transport them as long as long as they behave themselves. However, the passengers don't listen, and they all end up in the water.

42. *Stellaluna.* Written and illustrated by Janell Cannon. (Harcourt Brace Jovanovich, 1993.) When an owl attacks Stellaluna and her mother, the little fruit bat falls into a bird nest. She is adopted and raised with baby birds. The poor little bat tries to adapt to a bird's life, but it is a real challenge. She does not like the food the birds eat, has problems sleeping at night, and misses hanging upside down.

43. *Amazing Grace.* Written by Mary Hoffman. Illustrated by Caroline Binch. (Dial Books for Young Readers, 1991.) After Grace's classmates tell her that she cannot play the part of Peter Pan in a play because she is black and a girl, her nana takes her to a Shakespeare play where a black woman plays the part of Juliet. Grace is inspired and wins the lead role in the play.

44. *Horton Hatches the Egg.* Written and illustrated by Dr. Seuss. (Random House, 1940.) When an irresponsible bird named Mayzie wants to go on vacation, Horton agrees to hatch her egg. He keeps his word, though he must undergo many trials and tribulations, including being placed in a traveling circus. Horton sums it up by saying, "I meant what I said and I said what I meant, and an elephant's faithful, one hundred per cent!"

45. *Bread and Jam for Frances.* Written by Russell Hoban. Illustrated by Lillian Hoban. (Puffin, 1964.) Frances is a girl badger who wants to eat nothing but bread and jam. Her parents give in to her wishes and let her have her favorite food for all meals. Frances finally grows weary of this narrow diet and asks for spaghetti and meatballs.

46. *The Giving Tree.* Written and illustrated by Shel Silverstein. (Harper & Row, 1964.) This tender story is of a boy who grows into an old man while depending on the generosity of a tree. He eats her fruit, swings from her branches, and sits in her shade. When he grows older, he cuts the tree down to make it into a boat. As an old man he returns to sit on the tree, which is now only a stump.

47. *Big Red Lollipop.* Written by Rukhsana Khan. Illustrated by Sophie Blackall. (Penguin Group, 2010.) Rubina has been invited to a birthday party, the first ever for this immigrant girl. Her mother, Ami, insists she bring her younger sister, Sana, along with her. Rubina is embarrassed and has no luck explaining to her mother that this is not the American custom. Sana behaves badly at the party, demanding to win every game. Afterward, she even eats the big red lollipop from her older sibling's goodie bag. Later on, Sana is invited to a party, and her mother expects her to take her younger sister, Maryam, with her. Instead of seeking revenge, Rubina convinces their mother to let Sana go alone.

48. *There Was an Old Lady Who Swallowed a Fly.* Written and illustrated by Simms Taback. (Viking Press, 1997.) This funny old folktale is about an elderly woman who not only swallows a fly, but many things go into her ever-expanding stomach: a spider, bird, cat, dog, cow, and horse. A die-cut hole in the book allows the reader to see the contents of the old lady's stomach.

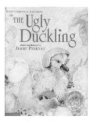

49. *The Ugly Duckling,* Written by Hans Christian Andersen. Adapted and illustrated by Jerry Pinkney. (HarperCollins, 1999.) This is the time-honored tale of a homely little duckling that is ostracized, leaves home, and triumphantly returns as a lovely swan. Pinkney's illustrations bring new energy to an already great story.

50. *Babe: The Gallant Pig.* Written by Dick King-Smith. Illustrated by Mary Rayner. (Knopf, 1985.) Babe is an orphan piglet who is adopted by farmer Hogget and his old sheepdog. The farmer, who was originally planning to eat Babe, discovers the pig has an amazing talent for sheepherding. Farmer Hogget enters him in the Grand Challenge Sheepdog Trials.

51. *Lon Po Po: A Red-Riding Hood Story from China.* Translated and illustrated by Ed Young. (Philomel Books, 1989.) This is a scary story about three sisters who outwit a wolf that wants to eat them. When the wolf sees that the children are home alone, he disguises himself as Po Po, their grandmother. In this variation on the Red Riding Hood tale, young Shang, Tao, and Paotze must defend themselves.

52. *The Day Jimmy's Boa Ate the Wash.* Written by Trinka Hakes Noble. Illustrated by Steven Kellogg. (Dial, 1980.) Jimmy's pet snake goes with him on a class trip to a farm. The boa slithers about and frightens the animals. Contrary to our expectations about boas, he does not eat any animals, but instead devours the laundry.

53. *Green Eggs and Ham.* Written and illustrated by Dr. Seuss. (Beginner Books, 1960.) A character called "Sam-I-Am" persistently pesters a grouch, asking him to taste his green eggs and ham. The grouch declines over and over again and finally gives in, tasting the meal and liking it. This classic tale contains only 50 words, among them the famous, "I do not like green eggs and ham. I do not like them, Sam-I-Am."

54. *Blackout.* Written and illustrated by John Rocco. (Hyperion Books for Children, 2011.) When the electricity goes out one summer night in the city, a family first uses flashlights and candles in their apartment, and then goes up on the roof to enjoy the bright stars. Down below the whole neighborhood comes alive and is out on the street having fun. The family plays a board game together, something they were too busy to do when the lights were on. When the power comes back on, the family decides to continue playing a game together by candlelight.

55. *Joseph Had a Little Overcoat.* Written and illustrated by Simms Taback. (Viking Press, 1999.) In this Yiddish tale, Joseph's coat becomes shabby. Instead of throwing it in the trash, he makes it into a jacket. When the jacket becomes tattered and torn, he makes it into a vest. Then he makes the vest into a scarf and then transforms the scarf into a necktie. The overcoat remnant becomes so small that the only thing that can be made of it is a button. Finally, Joseph is left with nothing.

56. *Lyle, Lyle, Crocodile.* Written and illustrated by Bernard Waber. (Houghton Mifflin, 1965.) Lyle, the friendly crocodile, lives with the Primms family in New York City. Their grouchy neighbor, Mr. Grumps, doesn't like Lyle because he scares his cat. When Mr. Grumps has Lyle placed in the zoo, Lyle escapes and returns home. There, he finds Mr. Grumps's house on fire. The crocodile saves the grouch, is hailed as a hero, and is again allowed to live with the Primms.

57. *My Father's Dragon.* Written by Ruth Stiles Gannett. Illustrated by Ruth Chrisman Gannett. (Random House, 1948.) Elmer Elevator, a 9-year-old boy, goes to a faraway place called Wild Island to rescue a baby dragon being held captive by wild animals. Elmer stows away on a ship and has to outwit several of the animals before he can reach the poor creature.

58. *Tar Beach.* Written and illustrated by Faith Ringgold. (Crown Publishers, 1991.) The year is 1939. A little girl named Cassie Louise Lightfoot dreams of flying high over the roof of her Harlem apartment building, her "tar beach," where her family and neighbors often assemble for picnics. She worries about her father not being able to find a job and how that makes her mother feel.

59. *The Boxcar Children.* Written by Gertrude Chandler Warner. Illustrated by L. Kate Deal. (Whitman, 1942.) An abandoned boxcar in the woods becomes home to four orphaned children, Henry, Jessie, Violet, and Benny. When they meet their wealthy grandfather, they decide to live with him. He relocates their boxcar home to his backyard so the children can use it as a playhouse. This book is the first in a series.

60. *The Velveteen Rabbit.* Written by Margery Williams. Illustrated by William Nicholson. (Doubleday, 1922.) The story centers on a boy who receives a velveteen rabbit for Christmas. He grows so fond of the toy that it magically comes to life. Even when it becomes shabby, the boy still loves the rabbit. When the boy gets sick and all his toys must be burned to disinfect his nursery, the rabbit sheds real tears and is made real.

61. *Clifford the Big Red Dog.* Written and illustrated by Norman Bridwell. (Scholastic, 1963.) Emily, an 8-year-old girl, chooses the runt from a litter of puppies to be her birthday gift. Because of her love, the tiny puppy grows into a dog so huge that he can hold a real, full-sized car in his mouth.

62. *Eloise.* Written by Kay Thompson. Illustrated by Hilary Knight. (Simon & Schuster, 1955.) Eloise is a precocious 6-year-old who has the run of New York City's Plaza Hotel. She keeps her British nanny busy and makes a general nuisance of herself by trying to assist the hotel staff.

63. *The Hundred Dresses.* Written by Eleanor Estes. Illustrated by Louis Slobodkin. (Harcourt Brace, 1944.) A poor Polish girl named Wanda Petronski wears the same faded blue dress to school each day. Her classmates tease and mock her claim of owning a hundred dresses kept in her modest home. They learn the truth about the dresses, and regret their actions, when Wanda does not come to school one day.

64. *Extra Yarn.* Written by Mac Barnett. Illustrated by Jon Klassen. (HarperCollins, 2012.) A young girl named Annabelle, who lives in a world of stark black and white, finds a box of colorful magical yarn. She knits a sweater first for herself, her dog, and a friend and then for everyone she knows. The box is mysterious and never runs out of yarn. Annabelle uses it for one project after another until the whole town is decorated with color. An evil archduke steals the box, but it runs out of yarn and he throws it into the sea. By magic, the box makes its way back to Annabelle and it is again full of colorful yarn.

65. *Ira Sleeps Over.* Written and illustrated by Bernard Waber. (Houghton Mifflin, 1972.) When Ira is invited to his first sleepover at his best friend Reggie's house, he worries about whether he should take his teddy bear along. His parents tell him not to worry, but his older sister teases him, convincing him to leave his stuffed animal behind. Later, Reggie tells a ghost story and the boys get scared. Reggie then pulls out his teddy bear, and Ira feels comfortable going next door to get his bear.

66. *Old Black Fly.* Written by Jim Aylesworth. Illustrated by Stephen Gammell. (Henry Holt & Company, 1992.) An annoying black fly makes an "alphabetical" trip through a house, flying in sequence from one thing to another. This rhyming book describes how the little insect eats some apple pie crust, bothers the baby, and drives everyone crazy.

67. *Rapunzel.* Written by the Brothers Grimm. Retold and illustrated by Paul O. Zelinsky. (Dutton Children's Books, 1997.) A beautiful girl with long blond hair is imprisoned by a witch in a tower. A prince calls to the girl to let down her hair and uses it to ascend the tower. When the wicked witch discovers the couple, she cuts off the girl's hair and casts the young man to the ground. Zelinsky's lush illustrations bring new life to this old German folktale.

68. *Ox-Cart Man.* Written by Donald Hall. Illustrated by Barbara Cooney. (Viking Press, 1979.) The focus of the book is the simple life and everyday buying and selling activities of a mid-19th-century colonial New England family. The story begins with a man and his family packing a cart with homemade goods. His daughter has knitted mittens, his wife has woven shawls, and his son carved a broom. The man travels to a nearby town to sell the items.

69. *The Stinky Cheese Man and Other Fairly Stupid Tales.* Written by Jon Scieszka. Illustrated by Lane Smith. (Viking Press, 1992.) In this collection, "The Stinky Cheese Man" parodies the classic gingerbread man story. Stinky runs away, but no one chases him because he smells so bad. This irreverent take on time-honored tales includes "The Really Ugly Duckling," "Jack's Bean Problem," and "The Other Frog Prince."

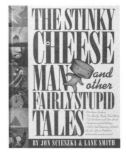

70. *Andy and the Lion.* Written and illustrated by James Daugherty. (Viking Press, 1938.) In this adaptation of Aesop's "Androcles and the Lion" fable, young Andy shows remarkable courage and kindness when he removes a thorn from a lion's paw on his way to school. When the circus comes to town, the very same lion escapes and puts everyone in danger. Fortunately, the wild beast remembers Andy, who saves the day.

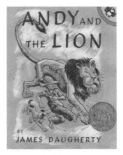

71. *Frederick.* Written and illustrated by Leo Lionni. (Pantheon, 1967.) Frederick is a dreamy little field mouse who writes poetry while the other mice gather nuts for winter. In the dark days ahead, when the food runs out, Frederick proves his worth by inspiring the dispirited mice with his poetry. Lionni's story shows how it is possible to help others in different ways.

72. *A Couple of Boys Have the Best Week Ever.* Written and illustrated by Marla Frazee. (Harcourt, 2008.) Eamon and James spend a week at a cottage at the beach. The cottage belongs to Eamon's grandparents, who try to interest the boys in nature activities. The boys are mostly interested in staying indoors and playing video games. On their last evening at the beach, they go outside and discover the joys of nature.

73. *The Doorbell Rang.* Written and illustrated by Pat Hutchins. (Greenwillow Books, 1986.) Ma has made a plate of 12 cookies for her two kids, Victoria and Sam, but children from the neighborhood keep on showing up at their door to share the treats. Victoria and Sam keep reallocating their remaining share of the cookies. Before they get to eat them, the doorbell rings again and again. When the doorbell rings a final time, it is Grandma with a new supply of cookies!

74. *The Gardener.* Written by Sarah Stewart. Illustrated by David Small. (Farrar Straus Giroux, 1997.) Set in 1935, this is a story told by Lydia Grace Finch in a series of letters to her family. She goes to live with her grumpy Uncle Jim in the city after her father loses his job. She learns to make bread and pursues her passion as a gardener. She grows a secret garden on the roof of Uncle Jim's bakery with the goal of bringing a smile to his face.

75. *The Hello, Goodbye Window.* Written by Norton Juster. Illustrated by Chris Raschka. (Hyperion Books for Children, 2005.) Some of a little girl's greatest joys at her grandparents' house are associated with saying hello and good-bye through the kitchen window. During a great visit with her Nana and Poppy, she shows how to climb up on the flower barrel, tap the window, press your face against it, and play peekaboo.

76. *Mr. Rabbit and the Lovely Present.* Written by Charlotte Zolotow. Illustrated by Maurice Sendak. (Harper & Row, 1962.) A girl and a rabbit spend a day together puzzling over what to get the girl's mother for her birthday. The girl tells Mr. Rabbit her mother likes the colors red, yellow, green, and blue. They cooperate in gathering bright pieces of fruit into a gift basket. They leave each other at nighttime with their mission accomplished.

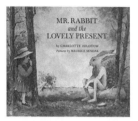

77. *How the Grinch Stole Christmas.* Written and illustrated by Dr. Seuss. (Random House, 1957.) In this classic story, the Grinch hatches a plan to ruin Christmas. This grouchy hermit tries to stop the holiday by stealing all of the presents and food from the residents of Whoville. The Whos are unfazed, and the Grinch realizes that "maybe Christmas doesn't come from a store. Maybe Christmas . . . perhaps . . . means a little bit more!"

78. *A Sick Day for Amos McGee.* Written by Philip C. Stead. Illustrated by Erin E. Stead. (Roaring Brook Press, 2010.) Amos, a zookeeper, comes to work every day to take care of his animal friends: an owl, elephant, tortoise, penguin, and rhinoceros. When a bad cold prevents him from visiting one day, his five buddies return the favor and take a bus to visit him in his little house. Amos plays chess with the elephant, races with the tortoise, and listens to the owl read him a bedtime story. The animals spend the night, snuggled up to Amos.

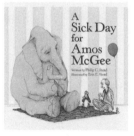

79. *John Henry.* Written by Julius Lester. Illustrated by Jerry Pinkney. (Dial Books, 1994.) Former slave John Henry, with his sledgehammer, challenges a steam drill to cut a tunnel through a mountain. He defeats the technology, but hammers so long and hard that his heart bursts. Passing away with a smile on his face, John Henry's core message is, "Dying ain't important. Everybody does that. What matters is how well you do your living." The story of this larger-than-life African American hero was based on a folk song.

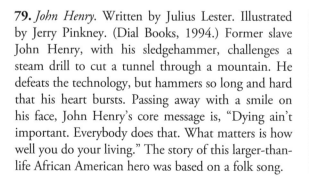

80. *Swamp Angel.* Written by Anne Isaacs. Illustrated by Paul O. Zelinsky. (Dutton Children's Books, 1994.) The Swamp Angel is a folklore heroine in the tradition of Paul Bunyan. At age 2, she builds her first log cabin. She wrestles a formidable bear, rescues a wagon train, and lassoes a tornado. These tall tales, set in Tennessee, are written in a southern dialect.

81. *Tuesday.* Written and illustrated by David Wiesner. (Clarion Books, 1997.) On a Tuesday under a full moon, a legion of frogs do a strange thing: they go airborne. Mounting lily pads, they startle birds and silently drift around as if they were on flying carpets. *Tuesday* is a surreal, whimsical, almost wordless picture book with stunning illustrations.

82. *Whistle for Willie.* Written and illustrated by Ezra Jack Keats. (Viking Press, 1964.) To a little boy named Peter, being able to whistle is a big deal. For one thing, he would love to be able to whistle for his dog. After many attempts at whistling, he finally succeeds. The moral of this simple story is that persistence pays off.

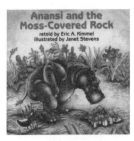

83. *Anansi and the Moss-Covered Rock.* Written by Eric A. Kimmel. Illustrated by Janet Stevens. (Holiday House, 1988.) Anansi the spider is a trickster. He finds a magic moss-covered rock in the jungle that has the power to put creatures to sleep while he robs them of their food. However, his trickery has not gone unnoticed, and a little deer outwits the spider, returning the food to its owners.

84. *Will I Have a Friend?* Written by Miriam Cohen. Illustrated by Lillian Hoban. (MacMillan, 1967.) Paul is about to start kindergarten, and, worried, he asks his dad, "Will I have a friend?" His father assures him he will. On the very first day, Paul and another boy bond over a toy that Paul brought to school. This is a perfect book for calming anxieties over starting school.

85. *Pecan Pie Baby.* Written by Jacqueline Woodson. Illustrated by Sophie Blackall. (Putnam Juvenile, 2010.) Gia's mom is pregnant and Gia is having trouble adjusting to the idea of having a new baby sister or brother in the family. Everyone talks endlessly of the impending birth, and Gia worries about losing the special bond she has with her mother. Her unhappiness is apparent when she announces at the Thanksgiving dinner: "I'm so sick of that ding-dang baby!" She is sent to her room for this outburst. Gia and her mother talk things over, and they both come to terms with the big change coming in their lives.

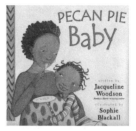

86. *Anansi the Spider: A Tale from the Ashanti.* Written and illustrated by Gerald McDermott. (Holt Rinehart & Winston, 1972.) In this retelling of a traditional West African story, Anansi the spider is saved from trouble by his six unique arachnid sons. But which son to reward? The conflicted father can't decide which son is most deserving of the prize, a glowing orb. Anansi gives it to Nyame, the God of All Things, for safekeeping until a decision is reached. In the interest of the family, the god elects to keep the orb in the sky with him. This folktale accounts for the existence of the moon.

87. *Grandpa Green.* Written and illustrated by Lane Smith. (Roaring Brook Press, 2011.) A boy narrates the story of his great-grandfather and the ornamental garden the elder created. The garden, filled with shapes of animals, people, and familiar objects, documents the essential milestones of the man's life. There is a cannon to commemorate his war service and the shape of a baby signifying his birth, which the boy says is from "a really long time ago, before computers or cell phones or television." When the old man sometimes forgets things, he has the garden to help him remember.

88. *Animals Should Definitely Not Wear Clothing.* Written by Judi Barrett. Illustrated by Ronald Barrett. (Atheneum, 1970.) A chicken wearing pants? A walrus in a suit and tie? A porcupine in a dress? Seeing funny pictures of animals in human garb shows us why animals are better off wearing their own ready-made clothing.

89. *A Bear Called Paddington.* Written by Michael Bond. Illustrated by Peggy Fortnum. (Houghton Mifflin, 1960.) Mr. and Mrs. Brown find a small unassuming bear named Paddington in a London railway station. Attached to his duffle coat is a note, which reads "Please look after this bear. Thank you." Paddington goes on to many adventures in England and becomes part of the Brown family.

90. *Chato's Kitchen.* Written by Gary Soto. Illustrated by Susan Guevara. (Putnam's, 1995.) A cat named Chato uses a welcome dinner to lure a new family of mice to his home. He invites another cat from the barrio to participate in the scheme and prepares a feast of fajitas, frijoles, salsa, and enchiladas. The mice, called "ratoncitos," are not fooled. They outsmart Chato by inviting a dog.

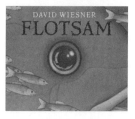

91. *Flotsam.* Illustrated by David Wiesner. (Clarion Books, 2006.) In this story, a boy finds an old-fashioned camera on the beach. When he develops the film within, it reveals pictures of a mysterious and fantastic undersea world. There are also pictures of a long line of children who have found the camera. Wisner's story needs no text: his vivid images tell the story.

92. *Crictor.* Written and illustrated by Tomi Ungerer. (Harper & Brothers, 1958.) A teacher's son gives her a pet boa constrictor named Crictor. When she takes the snake to school, the children love it. Crictor becomes a jump rope and uses his body to form numbers and letters. When the snake stops a burglary, he becomes a town hero.

93. *Frog and Toad Together.* Written and illustrated by Arnold Lobel. (Harper & Row, 1972.) The book opens with Toad making a list of things to do. It includes items such as wake up, go for a walk with Frog, eat lunch, and go to sleep. The two good friends do everything together. They do things such as share cookies, plant a garden, and fly a kite.

94. *Grandfather's Journey.* Written and illustrated by Allen Say. (Houghton Mifflin, 1993.) A Japanese American man writes about how his grandfather traveled back and forth between Japan and the United States because he loved both countries. The grandson and grandfather are alike in that if it were possible, the two would like to be in both countries at the same time.

95. *Henry and Mudge.* Written by Cynthia Rylant. Illustrated by Suçie Stevenson. (Bradbury Press, 1987.) This is the first in a series of books about a boy named Henry and a big dog named Mudge. Henry is an only child and has no one in his neighborhood to play with, so he asks for a dog. His parents get him Mudge, who becomes his constant companion. This is a great book for a beginning reader.

96. *Matilda.* Written by Roald Dahl. Illustrated by Quentin Blake. (Viking Kestrel, 1988.) Matilda is a prodigy and book lover who happens to have telekinetic powers. She uses this power to get revenge on the evil headmistress of her school, Miss Trunchbull. Matilda is supported by her beloved teacher, Miss Honey, but, unfortunately, not by her parents.

97. *Just in Case: A Trickster Tale and Spanish Alphabet Book.* Written and illustrated by Yuyi Morales. (Roaring Brook Press, 2008.) Señor Calavera is a skeleton on his way to Grandmother Beetle's birthday party. The ghost of Grandpa Zelmiro reminds him he needs a gift, and he decides to get Grandmother something for every letter of the alphabet. While Señor Calavera is riding his bike full of gifts to her house, he falls and ruins them, but arrives at the party with the best birthday present possible, his grandmother's departed husband.

98. *Sector 7.* Written and illustrated by David Wiesner. (Clarion Books, 1999.) In this visual tale, a boy is taken to Sector 7 to learn how clouds are made and circulated around the country. He visits this floating station in the sky while on a school trip to New York's Empire State Building. As with most of Wiesner's books, this is a virtually wordless story married to breathtaking imagery.

99. *Mirandy and Brother Wind.* Written by Patricia C. McKissack. Illustrated by Jerry Pinkney. (Knopf, 1988.) Mirandy is an African American girl in the rural South. She is excited about the upcoming junior cakewalk jubilee. Her mother tells her, "Whoever catches the Wind can make him do their bidding." Mirandy tries repeatedly to capture Brother Wind to get his help in winning the competition, but the wind eludes her.

100. *Ling & Ting: Not Exactly the Same!* Written and illustrated by Grace Lin. (Little, Brown Books for Young Readers, 2010.) Ling and Ting are identical Chinese American twin girls who look the same but whose personalities are very different. For one thing, Ling is rather placid, but Ting is fidgety. When the girls try to eat the dumplings they have made, Ting is a master of her chopsticks, while Ling flounders.

CHAPTER 3

Middle Readers (Ages 9–12)

It is not enough to simply teach children to read; we have to give them something worth reading.

—Katherine Paterson

1. Harry Potter (series). Written by J. K. Rowling. *Harry Potter and the Sorcerer's Stone* (Scholastic, 1998); *Harry Potter and the Chamber of Secrets* (Scholastic, 1999); *Harry Potter and the Prisoner of Azkaban* (Scholastic, 1999); *Harry Potter and the Goblet of Fire* (Scholastic, 2000); *Harry Potter and the Order of the Phoenix* (Scholastic, 2003); *Harry Potter and the Half-Blood Prince* (Scholastic, 2005); and *Harry Potter and the Deathly Hallows* (Scholastic, 2007). These seven immensely popular novels chronicle the adventures of wizards Harry Potter, Ronald Weasley, and Hermione Granger. They are students at Hogwarts School of Witchcraft and Wizardry. Harry battles Lord Voldemort, a dark wizard, who wants to rule the wizard world.

2. *Charlotte's Web*. Written by E. B. White. Illustrated by Garth Williams. (Harper & Row, 1952.) When Wilbur the lovable pig learns he is to be slaughtered for a Christmas dinner, his true friend Charlotte, a barn spider, saves his life. She spins words in her web extolling Wilbur's excellence and virtue.

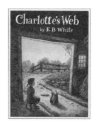

3. *Hatchet.* Written by Gary Paulsen. (Bradbury Press, 1987.) Thirteen-year-old Brian Robeson, a boy from the city, is the only survivor of a plane crash in the Canadian wilderness. He manages to survive for two months with only a hatchet to aid him. He learns to hunt, fish, and make a fire until he is rescued.

4. *One Crazy Summer.* Written by Rita Williams-Garcia. (Amistad, 2011.) Set in 1968, this is a story of three girls—Delphine, Vonetta, and Fern—in search of their mother, a poet, who left them behind. The Brooklyn girls travel to Oakland to visit their mother, Cecile, but she is unwilling to spend time with them. Over the course of four weeks, the girls are sent to attend daily programs and eat breakfast at a Black Panther Party center. "No one told y'all to come out here," Cecile says. "No one wants you out here making a mess, stopping my work." Eleven-year-old Delphine, the oldest girl, who looks after her sisters, tells this heartbreaking story.

5. *Wonderstruck.* Written and illustrated by Brian Selznick. (Scholastic Press, 2011.) In this novel of words and black-and-white drawings, Ben and Rose feel there is something missing in their lives. These two children have separate stories set 50 years apart, which ultimately converge. The boy's story is told in prose while the girl's story is communicated in pictures. Ben, who hails from Minnesota in the 1970s, longs for a father he never knew. Rose, a deaf girl from New Jersey in the 1920s, dreams of a mysterious actress. They both leave unhappy homes to take a journey that leads to New York City's American Museum of Natural History. *Wonderstruck*'s graphic format invites comparison to Selznick's earlier novel, *The Invention of Hugo Cabret.*

6. *Holes.* Written by Louis Sachar. (Farrar, Straus & Giroux, 1998.) Stanley Yelnats is a middle-school-aged boy who is falsely accused of stealing and is sent to Camp Green Lake, a cruel juvenile detention camp in Texas. As a character-building exercise, he and the other inmates are required by the warden to rise each morning and dig large holes in the desert. Stanley befriends Hector "Zero" Zeroni, who gets in trouble and runs away. Out of concern for Zero's safety, Stanley also escapes. The warden's real motive for all the digging is that he is searching for buried treasure.

7. *Island of the Blue Dolphins.* Written by Scott O'Dell. (Houghton Mifflin, 1960.) Set in the early 19th century, the book is based on a true story. A young Indian girl named Karana spends 18 years alone on an island off the coast of California. In her solitude, Karana learns to feed and clothe herself and to fight off predators.

8. *Mrs. Frisby and the Rats of NIMH.* Written by Robert C. O'Brien. Illustrated by Zena Bernstein. (Atheneum, 1971.) Mrs. Frisby, a widowed field mouse, attempts to move her sick son before spring planting. She finds a group of rats that were once part of an experimental group at NIMH, the National Institute of Mental Health, who are about to set up their own society. The highly intelligent rats move her house to a location safe from the plough.

9. *A Wrinkle in Time.* Written by Madeleine L'Engle. (Farrar Straus & Giroux, 1962.) The Murry family go on a dangerous mission to find their physicist father. In this science fiction/fantasy novel, the father goes missing after working on a mysterious project called a tesseract, a space-time portal.

10. *Maniac Magee.* Written by Jerry Spinelli. (Scholastic, 1990.) Jeffery Lionel "Maniac" Magee is a Caucasian orphan boy who becomes a local legend because of his amazing athletic abilities. Having lost his parents in a trolley accident when he was 3 years old, he went to live with his Aunt Dot and Uncle Dan, but ran away after eight years because of problems in their relationship. For a time, Maniac is homeless and lives at the zoo. Amanda Beale, an African American girl, befriends him. Her family takes him in, but he is pressured to leave their home in this racially segregated Pennsylvania town.

11. *Tuck Everlasting.* Written by Natalie Babbitt. (Farrar, Straus, Giroux, 1975.) Winnie Foster, a 10-year-old girl, learns about a family in the woods who never grow older because they drink from a fountain of youth. A mysterious man also knows the Tuck family secret and is determined to use it to make a fortune.

12. *Anne of Green Gables.* Written by L. M. Montgomery. (L. C. Page, 1908.) Eleven-year-old Anne Shirley is an orphaned Canadian girl who is sent to live with a family on Prince Edward Island. Although they originally asked the orphanage to send them a boy, they take pity on the red-haired girl and keep her. Anne adapts to farm life and ultimately brings joy to everyone around her.

13. *Wonder.* Written by R. J. Palacio. (Knopf Books for Young Readers, 2012.) Until fifth grade, when he attends school for the first time, Auggie Pullman has been homeschooled because of profound facial disfigurations. Middle school is a challenge under any circumstances, but Auggie's father feels that his attending Beecher Prep is like sending a lamb to the slaughter. Not unexpectedly, a bully targets him. People look at Auggie in shock or avoid looking at him altogether. Few see that he is mostly an ordinary boy. Auggie and his family members and classmates take turns narrating the story. Everyone is affected in some way by Auggie's struggle.

14. *Bridge to Terabithia.* Written by Katherine Paterson. Illustrated by Donna Diamond. (Crowell, 1977.) A tomboy named Leslie and an artistic boy named Jesse become friends after she wins a footrace against him. Together, they invent a secret land named Terabithia, a magic kingdom where they rule as king and queen. When Leslie accidentally drowns, Jesse is able to cope with it because of the strength she gave him in their friendship.

15. *The Phantom Tollbooth.* Written by Norton Juster. Illustrated by Jules Feiffer. (Random House, 1961.) A bored young boy named Milo drives his toy car through a tollbooth to the enchanted Kingdom of Wisdom. In this modern fairy tale, Milo encounters strange characters and has many adventures. When he drives back through the tollbooth, he finds he has only been gone for an hour.

16. *Shiloh.* Written by Phyllis Reynolds Naylor. (Atheneum, 1991.) When Marty finds a beagle that has been abused by his neighbor, he decides to steal and hide the dog. He names the dog Shiloh. When his scheme is discovered, he must give the dog back. After Marty spots the neighbor shooting deer out of season, he blackmails the unsavory man into selling Shiloh to him. *Shiloh* is the first book in a trilogy.

17. *Little Women.* Written by Louisa May Alcott. (Roberts Brothers, 1868.) Set in 19th-century Massachusetts, this novel follows the lives of four sisters, each of them coming of age and struggling to define themselves. Beautiful Meg is the oldest sister, Jo is considered to be boyish, Beth is shy, and Amy March, the youngest, is interested in art.

18. *Sarah, Plain and Tall.* Written by Patricia Mac-Lachlan. (HarperCollins, 1985.) Jacob Witting is a widower. He can't manage taking care of his farm and two children, Anna and Caleb, so he places an ad in an eastern newspaper for a mail-order bride. Sarah Wheaton, who describes herself as "plain and tall," accepts his proposal and comes to the prairie to become his wife. Sarah becomes homesick, but Anna and Caleb want her to remain with them.

19. *Treasure Island.* Written by Robert Louis Stevenson. (Cassell and Company, 1883.) *Treasure Island* is the preeminent pirate adventure story. Told from the perspective of a boy named Jim Hawkins, the book is filled with mutiny, treachery, and intrigue and features unforgettable scoundrels such as Long John Silver.

20. *Ella Enchanted.* Written by Gail Carson Levine. (HarperCollins, 1997.) This novel is an imaginative retelling of the story of Cinderella. At Ella's birth, a misguided fairy makes her lastingly obedient. Though Ella cannot disobey an order, she is strong willed and struggles to break the curse. Ella goes on a quest and must contend with wicked stepsisters, but will she live happily ever after with a handsome prince?

21. *From the Mixed-Up Files of Mrs. Basil E. Frankweiler.* Written and illustrated by E. L. Konigsburg. (Atheneum, 1967.) Claudia and her younger brother Jamie run away from their suburban life to live in the Metropolitan Museum of Modern Art. During their adventure, they meet the strange Mrs. Basil E. Frankweiler. When the runaway children visit Frankweiler at her home, she puts them to work going through her files to find the secret of a marble statue of an angel.

22. *The Great Gilly Hopkins.* Written by Katherine Paterson. (Crowell, 1978.) Gilly is an angry 11-year-old girl who has been moved from one foster home to another. When she is placed in the Trotter home, she escapes, hoping to live with her biological mother, Courtney Rutherford Hopkins. After meeting her mother, Gilly realizes that she is better off with her foster family.

23. *When You Reach Me.* Written by Rebecca Stead. (Wendy Lamb Books, 2009.) Set in Manhattan in 1979, this is a coming-of-age time-travel story about sixth-grader Miranda Sinclair. After her best friend Sal is punched in the face by a boy named Marcus, Miranda's life takes a turn for the worse. Then she begins receiving mysterious notes that somehow predict the future.

24. *Harriet the Spy.* Written and illustrated by Louise Fitzhugh. (Harper & Row, 1964.) Harriet, who wants to be a spy and a writer, observes and takes copious notes about everything. Dressed in a hooded sweatshirt, she secretly eavesdrops. Problems arise after her classmates get her notes and read what she has written. The children launch a "Spy Catcher Club" to repay what they see as Harriet's mean behavior, and she becomes an outcast.

25. *The Lion, the Witch, and the Wardrobe.* Written by C. S. Lewis. Illustrated by Pauline Baynes. (MacMillan, 1950.) Four children: Peter, Susan, Edmund, and Lucy Pevensie, find a wardrobe that leads to a magic world called Narnia. In this world, Aslan the Lion, assisted by the Pevensie children, frees the inhabitants from the spell of the White Witch. The lion dies for the sins of the children, but rises from the grave. This is the first in the famous series of books called the Chronicles of Narnia.

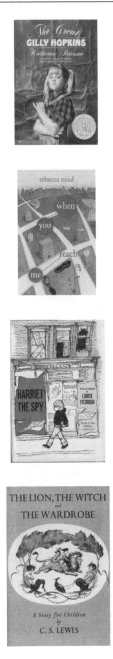

26. *The Secret Garden.* Written by Frances Hodgson Burnett. Illustrated by Tasha Tudor. (Lippincott, 1912.) Three children: Mary, Colin, and Dickon, spend time in a neglected, walled garden and bring it back to life. Like the garden, the children are rejuvenated. Colin, for example, begins the story bound to a wheelchair, and by its end he is running about.

27. *Johnny Tremain.* Written by Esther Forbes. (Houghton Mifflin, 1943.) Johnny is a silversmith's apprentice just prior to the American Revolution who burns his hand while working on an order for John Hancock. His crippled hand requires him to look for a new trade, and his attention turns to politics. Johnny helps in the Boston Tea Party and warns the colonists at Lexington with Paul Revere.

28. *Where the Red Fern Grows.* Written by Wilson Rawls. (Doubleday, 1961.) In the Ozark Mountains during the Great Depression, a young boy named Billy earns the money to buy two puppies, which he names Old Dan and Little Ann. He teaches the coonhounds to become champion hunters. Billy and the dogs hunt raccoons almost every night. One night ends tragically when the dogs get in a fatal fight with a mountain lion.

29. *Alice's Adventures in Wonderland.* Written by Lewis Carroll. Illustrated by John Tenniel. (MacMillan, 1865.) A little girl named Alice sees a clothed white rabbit with a pocket watch run by her. She follows him, famously falls down a rabbit hole, and journeys through a strange fantasyland. Along the way she has many adventures, such as meeting the Cheshire Cat and being a guest at a mad tea party.

30. *The Book of Three.* Written by Lloyd Alexander. (Holt Rinehart & Winston, 1964.) This is an adventure story of a young hero named Taran, the assistant pig keeper, who fights the forces of evil in the mythical land of Prydain. The book borrows heavily from Gaelic and Welsh mythology and is the first of a five-part series called the Chronicles of Prydain.

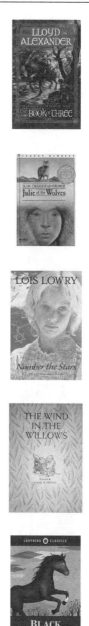

31. *Julie of the Wolves.* Written by Jean Craighead George. Illustrated by John Schoenherr. (Harper & Row, 1972.) When Julie is threatened by an impending arranged marriage, the Eskimo girl runs away into the Alaskan wilderness. The 13-year-old girl gets lost on the tundra and is protected by a wolf pack.

32. *Number the Stars.* Written by Lois Lowry. (Houghton Mifflin, 1989.) A Danish 10-year-old named Annemarie Johansen helps to hide her Jewish friend from the Nazis during World War II. During the German occupation of Denmark, Annemarie's family allows her best friend, Ellen Rosen, to move in to escape being sent to a death camp.

33. *The Wind in the Willows.* Written by Kenneth Grahame. Illustrated by Ernest H. Shepard. (Charles Scribner's Sons, 1908.) This classic tells of the adventures of Mole, Rat, Badger, and Toad on a riverbank and in the English countryside. Toad tends to drive the action, as when he steals a motorcar and is sent to jail.

34. *Black Beauty.* Written by Anna Sewell. (Jarrold & Sons, 1877.) This is the well-known first-person autobiography of a horse. *Black Beauty* recounts many episodes of both cruelty and compassion, beginning with Black Beauty's life as a colt. Sewell shows empathy for a horse that has had a long life with many different masters.

35. *The Adventures of Tom Sawyer.* Written by Mark Twain. (American Publishing Company, 1876.) This iconic novel is about a mischievous young boy growing up along the Mississippi River in the early 19th century. Tom skips school, tricks friends into doing his work, falls in love with Becky Thatcher, and witnesses a murder.

36. *The Borrowers.* Written by Mary Norton. Illustrated by Beth and Joe Krush. (Harcourt Brace, 1953.) A family of little people lives under the kitchen floor of a country house and borrows what they need to survive. Pod, Homily, and their daughter, Arrietty, are miniature people that recycle items from the full-sized family above. Postage stamps become pictures on the wall. Matchboxes become storage containers. What happens when the tiny folks are finally seen?

37. *Charlie and the Chocolate Factory.* Written by Roald Dahl. Illustrated by Joseph Schindelman. (Knopf, 1964.) Poor but deserving Charlie Bucket, along with four spoiled children, win a tour and a lifetime supply of chocolate from Willie Wonka's chocolate factory. During the tour, the spoiled brats each get their just deserts, but Charlie becomes heir to the factory.

38. *Because of Winn-Dixie.* Written by Kate DiCamillo. (Candlewick Press, 2000.) The opening line of the novel says it all, "My name is India Opal Buloni, and last summer my daddy, the preacher, sent me to the store for a box of macaroni-and-cheese, some white rice, and two tomatoes and I came back with a dog." Opal prevents the big stray dog from being sent to the pound. She immediately names him Winn-Dixie, after the grocery store where she finds him.

39. *The Cricket in Times Square.* Written by George Selden. Illustrated by Garth Williams. (Farrar, Straus & Giroux, 1960.) Chester the musical cricket ends up in Times Square after accidentally boarding a train from Connecticut. He lives at a newsstand and befriends streetwise Harry the cat and Tucker the mouse. They show Chester the sights of New York City, and he is overwhelmed.

40. *The Incredible Journey.* Written by Sheila Burnford. Illustrated by Carl Burger. (Atlantic Monthly Press, 1960.) Three house pets attempt a long and dangerous trip through the wilds of Canada. A bull terrier, a Siamese cat, and a Labrador retriever fight wild animals and a harsh terrain to search for their cherished masters.

41. *The Jungle Book.* Written by Rudyard Kipling. Illustrated by John Lockwood Kipling. (Macmillan, 1894.) *The Jungle Book* is a collection of stories creating a magical world in which animals can talk and reason. In "Mowgli's Brothers," a boy raised by wolves in the Indian jungle has to fight the tiger Shere Khan. In "Rikki-Tikki-Tavi," a heroic mongoose battles two cobras, Nag and Nagaina, who have the run of the garden.

42. *Okay for Now.* Written by Gary D. Schmidt. (Clarion Books, 2011.) Doug Swieteck has just moved to a new town. Struggling to survive his abusive family and overcome the general perception that he is a delinquent, 14-year-old Doug finds a friend in a green-eyed girl named Liv Spicer, who helps him get a job delivering groceries for her father. His life is transformed when he discovers an Audubon book in the library. Inspired by its artistry, he is encouraged by the librarian, who offers to teach him how to draw. With the help and kindness of a few people, Doug starts to become the master of his own fate.

43. *Mr. Popper's Penguins.* Written by Richard and Florence Atwater. Illustrated by Robert Lawson. (Little, Brown & Company, 1938.) Mr. Popper, a mild-mannered housepainter, comes into possession of two zany penguins that soon have 10 chicks. When the poor man can no longer afford to feed the flock of penguins, he takes them on the road as a circus act.

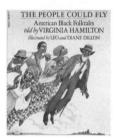

44. *Redwall.* Written by Brian Jacques. Illustrated by Gary Chalk. (Philomel Books, 1986.) When an evil rat known as Cluny the Scourge and his horde attack Redwall Abbey, a brave young mouse known as Matthias goes on a quest to recover the legendary sword of Martin the Warrior to help the Redwallers. The sword is hidden somewhere in the abbey.

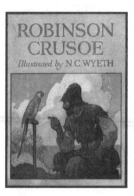

45. *The People Could Fly: American Black Folktales.* Written by Virginia Hamilton. Illustrated by Leo and Diane Dillon. (Knopf, 1985.) Twenty-four stories of strength and courage, told first by slaves and passed down through the years in a rich oral tradition, are retold here in print. This anthology of American folktales is a testimony to the triumph of the human spirit over slavery.

46. *Robinson Crusoe.* Written by Daniel Defoe. (W. Taylor, 1719.) Robinson Crusoe is the world's most famous castaway. The book's original, unedited title tells it all: "The Life and Strange Surprising Adventures of Robinson Crusoe, of York, Mariner: Who lived Eight and Twenty Years, all alone in an un-inhabited Island on the Coast of America, near the Mouth of the Great River of Oroonoque; Having been cast on Shore by Shipwreck, wherein all the Men perished but himself. With An Account how he was at last as strangely deliver'd by Pirates."

47. *Stuart Little.* Written by E. B. White. Illustrated by Garth Williams. (Harper & Row, 1945.) Stuart Little, a refined little mouse, journeys into the world to find a wren named Margalo, a dear friend who stayed a few days in his family's garden. Margalo fled when she was warned that a cat intended to eat her. Stuart protects Margalo from a cat. She returns the kindness by saving Stuart when he is trapped in a garbage can.

48. *The Whipping Boy.* Written by Sid Fleischman. Illustrated by Peter Sís. (Greenwillow Books, 1986.) As in *The Prince and the Pauper*, Prince Brat and his whipping boy, Jemmy, inadvertently trade places. The prince runs away, taking Jemmy with him, and they get entangled with dangerous outlaws.

49. *Winnie-the-Pooh.* Written by A. A. Milne. Illustrated by Ernest H. Shepard. (Dutton, 1926.) This book describes the adventures of Winnie-the-Pooh, a lovable teddy bear; Piglet, a small toy pig; Eeyore, a toy donkey; Owl, a real owl; and Rabbit, a real rabbit.

50. *The BFG.* Written by Roald Dahl. Illustrated by Quentin Blake. (Jonathan Cape, 1982.) The BFG, a Big Friendly Giant, collects good dreams and gives them to children. One night when a little orphan girl named Sophie spots him blowing something in the window down the street, he kidnaps her and takes her to giant land. BFG, unlike the other giants, does not eat children, and the two become friends. Sophie convinces BFG to meet the queen of England when they hatch a plot to capture the child-eating giants and bring them to London.

51. *Anastasia Krupnik.* Written by Lois Lowry. Illustrated by Diane deGroat. (Houghton Mifflin, 1979.) Spunky fourth-grader Anastasia's everyday problems growing up in a Boston suburb are the subject of this book, the first in a series. At the end of each chapter Anastasia makes a list of her likes and dislikes, which has the effect of charting her personal growth. The

novel features Anastasia's reactions to the birth of her baby brother and the death of her grandmother.

52. *The Wonderful Wizard of Oz.* Written by L. Frank Baum. Illustrated by W. W. Denslow. (George M. Hill Company, 1900.) Dorothy is swept up in a tornado and deposited in the mystical Land of Oz. She runs afoul of a wicked witch when her Kansas farmhouse falls out of the sky and kills the witch's sister. She joins with a scarecrow, tin woodman, and cowardly lion to see the wizard. After defeating the wicked witch, Dorothy returns to Kansas with the words "There's no place like home."

53. *Are You There God? It's Me, Margaret.* Written by Judy Blume. (Bradbury, 1970.) Margaret talks with God often about her adolescent worries. Among her concerns is her religious identity: her mother is Christian and her father is Jewish. The book also deals with issues common to many preteen girls, such as Margaret getting her first bra and having her first period.

54. *Bud, Not Buddy.* Written by Christopher Paul Curtis. (Delacorte Books for Young Readers, 1999.) Bud is an African American orphan growing up during the Great Depression. After abusive foster homes (most recently, he was locked in a shed with hornets), Bud decides to run away. He embarks on a quest to find Herman E. Calloway, who has a jazz band and may be his father. When Bud finally finds Harry, the man does not believe Bud is his son.

55. *Bunnicula: A Rabbit-Tale of Mystery.* Written by Deborah Howe and James Howe. Illustrated by Alan Daniel. (Atheneum, 1979.) The Monroe family found Bunnicula at a movie theater where Dracula was playing. Bunnicula turns out to be a bunny that sucks the juice out of vegetables. The book is narrated by Chester, the family cat, who believes that Bunnicula is a vampire. Chester convinces Harold, the family dog, to help him keep the family safe.

56. *Dear Mr. Henshaw.* Written by Beverly Cleary. Illustrated by Paul O. Zelinsky. (HarperCollins, 1983.) For a school project, Leigh Botts writes a series of questions to his favorite author, Boyd Henshaw. The writer replies with some questions of his own. In his letters, Mr. Henshaw prompts Leigh to come to terms with some issues, such as adjusting to his parents' divorce, being the new kid in school, and having food stolen from his lunch bag.

57. *The Egypt Game.* Written by Zilpha Keatley Snyder. Illustrated by Alton Raible. (Atheneum, 1967.) While her mother tours with a band, April is sent to live with her grandmother. Unhappy with her situation, April makes friends with Melanie, another girl in the apartment building. April and Melanie, who share an interest in ancient Egypt, create an imaginative game. Other children join in, and strange things begin to happen. The game leads them into a criminal investigation.

58. *Heidi.* Written by Johanna Spyri. Translated from German by Helen B. Dole. (Ginn and Company, 1899.) Heidi is a young girl who lives with her reclusive grandfather in the Swiss Alps, bringing joy into his lonely life. Heidi is taken to Frankfurt to live with an older girl named Clara, who is confined to a wheelchair. Heidi's influence on Clara leads to her walking.

59. *Splendors and Glooms.* Written by Laura Amy Schlitz. (Candlewick, 2012.) A master puppeteer in dark Dickensian London, Gasper Grisini, is hired to perform at Clara Wintermute's 12th birthday party. When lonely Clara invites Grisini's two orphaned apprentices, Lizzie Rose and Parsefall, for tea, they are in awe of the opulent Wintermute home. When Clara goes missing, Grisini is suspected of kidnapping her and is nowhere to be found. Lizzie Rose and Parsefall leave the city in search of Clara. An ancient witch named Cassandra, who has a score to settle with Grisini, assists the children in their quest.

60. *The Indian in the Cupboard.* Written by Lynne Reid Banks. Illustrated by Brock Cole. (Doubleday, 1981.) A Native American figurine is brought to life when a young boy first places him inside and then unlocks an old cupboard using a magic key. The Indian is an Iroquois from the 18th century. When a miniature cowboy is introduced, the tiny men fight, and the cowboy is wounded. *The Indian in the Cupboard* is the first book in a series.

61. *Little House in the Big Woods.* Written by Laura Ingalls Wilder. Illustrated by Garth Williams. (Harper & Brothers, 1932.) This is a portrait of a pioneering family's wholesome, hardworking, and rewarding life in the big woods on the Wisconsin frontier. Laura Ingalls's classic story is based on her own childhood.

62. *Out of the Dust.* Written by Karen Hesse. (Scholastic, 1997.) When Billie Jo's mother dies of a tragic accident, she and her grieving father must survive in the Oklahoma Dust Bowl of the 1930s. The same accident that kills her mother leaves Billie Jo's hands permanently scarred and in pain, affecting her ability to play the piano.

63. *Inside Out and Back Again.* Written by Thanhha Lai. (HarperCollins, 2011.) Ten-year-old Hà and her family are forced to flee their home in Saigon when it falls to the North Vietnamese. The child refugee, whose father went missing during the war, copes with alienation and strange customs in her new Alabama home. Making social mistakes such as wearing a flannel nightgown to school adds to the prejudice, rejection, and bullying she faces. "No one would believe me, but at times I would choose wartime in Saigon over peacetime in Alabama," Hà laments. This portrait of an outcast is written in short free-verse poems.

64. *Tales of a Fourth Grade Nothing.* Written by Judy Blume. Illustrated by Roy Doty. (Dutton, 1972.) Being around his demanding, 2-year-old brother, Fudge, makes Peter feel like a nothing. Though Fudge throws temper tantrums, scribbles on Peter's homework, insists on being involved with everything, and even takes off with Peter's turtle, their parents do nothing to stop him.

65. *My Side of the Mountain.* Written and illustrated by Jean Craighead George. (Dutton, 1959.) Sam Gribley runs away from his New York City apartment all the way to the Catskill Mountains. The 12-year-old lives in a large hollowed-out tree in the wilderness. Sam survives blizzards, uses the resources of the local library, and learns to live off the land. His companions are a weasel and a falcon.

66. *The Watsons Go to Birmingham—1963.* Written by Christopher Paul Curtis. (Yearling, 1995.) With tensions rising in the civil rights movement, the Watson family travels from Flint, Michigan, to visit Grandma Sands in Birmingham, Alabama. The trip is prompted by concern for the Watsons' oldest boy, who was beginning to get in trouble in Flint. The Watsons believed Birmingham would be a safer environment until Grandma's church is bombed, an actual historical event.

67. *Little House on the Prairie.* Written by Laura Ingalls Wilder. (Harper & Brothers, 1935.) In *Little House on the Prairie*, the sequel to *Little House in the Big Woods*, the Ingalls family travels by covered wagon from the Wisconsin woods to Indian Territory on the Kansas prairie. There they build a log cabin and settle in, but get caught in the middle of a conflict between the U.S. government and the Osage Indians.

68. *Misty of Chincoteague.* Written by Marguerite Henry. Illustrated by Wesley Dennis. (Rand McNally, 1947.) Phantom, part of a band of wild horses that lives on the Virginia coastal island of Chincoteague, is captured in a frenzied roundup. Her colt, named Misty, is also captured in the roundup. The book focuses on the story of a young boy and girl's efforts to raise Misty.

69. *Ramona Quimby, Age Eight.* Written by Beverly Cleary. Illustrated by Jacqueline Rogers. (HarperCollins, 1981.) The sixth book in the Ramona series features third-grader Ramona, now at a new school. Among other things, she breaks an egg on her head, thinking her mom hard boiled it, and is sent to the office. Her family learns to adjust to her father's going back to college.

70. *Pippi Longstocking.* Written by Astrid Lindgren. Illustrated by Louis S. Glanzman. (Viking Press, 1950.) Pippi is an unconventional 9-year-old girl with amazing physical strength. She lives with a horse and a monkey in a house on the edge of a Swedish town. She can lift her horse with one hand and handle herself with bullies. Pippi, the daughter of a sea captain, was raised aboard ship among buccaneers.

71. *Stone Fox.* Written by John Reynolds Gardiner. Illustrated by Marcia Sewall. (Crowell, 1980.) Little Willy enters a dogsled race in hopes of keeping his ill grandfather from losing his potato farm. He is matched against the legendary Stone Fox, who has never lost a race.

72. *Where the Sidewalk Ends.* Written and illustrated by Shel Silverstein. (Harper & Row, 1974.) This is an excellent collection of poems and drawings, which deal with common childhood issues. Some of the poems are sad, but most are funny, as with the crocodile that goes to the dentist.

73. *Sounder.* Written by William H. Armstrong. Illustrated by James Barkley. (Harper & Row, 1969.) When his sharecropper father is imprisoned for stealing food to feed his family, a poor southern boy endures hardship. As the sheriff carts his father off to jail, one of his deputies shoots Sounder, the family dog, with a shotgun. The dog lives but is disfigured. When he goes to live with an old teacher, the boy learns to read.

74. *D'Aulaires' Book of Greek Myths.* Written and illustrated by Ingrid and Edgar Parin D'Aulaire. (Doubleday, 1962.) This elaborately illustrated compendium describes all the major gods and goddesses of ancient Greece. The classic stories are made fresh, and the drawings are beautiful in this action-packed introduction to the foundations of Western culture.

75. *Turtle in Paradise.* Written by Jennifer L. Holm. (Random House Books for Young Readers, 2010.) When her mother gets a job as a live-in housekeeper with an employer who won't accept children, Turtle is sent to live with relatives in Key West, Florida. The 11-year-old leaves her home in Depression-era New Jersey and enters a world of rowdy boy cousins she's never seen before. Tough like the shell of a turtle, she flourishes in this new environment. "Folks have always told me that I look like Momma," Turtle says. "Our eyes are different, though. I think the color of a person's eyes says a lot about them. Mama has soft blue eyes and all she sees are kittens and roses. My eyes are gray as soot, and I see things for what they are."

76. *Esperanza Rising.* Written by Pam Muñoz Ryan. (Scholastic, 2000.) This story of Mexican farmworkers struggling in the United States during the Great Depression focuses on Esperanza Ortega, whose father is murdered by Mexican bandits. After the crime, her mother takes her to California. Esperanza's family, wealthy in Mexico, now lives in a shack. They are resented in their new community because of their past privilege.

77. *Frindle.* Written by Andrew Clements. Illustrated by Brian Selznick. (Aladdin Paperbacks, 1996.) Fifth-grader Nick Allen comes up with a new name for an old object. He decides that instead of using the word "pen," he will begin calling it a "frindle." His teacher doesn't like the idea, but the new word becomes so popular that it is eventually included in the dictionary.

78. *Homer Price.* Written and illustrated by Robert McCloskey. (Viking Press, 1943.) Homer is an ordinary, mild-mannered boy who has many unusual adventures. He helps capture bandits with the help of his pet skunk Aroma, is involved with the winding of the world's largest ball of string, and copes with an out-of-control doughnut-making machine in his uncle's diner.

79. *Ninth Ward.* Written by Jewell Parker Rhodes. (Little, Brown Books for Young Readers, 2010.) Lanesha and her elderly caretaker, Mama Ya-Ya, face Hurricane Katrina as it devastates their New Orleans home. Lanesha was born with a caul, a bloody membrane, which Mama Ya-Ya, the midwife, removed from her face. Both Lanesha and Mama Ya-Ya are imbued with second sight. While Mama Ya-Ya predicts the arrival of the horrible storm, 12-year-old Lanesha has the ability to see ghosts, including the spirit of her teenaged mother, who died giving birth to her. When they are told they must evacuate, Mama Ya-Ya sees that she will not survive. Brave Lanesha survives the rising water in a rowboat.

80. *The Little Prince.* Written and illustrated by Antoine de Saint-Exupéry. (Reynal & Hitchcock, 1943.) The book's narrator is an artist and pilot who crashes his plane in the Sahara Desert. He meets a little prince from another planet who asks him to draw a sheep. The prince is on earth because he wants to explore other planets and cure his loneliness.

81. *Hoot.* Written by Carl Hiaasen. (Knopf, 2002.) Roy, a newcomer to Florida, immediately becomes a target of a bully. Roy breaks the bully's nose and fails to get the bully to agree to a truce. Roy soon befriends a barefoot boy named Mullet Fingers and joins his quest to save some burrowing owls from destruction. The boys plan to upset the construction of a pancake restaurant over the home of this endangered species.

82. *The Invention of Hugo Cabret.* Written and illustrated by Brian Selznick. (Scholastic, 2007.) Hugo secretly lives in the walls of a Paris train station, where he tends to its clocks. He steals everything he needs to survive and do his work. Hugo owns a damaged mechanical man, which once belonged to his father. His ultimate goal is to make it work again. Part novel and part picture book, the inspiration for *Hugo Cabret* was the true story of a French pioneer filmmaker.

83. *James and the Giant Peach.* Written by Roald Dahl. Illustrated by Nancy Ekholm Burkert. (Knopf, 1961.) James, an orphan who lives with two abusive aunts, accidentally spills magic crystals on a withering peach tree. A peach grows to the size of a house, with talking insects inside. James and his insect friends cut the peach loose, and it rolls into the sea. Out in the ocean, the peach is attacked by sharks and then saved by seagulls that lift the giant peach up and away to safety.

84. *Peter Pan.* Written by J. M. Barrie. Illustrated by F. D. Bedford. (Charles Scribner's Sons, 1911.) Peter Pan is a boy who can fly and who never grows old. As the leader of a gang of lost boys, his life is a nonstop adventure in Neverland. Originally published as *Peter and Wendy*, the story focuses on Peter's relationships with Wendy Darling, her brothers, Tinker Bell, and Captain Hook. Peter invites Wendy to Neverland after she reattaches his lost shadow.

85. *A Long Way from Chicago.* Written by Richard Peck. (Dial Press, 1998.) Two children, Joey and Mary Alice Dowdel, spend a series of vacations with their eccentric grandmother in rural Illinois. The book, set in the 1930s and 1940s, is a collection of short stories. In the first story, their grandmother is holding an open house for a man who has just died. When the coffin begins to move, Grandma shoots it with her shotgun. It turns out that a cat moved the coffin.

86. *Mary Poppins.* Written by P. L. Travers. Illustrated by Mary Shepard. (Gerald Howe, 1934.) Blown in by a strong wind, an amazing English nanny arrives in the household of the Banks family and takes on the job of caring for their children, Jane, Michael, John, and Barbara. Contrary to the popular Disney film version of this story, the actual Mary Poppins depicted in the book is stern, but still magical.

87. *Crispin: The Cross of Lead.* Written by Avi. (Hyperion Books, 2002.) Accused of a crime he did not commit, a 13-year-old peasant boy is forced to go on the run in 14th-century England. He has no possessions except a cross of lead given to him by the village priest. The cross belonged to his mother and reveals his true name to be Crispin. This is the first book in a trilogy.

88. *The Summer of the Swans.* Written by Betsy Byars. Illustrated by Ted Coconis. (Viking Press, 1970.) Sara loves her younger, mentally impaired brother, Charlie, and takes him to visit the swans that have settled on the neighborhood pond. One night, Charlie awakens and gets lost while searching for the beautiful birds, stumbling into a ravine. Fourteen-year-old Sara and a friend search the woods for the terrified boy.

89. *Ramona the Pest.* Written by Beverly Cleary. Illustrated by Louis Darling. (W. Morrow, 1968.) In the second book in the series, Ramona starts kindergarten. She discovers the joys and challenges presented by her teacher Miss Binney, as well as the temptations of her new and interesting classmates. Ramona likes her classmate Davy so much she keeps trying to kiss him, and she is so fascinated by Susan's red springy curls she just has to pull them.

90. *The Dreamer.* Written by Pam Muñoz Ryan. Illustrated by Peter Sís. (Scholastic Press, 2010.) This is the fictional biography of Chilean poet Pablo Neruda. Neruda, born with the name Neftali Reyes, is a sensitive boy with a stutter who perseveres with his poetry despite strong opposition from his father. As Neftali grows up, he becomes aware of social injustice, particularly the predicament of the indigenous Mapuche people. This shy boy, who goes on to become one of the greatest poets of the 20th century, adopted a pseudonym to hide his antigovernment writing from his domineering father and the authorities. In his formative years, Neftali is seen wandering and dreaming at the seashore and in the lush rain forest. These scenes are skillfully depicted in Peter Sís's delicate drawings.

91. *The Swiss Family Robinson.* Written by Johann David Wyss. (Frederick Warne and Co., 1888.) After a great storm, a ship runs aground on a reef near a tropical island. The family aboard the ship discovers the crew has abandoned them. They unload the ship's provisions, including tools, books, guns, and livestock, and ferry it to shore. They eventually build a tree house, complete with a library. Modeled after the novel *Robinson Crusoe*, the novel describes the shipwrecked family's resourcefulness.

92. *Abel's Island.* Written by William Steig. (Farrar, Straus & Giroux, 1976.) Abel and his wife Amanda are mice caught in a fierce rainstorm. Abel is swept away by the water and transported downstream, where he is stranded on a deserted island. Struggling to survive harsh conditions and predators, he repeatedly tries to leave the island to return to his wife.

93. *Dead End in Norvelt.* Written by Jack Gantos. (Farrar, Straus & Giroux, 2011.) Young Jack gets grounded for an entire summer. He is only allowed out to help Miss Volker, an arthritic neighbor who writes obituaries and history for the local newspaper and who needs a typist. The elderly woman gives the spirited boy a valuable education on social reformers who stood up for worker rights. This autobiographical novel is set in the summer of 1962 in Norvelt, Pennsylvania, a small town built during the New Deal.

94. *Al Capone Does My Shirts.* Written by Gennifer Choldenko. (Putnam Juvenile, 2004.) In 1935, Moose Flanagan and his family move to Alcatraz Island, the location of the prison where the infamous mob boss Al Capone is locked up and where Moose's father has a job. The boy's autistic sister, Natalie, is supposed to go to the Esther P. Marinoff School, a special school in San Francisco. When the school rejects Natalie, 12-year-old Moose secretly writes a note to Al Capone asking him to help Natalie get admitted to the school.

95. *The Black Stallion.* Written by Walter Farley. (Random House, 1941.) Alec Ramsay and a wild black stallion are stranded together on a desert island and develop a lifelong bond. After he is rescued, Alec begins training the stallion as a racehorse. This is the first in a series of books.

96. *Among the Hidden*. Written by Margaret Peterson Haddix. (Simon & Schuster Books for Young Readers, 2000.) In this totalitarian future, it is a crime for a family to have more than two children. Twelve-year-old Luke, an illegal third child, must spend his days in hiding. He is eventually confined to the attic, a lonely life, until he secretly meets Jen, another hidden child like him.

97. *Caddie Woodlawn*. Written by Carol Ryrie Brink. Illustrated by Trina Schart Hyman. (MacMillan, 1935.) This novel about pioneer life in the 1860s features an 11-year-old tomboy named Caroline Augusta Woodlawn. Caddie, who would rather hunt and explore in the Wisconsin wilderness than assume her expected domestic role, makes friends with the Native Americans.

98. *The Arrival*. Illustrated by Shaun Tan. (Arthur A. Levine Books, 2007.) This graphic novel is the story of a man's journey to a strange new country. The artistry of this wordless book captures the wonder and confusion this immigrant feels as he arrives in a city. Instead of a familiar alphabet, he encounters an incomprehensible system of symbols that appears to function as words.

99. *Nothing but the Truth*. Written by Avi. (Orchard Books, 1992.) In this documentary novel, Phillip Malloy is suspended from school for humming along with the national anthem. Events regarding this minor school infraction spin out of control, locally and then nationally, when the incident becomes a political news story about patriotism. The school district scapegoats his teacher, Miss Narwin, who is an excellent instructor.

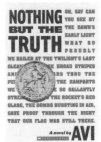

100. *All-of-a-Kind Family.* Written by Sydney Taylor. Illustrated by Helen John. (Yearling, 1951.) In a close-knit family, five young sisters—Ella, Henny, Sarah, Charlotte, and Gertie—experience New York City in the early part of the 20th century. They are a poor immigrant family living in New York's Lower East Side, a hub of Jewish culture.

CHAPTER 4

Young Adults (Ages 13–17)

A book must be the ax for the frozen sea within us.

—Franz Kafka

1. *The Giver*. Written by Lois Lowry. (Houghton Mifflin, 1994.) At age 12, Jonas is given his life assignment from the committee of elders to become the receiver of memories along with one other member of his community. Jonas learns a horrible truth about his society, realizing that he is living in a world that has eliminated all pain, fear, war, hatred, and freedom.

2. *Code Name Verity*. Written by Elizabeth Wein. (Hyperion Books, 2012.) The Gestapo captures a young female undercover agent, code name Verity, after her spy plane crashes on an unauthorized flight into France during World War II. As a reprieve from torture, she is forced to write a confession. Verity writes about the British war effort and her strong friendship with Maddie, the pilot of the plane, who Verity believes died in the crash. Though they are from different Scottish social classes, Verity conveys how the war brought them together to become the most devoted of friends. In this complex story, nothing is as it first seems.

3. *The Hobbit.* Written by J. R. R. Tolkien. (George Allen & Unwin, 1937.) This novel follows the adventures of Bilbo Baggins on his journey to reclaim stolen treasure from Smaug the dragon. He and his companions must overcome many dangerous challenges. *The Hobbit* is the precursor to the Lord of the Rings trilogy.

4. *Roll of Thunder, Hear My Cry.* Written by Mildred Taylor. (Dial Press, 1976.) This book focuses on the prejudice and poverty that young Cassie Logan and her family face in Depression-era Mississippi. The Logan family struggles to maintain both their land and their dignity.

5. The Lord of the Rings (trilogy series). Written by J. R. R. Tolkien. *The Fellowship of the Ring; The Two Towers; The Return of the King.* (George Allen & Unwin, 1954–1955.) The trilogy begins in the Shire, where the hobbit Frodo Baggins inherits a dangerous and powerful ring from his cousin Bilbo Baggins. The ring was forged by the dark lord Sauron to dominate Middle-earth and corrupt all who wear it. Frodo accepts the task of destroying it. He and his companion Samwise Gamgee go on a treacherous journey to rid the world of the evil ring in the fire of Mount Doom.

6. *Pride and Prejudice.* Written by Jane Austen. (T. Egerton, Whitehall, 1813.) Intelligent and high-spirited Elizabeth Bennet, the second of five unmarried daughters, deals with manners, morality, and romance in wealthy 19th-century English society. The novel is a portrait of an aristocratic world of money and social status where Elizabeth hopes to marry for love.

7. *A Monster Calls: Inspired by an Idea from Siobhan Dowd.* Written by Patrick Ness. Illustrated by Jim Kay. (Candlewick, 2011.) Conor O'Malley's mother is dying of cancer. Bullies are harassing him in school. He's been having a truly frightening nightmare ever since his mother started her therapy. And a monster that resembles a yew tree from his backyard has been visiting the 13-year-old boy. The monster says he will tell him three true tales. In return, Conor must tell the enormous creature the truth that has been haunting him or face being eaten. The idea for the novel came from award-winning author Siobhan Dowd, who died of cancer before she could write the book herself.

8. *The Call of the Wild.* Written by Jack London. (MacMillan, 1903.) This novella, set in the time of the Alaskan gold rush, is an adventure story featuring the struggles of a dog named Buck. He starts out as a domesticated pet, but is sold into a harsh and cruel life of being tethered to a sled.

9. *The Chocolate War.* Written by Robert Cormier. (Pantheon, 1974.) This novel deals with the misuse of power at a boys' Catholic high school in New England. Archie Costello, the leader of a school gang, targets Jerry Renault because he is a nonconformist. The ambitious acting headmaster of the school colludes with Archie to use the boy's gang influence to dramatically increase this year's chocolate sales.

10. *Skellig.* Written by David Almond. (Delacorte Press, 1999.) When Michael and his family move into a rundown house, he discovers a mysterious old man in poor health lying in the garage. Michael notices what might be a pair of wings on the stranger's back.

11. *To Kill a Mockingbird.* Written by Harper Lee. (Lippincott, 1960.) This novel is set in the Deep South during the 1930s and is told from the perspective of a young girl nicknamed "Scout" Finch. Her father, Atticus Finch, is a lawyer who courageously defends a black man accused of raping a white woman. "It was times like these when I thought my father, who hated guns and had never been to any wars, was the bravest man who ever lived," says Scout about her father.

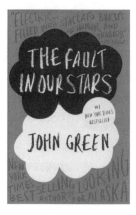

12. *The Fault in Our Stars.* Written by John Green. (Dutton Juvenile, 2012.) Two irreverent and ill teenagers, Hazel and Augustus, meet in a cancer support group and soon fall deeply in love. Hazel, the narrator of the story, has advanced thyroid cancer and must travel with an oxygen tank. Augustus is a former basketball star whose cancer is in remission, but who has already lost his right leg to the disease. The couple's favorite book is an unflinching novel about cancer written by an American recluse who lives in Amsterdam and whose daughter was a cancer victim. Augustus arranges for them to travel to Amsterdam to meet the author, but the author is rude and the meeting is a disaster. Afterward, Augustus reveals that his cancer has returned and has metastasized to other parts of his body.

13. *Walk Two Moons.* Written by Sharon Creech. (HarperCollins, 1994.) While on a cross-country trip with her grandparents, 13-year-old Sal tries to understand and deal with her mother's disappearance. She tells her grandparents a similar story of her friend Phoebe, whose mother also left home.

14. *The Witch of Blackbird Pond.* Written by Elizabeth George Speare. (Houghton Mifflin, 1958.) This novel is set in Connecticut in 1687. Kit Tyler is accused of witchcraft when she befriends an old woman known as the Witch of Blackbird Pond. The stern Puritans have been suspicious of Kit from the time she arrived from her island home in the Caribbean.

15. *Son.* Written by Lois Lowry. (Houghton Mifflin Books for Children, 2012.) *Son* returns to the dystopian world of *The Giver*, where newborn children are considered to be no more than manufactured products. Into this loveless society, 14-year-old Claire gives birth to a boy by Caesarean section. The authorities forget to give her the pills that insulate her from feeling, and she feels an intense desire to find her boy. Another critical mistake is made when Claire is accidentally told her child's number, and with this information she finds him. Over the course of the book, Claire goes to extreme lengths to locate and protect her offspring. *Son* is the fourth and final book in the Giver series.

16. *The Outsiders.* Written by S. E. Hinton. (Viking Press, 1967.) Two rival groups, divided by their socioeconomic status, have violent clashes that end in murder. Ponyboy Curtis belongs to a lower-class group of teenagers who call themselves Greasers because of their long, greasy hair. They feel like outsiders. Ponyboy feels that the rich gang called Socs (short for Socials) can get away with anything because they have money.

17. *A Wizard of Earthsea.* Written by Ursula Le Guin. Illustrated by Ruth Robbins. (Parnassus Press, 1968.) Ged, a prideful young man born with a great aptitude for magic, undergoes the process of becoming a wizard. He learns a little from his aunt, the village witch, and then becomes apprenticed to a master wizard. Ged accidentally summons a shadow from the land of the dead that nearly destroys him.

18. *The Catcher in the Rye.* Written by J. D. Salinger. (Little, Brown & Company, 1951.) This celebrated novel covers two days in the life of Holden Caulfield, a teenager who has been expelled from prep school and wanders into New York City. Caulfield is the archetypal alienated teenager, rebelling against authority.

19. *Between Shades of Gray.* Written by Ruta Sepetys. (Philomel, 2011.) This novel is about Soviet atrocities committed against the Baltic peoples and a teenage girl's hope, strength, and perseverance in the face of unimaginable cruelty and hardship. In the aftermath of Russia's 1939 invasion of Lithuania, Lina Vilkas and her family are arrested, stuffed into cattle cars, and sent to labor camps in Siberia. Branded as fascist sympathizers, they are ripped from their comfortable home and forced to endure extreme conditions and fight for their lives. In her old life, 15-year-old Lina was going to attend art school. Now she makes documentary drawings that include secret clues regarding their location in the hope that the drawings will make their way to the Soviet camp where her father is being held.

20. *Catherine, Called Birdy.* Written by Karen Cushman. (Clarion Books, 1994.) Catherine, called Birdy because she keeps caged birds in her room, is the daughter of a poor knight. She tries to avoid marriage, especially when she sees her father trying to "sell me like a cheese to some lack-wit seeking a wife." Catherine writes in her diary her frustration about her mother's attempts to make her into a proper young noblewoman.

21. *Lord of the Flies.* Written by William Golding. (Faber & Faber, 1954.) *Lord of the Flies* is a lesson in how quickly the structure and restraints of civilization can fall away. When a plane crashes on a deserted island, the only survivors are British schoolboys, who initially try to pull together and govern themselves. Soon there are power struggles, and they descend into savagery.

22. *The True Confessions of Charlotte Doyle.* Written by Avi. (Orchard Books, 1990.) During a transatlantic voyage from England to America, Charlotte warns Captain Jaggery of a planned mutiny. Two sailors end up dead by the captain's hand. Charlotte regrets her mistake and joins the crew, promising to expose the captain at the end of the voyage.

23. *The Westing Game.* Written by Ellen Raskin. (E. P. Dutton, 1978.) Sixteen heirs to millionaire Samuel W. Westing come together to hear the reading of the will. They are given clues to lead them to their inheritance. The sixteen are divided into eight pairs with different clues. Whoever solves the puzzle gets the fortune.

24. *The Bell Jar.* Written by Sylvia Plath. (Harper & Row, 1971.) A struggling and gifted young writer has a breakdown and ends up in a mental hospital. In this autobiographical novel, Esther Greenwood cannot cope with the world, and she feels like she is living in a bell jar cut off from everyone.

25. *Fallen Angels.* Written by Walter Dean Myers. (Scholastic, 1988.) Fresh out of Harlem High School, Richie Perry's time in Vietnam introduces him to the horror and uselessness of war as he learns to kill and sees his comrades die. Throughout the novel, he questions why the United States is in Vietnam.

26. *The House of the Scorpion.* Written by Nancy Farmer. (Atheneum Books for Young Readers, 2002.) In the future, the organs of clones are harvested to keep the wealthy alive. Matt is a young clone of the world's biggest drug kingpin, the 142-year-old El Patrón, who runs a drug empire located between the United States and Mexico. When El Patrón needs a new heart, Matt is expected to be the donor.

27. *The Moves Make the Man.* Written by Bruce Brooks. (Harper & Row, 1984.) In North Carolina in the early 1960s, a friendship grows between Jerome Foxworthy, a black basketball player, and Bix Rivers, an emotionally troubled white baseball player. Jerome, the first black in an all-white school, teaches Bix his basketball moves. Bix improves, but he does not fake or make basketball moves, equating them with falsehood.

28. *The Absolutely True Diary of a Part-Time Indian.* Written by Sherman Alexie. Illustrated by Ellen Forney. (Little, Brown Books for Young Readers, 2007.) A talented Native American teenager named Arnold Spirit, born with medical problems and teased by bullies, leaves his reservation to attend a rich, all-white school. Besides the team mascot, Arnold is the only Indian at the school.

29. *M. C. Higgins the Great.* Written by Virginia Hamilton. (MacMillan, 1974.) Mayo Cornelius's family has lived on Sarah's Mountain in Kentucky ever since Sarah, his great-grandmother, went there as a runaway slave. Now a slagheap left from strip mining threatens his home. This novel is about not only protecting the environment but also standing up for what you believe.

30. *The Dark Is Rising.* Written by Susan Cooper. (Atheneum, 1973.) On his 11th birthday, Will Stanton learns that he is the last of the Old Ones, people dedicated to fighting the evil forces of the dark. With this comes special powers and responsibilities. In order for good to prevail, Will must join together six magical signs: wood, bronze, iron, water, fire, and stone. This novel is the first in a series.

31. *Jacob Have I Loved.* Written by Katherine Paterson. (Crowell, 1980.) Sara Louise, the more boyish of a set of identical twins, helps her father on his boat during crabbing season. Throughout the novel, she struggles to find her identity, as well as combat her feelings of jealousy toward her prettier, more talented, and more conventionally feminine twin sister Caroline.

32. *Eva.* Written by Peter Dickinson. (Delacorte Press, 1988.) After 13-year-old Eva is terribly injured in a car accident, she wakes up in the hospital to learn that she has been given the body of a chimpanzee. When her new body brings with it instincts and subconscious memories of the chimpanzee, Eva becomes an advocate for animal rights, eventually going to live among regular chimps on an experimental island.

33. *The Joy Luck Club.* Written by Amy Tan. (G. P. Putnam, 1989.) In 1949, four Chinese American women form the Joy Luck Club. Over the years, they meet regularly in San Francisco and play the Chinese game of mah-jongg. The novel is comprised of 16 related stories that focus on the immigrant women and their daughters. The women are haunted by their early lives in China.

34. *My Brother Sam Is Dead.* Written by James Lincoln Collier and Christopher Collier. (Four Winds, 1974.) Tim Meeker, the narrator of this American Revolutionary War story, comes from a town and a family that are loyal to Britain. When his brother Sam returns from Yale, he announces that he has joined the Continental army to fight the British. Tim's father and brother die serving opposite sides of the war.

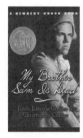

35. *Chime.* Written by Franny Billingsley. (Dial, 2011.) In a Victorian-era English village in the land of Swampsea, Briony is a teenage witch who would face certain death if her paranormal secret were discovered. Believing she is the cause of terrible accidents, including her stepmother's death and her twin sister's brain damage, she is riddled with guilt and self-hatred. Briony has the ability to communicate with the spirits who haunt the swamps. She becomes romantically involved with a boy named Eldric when he and his engineer father become lodgers in her home, where she lives with her clergyman father and sister. When the Industrial Revolution arrives in Swampsea and Eldric's father starts draining the swamp, the spirits retaliate.

36. *The Adventures of Huckleberry Finn.* Written by Mark Twain. (Charles L. Webster & Company, 1885.) Huckleberry Finn goes on the run after he fakes his own murder to escape from his abusive father. He sets off down the Mississippi River with his friend Jim, an escaped slave. This seminal work is a sequel to *The Adventures of Tom Sawyer.*

37. *The Color Purple.* Written by Alice Walker. (Harcourt Brace Jovanovich, 1982.) Celie is a poor black southern girl who writes a series of letters to God. These letters and others trace her evolution from self-hatred, born of brutal treatment by men, to the discovery of a woman's love.

38. *Animal Farm.* Written by George Orwell. (Secker & Warburg, 1945.) In this biting satire about Soviet communism, new tyranny replaces old in an uprising of farm animals against their human masters. The pig leaders adopt Seven Commandments of Animalism, including "All animals are equal." After a number of years, the commandments devolve into a single "All animals are equal, but some animals are more equal than others."

39. *The Astonishing Life of Octavian Nothing, Traitor to the Nation.* Volume 1, *The Pox Party.* Written by M. T. Anderson. (Candlewick Press, 2006.) In American Revolution–era Boston, a black youth named Octavian is given a classical education as part of an experiment to determine if Africans are an inferior race. He sees the hypocrisy of those who fight for liberty but continue to sanction slavery.

40. *The Book Thief.* Written by Markus Zusak. (Knopf, 2006.) Set in Nazi Germany, this is the story of young Liesel Meminger, who steals books and tells stories to help sustain her foster family and the Jewish man they are hiding. Liesel makes friends with Rudy Steiner, a neighborhood boy who falls in love with her.

41. *Aristotle and Dante Discover the Secrets of the Universe.* Written by Benjamin Alire Sáenz. (Simon & Schuster Books for Young Readers, 2012.) Ari and Dante are 15-year-old gay loners, both of Mexican American heritage but with distinctly different inclinations. Dante is quick to laugh, sure of himself and his homosexuality, while Ari is reticent about his sexual identity and is constantly angry. When they meet at a community pool one summer, Dante offers to teach Ari how to swim. They have a good laugh, and the friendship is formed when they realize that their namesakes are great philosophers. Ari, the narrator of the story, finally admits the depth of love he has for his friend after Dante is hospitalized after a gay-bashing incident.

42. *The Ear, the Eye, and the Arm.* Written by Nancy Farmer. (Orchard Books, 1994.) Tendai, Rita, and Kuda, the children of Zimbabwe's chief of security, are privileged people who lead dull and sheltered lives inside the family compound. When they venture out into the city, they are kidnapped. Three mutants, whose exposure to nuclear waste has given them unique powers, form the Ear, the Eye, and the Arm detective agency. They are called in to search for the children.

43. *Fahrenheit 451.* Written by Ray Bradbury. (Ballantine Books, 1953.) This prophetic novel envisions a world where people get all the media they need from visual images. Books are banned and firemen burn them. The title of this classic dystopian book refers to the temperature at which paper burns.

44. *The Golden Compass.* Written by Philip Pullman. (Knopf, 1996.) In a parallel universe, 12-year-old Lyra Belacqua fights the evil that is stealing children and experimenting on them. The experiments separate children from their "daemons," the manifestations of their souls in animal form. *The Golden Compass* is the first book in the His Dark Materials trilogy.

45. *Frankenstein.* Written by Mary Wollstonecraft Shelley. (Lackington, Hughes, Harding, Mavor & Jones, 1818.) Dr. Victor Frankenstein had hoped to construct a beautiful creature in his laboratory, but it ended up a hideous monster. The monster disappears, becomes educated, and eventually starts killing people. The creature demands that a female companion like itself be created. This book is often considered the first true science fiction novel.

46. *The Grapes of Wrath.* Written by John Steinbeck. (Viking Press, 1939.) This novel shows the hard reality of an America deeply mired in the Great Depression and divided between haves and have-nots. The book focuses on the odyssey of the Joads, a traveling homeless family, as they cope with poverty and exploitation by California farmers.

47. *Kidnapped.* Written by Robert Louis Stevenson. (Cassell & Company, 1886.) David Balfour, an orphan, discovers that he has a wealthy family and is the rightful heir to its fortune. He visits his rich Uncle Ebenezer, who controls the Balfour money. He has David kidnapped and imprisoned aboard a ship.

48. *The Great Gatsby.* Written by F. Scott Fitzgerald. (Charles Scribner's Sons, 1925.) *The Great Gatsby* is widely regarded as the Great American Novel. With the Roaring Twenties and the Prohibition era providing the backdrop, it is the story of the greed and excess of millionaire Jay Gatsby and his love for the beautiful Daisy Buchanan.

49. *Homecoming.* Written by Cynthia Voigt. (Atheneum, 1981.) Four children—Dicey, James, Maybeth, and Sammy Tillerman—are abruptly abandoned by their mentally ill mother in a car at a Connecticut shopping mall. When it becomes clear that their mother is not coming back, they go on a perilous walking trip to find Great-Aunt Cilla. When they find that she has passed away, their journey continues.

50. *Jane Eyre.* Written by Charlotte Brontë. (Smith, Elder & Co., 1847.) *Jane Eyre* tells the story of Jane's maturation and growth to adulthood. At the novel's beginning, Jane is a 10-year-old orphan living with a family that dislikes her. Undaunted, she does very well in school and becomes a governess for Edward Rochester. She fall in love with him, and he misleads her. In Gothic style, Brontë creates an atmosphere of mystery and suspense.

51. *Divergent.* Written by Veronica Roth. (Katherine Tegen Books, 2011.) In a dystopian future, Chicago is divided into five factions, each dedicated to a different virtue: Abnegation (the selfless), Amity (the peaceful), Candor (the honest), Dauntless (the brave) and Erudite (the intelligent). Beatrice Prior, like all 16-year-olds, must take a test to determine where she belongs, a decision that will dictate every aspect of her life. Something goes terribly wrong with Beatrice's test. Because she doesn't neatly fit any one faction, she is at risk of being labeled "divergent" and a danger to this supposedly perfect society. War between the factions is on the horizon as Beatrice makes her momentous choice. *Divergent* is the first book in a trilogy.

52. *The Midwife's Apprentice.* Written by Karen Cushman. (Clarion Books, 1995.) In 14th-century England, a homeless, nameless girl is found in a dung pile and is apprenticed to the town midwife. The girl matures and finds her calling and her place in the world, delivering babies.

53. The Hunger Games (trilogy series). Written by Suzanne Collins. *The Hunger Games, Catching Fire*, and *Mockingjay*. (Scholastic, 2008–2010.) The Hunger Games trilogy takes place in the postapocalyptic future in the country of Panem, which exists in place of what was once the United States. Panem is comprised of 12 poor districts, ruled by a wealthy, technologically advanced, and thoroughly hated "Capital." Each year one boy and one girl from every district, between the ages of 12 and 18, are selected by lottery and forced to fight to the death in the televised Hunger Games. The story focuses on Katniss Everdeen, the narrator of the tale and representative of her district. In the first book, when the people see how Katniss stands up to the Capital rulers, a rebellion starts. The second and third books follow Katniss and the rebellion.

54. *Shabanu, Daughter of the Wind.* Written by Suzanne Fisher Staples. (Knopf, 1989.). Shabanu describes her life as a member of a nomadic tribe in Pakistan. Torn between her independence and her allegiance to her family, Shabanu is pledged to marry an older man whose money will bring honor to the family.

55. *One-Eyed Cat.* Written by Paula Fox. (Bradbury Press, 1984.) Eleven-year-old Ned Wallis, a pastor's son, sneaked an air rifle out of the attic at night while everyone was sleeping. He believes that he shot out the eye of a stray cat with his air rifle and is haunted by guilt. The one-eyed cat is thin and sick and can't hunt, and Ned worries that it will not survive the winter.

56. *Slaughterhouse-Five.* Written by Kurt Vonnegut. (Delacorte, 1969.) Billy Pilgrim is an American soldier who is captured by the Germans during the Battle of the Bulge. Kept in a slaughterhouse in Dresden, Billy is one of the few survivors of an Allied firebombing that killed 135,000 German civilians. He begins to travel in time and is kidnapped by aliens from another planet.

57. *Monster.* Written by Walter Dean Myers. (HarperCollins, 1999.) A Harlem convenience store owner is killed in a robbery gone wrong. Sixteen-year-old Steve Harmon, the supposed lookout for the crime, is arrested and put on trial, where the district attorney labels him a "monster" before the jury. Steve's story is conveyed through journal entries and a movie script he writes during his time in jail.

58. *The Slave Dancer.* Written by Paula Fox. Illustrated by Eros Keith. (Bradbury Press, 1973.) Jessie Bollier is kidnapped and brought aboard a slave ship bound for Africa. To his horror, the boy finds that his job is to play his flute so the slaves will "dance" as exercise to keep their bodies healthy and suitable for sale.

59. *Weetzie Bat.* Written by Francesca Lia Block. (Harper & Row, 1989.) This is the story of unconventional Weetzie Bat and her friend Dirk, both searching for love in Los Angeles. Weetzie is granted three wishes by a genie. The wishes change her life in unexpected ways.

60. *The Sword in the Stone.* Written by T. H. White. Illustrated by Robert Lawson. (Collins, 1938.). The novel tells the story of the education of Arthur, the young future king, under the wise mentorship of Merlin the magician. Arthur is prepared for the day when he can draw forth the sword from the magic stone, which is inscribed, "Whoso Pulleth out This Sword of This Stone and Anvil, Is Rightwise King Born of All England."

61. *Twenty Thousand Leagues under the Sea.* Written by Jules Verne. (Pierre-Jules Hetzel, 1870.) The legendary Captain Nemo and the Nautilus, his futuristic submarine, are the source of adventure in this science fiction classic. The story begins with a sailing ship damaged in a battle with a sea monster. The sailors are thrown overboard and are rescued by Nemo's submarine.

62. *Watership Down.* Written by Richard Adams. (MacMillan, 1972.) A band of rabbits in the English countryside flee the destruction of their warren by a land developer. The heroic rabbits encounter many perils along the way in search of a new home. They stop at a strange warren where the rabbits are well fed by the local farmer, but realize it is a trap and that the farmer has set snares to catch them.

63. *The Scorpio Races.* Written by Maggie Stiefvater. (Scholastic Press, 2011.) The Scorpio race is run every November in the island town of Thisby. People participate in this often deadly event by first capturing and then riding wild, flesh-eating horses that come from the sea. Nineteen-year-old Sean, stoic and silent, has a way with the beasts and has won the race the previous four times. Puck Connolly is the first female to enter the race and plans to compete with an ordinary horse. Puck never expected to be in this position—she lost both her parents in this brutal race—but needs the money prize to keep what's left of her impoverished family together. As Puck and Sean train for the race, a friendship develops and grows into romance.

64. *The Yearling*. Written by Marjorie Kinnan Rawlings. Illustrated by N. C. Wyeth. (Scribners, 1938.) Set in the Florida Everglades, this novel focuses on Jody Baxter and a fawn named Flag that he loves. When the deer grows to maturity, Jody's simple backwoods family can no longer afford to feed it, and his parents order him to shoot Flag. When he can't kill the deer, his mother shoots and wounds it, and Jody is forced to finish the job. In anger, Jody runs away.

65. *Blink & Caution*. Written by Tim Wynne-Jones. (Candlewick Press, 2011.) Blink and Caution are two young runaways surviving on the streets of Toronto. Blink is a street punk with a facial tic escaping from an abusive home. Caution is on the run from her drug-dealing boyfriend after stealing money from him. She is consumed by guilt because of her responsibility for a fatal accident involving her brother. Foraging through breakfast leftovers in a luxury hotel, Blink witnesses a fake kidnapping. The 16-year-olds team up and decide to use the "kidnapping" to their advantage.

66. *Z for Zachariah*. Written by Robert O'Brien. (Atheneum, 1975.) Two survivors of a nuclear holocaust are brought together in a peaceful valley. Sixteen-year-old Ann Burden, one of the survivors, narrates the story in the form of a diary. The other survivor is John R. Loomis, a university chemist who helped design a radiation safety suit. After Ann nurses John back from a near-fatal illness, she concludes that he is a murderer.

67. *1984*. Written by George Orwell. (Harcourt, Brace, 1949.) The protagonist of the novel, Winston Smith, works for the Ministry of Truth. His job is to rewrite the past in support of the current regime. Winston prefers the truth and secretly hates the regime. More than any novel, *1984* is synonymous with the idea of a dystopian future. Words and phrases from the book such as "Orwellian" and "Big Brother" have become everyday vocabulary.

68. *Across Five Aprils.* Written by Irene Hunt. Illustrated by Albert John Pucci. (Follett Publishing, 1964.) In Illinois during the Civil War era, young Jethro Creighton grows from a boy to a man when he is left to take care of the family farm and must contend with brothers fighting on opposite sides of the war. The Creighton family is harassed because one of its sons is in the Confederate army.

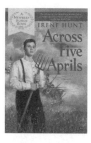

69. *Catch-22.* Written by Joseph Heller. (Simon & Shuster, 1961.) This antiwar novel features antihero protagonist Captain John Yossarian. Responsible for coining the expression "Catch-22" for a no-win situation, Heller sets this funny, horrific story in an island camp off the coast of Italy during World War II. The novel focuses on the experiences of Yossarian and the other airmen in the camp as they put in their time and try to keep their sanity.

70. *American Born Chinese.* Written by Gene Luen Yang. (First Second, 2007.) *American Born Chinese* is a graphic novel with three different but interwoven plotlines. They involve Jin Wang, the only Chinese American at his new school, who just wants to fit in; Monkey King, the Chinese god and folk hero; and Danny, a Caucasian, embarrassed by his stereotypical Chinese cousin Chin-Kee.

71. *Before We Were Free.* Written by Julia Alvarez. (Knopf, 2002.) Secret police in the Dominican Republic terrorize Anita, a teenage girl, and her family, who are involved in the attempt to overthrow the country's dictator. When her father and brother are hauled away by the secret police, Anita and her mother must flee.

72. *The Devil's Arithmetic.* Written by Jane Yolen. (Viking Kestrel, 1988.) Hannah, a Jewish girl from New Rochelle, New York, gains a new appreciation for learning about the past when she is transported back in time to World War II Poland. Sent to a Nazi concentration camp, she saves the life of a girl in the camp. When Hannah is brought back to the present, she realizes that the girl she saved is her old Aunt Eva.

73. *Beloved.* Written by Toni Morrison. (Knopf, 1987.) In the Reconstruction era in Ohio, Sethe cannot escape her memories of being a slave. She is literally haunted by the spirit of her deceased infant daughter, whom she murdered many years earlier in order to save her from a life of slavery.

74. *The Cay.* Written by Theodore Taylor. (Doubleday, 1969.) When a German submarine torpedo hits his ship during World War II, Phillip receives a blow on the head that blinds him. Phillip, a white teenage boy, and Timothy, an elderly black man, are stranded together on a tiny Caribbean island. Their relationship evolves from disdain to friendship.

75. *The Changeover: A Supernatural Romance.* Written by Margaret Mahy. (Scholastic, 1984.) When Laura's little brother Jacko becomes deathly sick because evil forces are attacking him, she realizes that she needs to change over into a witch to save him. A male witch at her school named Sorry Carlisle assists her.

76. *A Christmas Carol.* Written by Charles Dickens. (Chapman & Hall, 1843.) Miserly, mean-spirited Ebenezer Scrooge receives a visitation from the ghost of his dead partner, Jacob Marley, who tells him to expect a visit from three spirits. In this novella, the spirits give Scrooge a glimpse of his past, present, and future. He becomes overwhelmed by the desire to redeem his selfish and greedy ways and to honor Christmas with all his heart.

77. *Never Fall Down.* Written by Patricia McCormick. (Balzer & Bray, 2012.) *Never Fall Down* is based on the true story of peace advocate Arn Chorn-Pond, whose life is forever changed when the brutal Khmer Rouge strip him from his family, sending him at age 11 to work in a Cambodian labor camp. To survive, he learns to play a musical instrument and discovers that the music is used not only to entertain his captors, but to cover up the sounds of mass killing. When the Khmer Rouge herd everyone into camps known as "killing fields," millions perish from starvation, disease, and murder. When Vietnam invades Cambodia, Arn is forced to join the Khmer Rouge army.

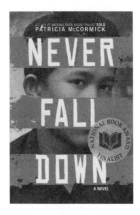

78. *The Curious Incident of the Dog in the Night-Time.* Written by Mark Haddon. (Doubleday, 2003.) The unusual narrator of this mystery novel is Christopher Boone, a high-functioning autistic 15-year-old boy. Christopher loves prime numbers but is baffled by facial expressions. When he finds Mrs. Shears's large black poodle with a fork in it, he follows the clues of the murder into areas well outside his comfort zone.

79. *Dragonwings.* Written by Laurence Yep. (Harper & Row, 1975.) *Dragonwings* is told through the eyes of a young Chinese boy, Moon Shadow, who leaves his mother in China to join his father, Windrider, in America. Moon Shadow helps his father run a laundry in San Francisco and fulfill his dream of making a flying machine.

80. *Ender's Game.* Written by Orson Scott Card. (Tor Books, 1985.) *Ender's Game* is a science fiction novel about humans at war with an alien insect species called Buggers. Ender Wiggin, a very talented boy, is taken to a training center to undertake increasingly difficult mock battle games. He is such a tactical genius that he skips several years of school. For his final test simulation, Ender is in for a big surprise.

81. *Gathering Blue.* Written by Lois Lowry. (Houghton Mifflin, 2000.) Kira is a disabled girl in a harsh and primitive future society that normally leaves the disabled to die. Because she has a unique skill at embroidery, the ruling council spares her life in order for her to update a beautiful robe depicting their society's history. Kira not only learns the art of dyeing thread but discovers some terrible truths about her village. *Gathering Blue* is the second novel in the Giver quartet.

82. *Eragon.* Written by Christopher Paolini. (Knopf, 2003.) Eragon, a farm boy, one day finds a dragon's egg. He secretly raises the dragon, Saphira, and learns to become a dragon rider. When King Galbatorix's servants kill his uncle and destroy his home, Eragon seeks revenge.

83. *The First Part Last.* Written by Angela Johnson. (Simon & Schuster Books for Young Readers, 2003.) Bobby is an African American teenager struggling to raise his infant on his own. His friends do not understand what he is doing, his parents are supportive but refuse to take over the work, and Nia, the infant's mother, is unable to help because she is in a coma.

84. *Heart of Darkness.* Written by Joseph Conrad. (William Blackwood, 1902.) Marlow tells a story about a trip he took down the Congo River in search of an ivory agent named Kurtz who disappeared without a trace. Besides being an adventure story, this novella is a critique of European colonialism and a statement about the darkness in the heart of civilized men.

85. *Go Tell It on the Mountain.* Written by James A. Baldwin. (Knopf, 1953.) John Grimes has a difficult relationship with his disciplinarian father, Gabriel, who is a Harlem preacher. John hates his puritanical father and dreams of running away. In this novel set during the Depression, the secrets and sins of a tormented black family are revealed.

86. *Gossamer.* Written by Lois Lowry. (Houghton Mifflin, 2006.) There are benevolent creatures that make nightly visits to people's homes. By touching objects around the home, they collect memory fragments such as colors, words, and sounds, combining them into dreams. They impart their creations to humans and pets. In this novel, the dream givers work to strengthen a lonely woman and a damaged boy, giving them protection from bad dreams.

87. *Sweet Whispers, Brother Rush.* Written by Virginia Hamilton. (Philomel, 1982.) Brother Rush, the ghost of her uncle, visits 14-year-old Sweet Teresa Pratt, nicknamed Tree. He reveals heartbreaking secrets about her family that connect Tree's childhood to the present.

88. *The Merry Adventures of Robin Hood.* Written by Howard Pyle. (Scribners, 1883.) Robin Hood becomes an outlaw and has many adventures with his Merry Men. These familiar stories tell of Robin's good-natured fights with Little John and Friar Tuck and of Robin being pardoned by King Richard.

89. *The Hitchhiker's Guide to the Galaxy.* Written by Douglas Adams. (Harmony Books, 1979.) This science fiction spoof is about a man, Arthur Dent, who escapes from Earth moments before it is destroyed by an alien construction team planning to build a galactic bypass. Arthur hitchhikes through the galaxy with his friend Ford Prefect, who is gathering information for a guidebook.

90. *The Scarlet Letter.* Written by Nathaniel Hawthorne. (Ticknor, Reed & Fields, 1850.) Set in Salem, Massachusetts, during the 1640s, this is the story of Hester Prynne. After an adulterous affair, she gives birth to a daughter and struggles to create a new life after being forced to wear the scarlet letter *A* as a symbol for her sin.

91. *Hoops.* Written by Walter Dean Myers. (Delacorte, 1981.) Lonnie is a Harlem teenager with a bright future. An excellent basketball player, he practices hard to get into the city tournament. Cal, his coach, is a former professional player and a man with a shady past. Before the championship, Cal gets a call from bettors who tell him to keep Lonnie on the bench and lose the tournament.

92. *No Crystal Stair: A Documentary Novel of the Life and Work of Lewis Michaux, Harlem Bookseller.* Written by Vaunda Micheaux Nelson. (Lerner Publishing Group, 2012.) Despite being told by a white banker "Negroes don't read," Lewis Michaux succeeds in opening a bookstore in Harlem that grows to become an intellectual and cultural center. Specializing in African American literature, he starts the store with only 500 dollars, an inventory of five books, and faith in the idea that the black community is hungry for knowledge, particularly of its own heritage. Michaux's bookstore, launched during the Great Depression, becomes an important meeting place during the civil rights era.

93. *The Pigman.* Written by Paul Zindel. (Harper-Teen, 1968.) John Conlan and Lorraine Jensen, two high-school sophomores, strike up a close friendship with Mr. Pignati, a lonely old man. They visit him every day after school. When Mr. Pignati suffers a heart attack, they agree to watch his house until he recovers. While he is hospitalized, they betray him by inviting friends to his house, ransacking it in a drunken party, and even destroying his deceased wife's cherished collection of porcelain pigs.

94. *Thirteen Reasons Why.* Written by Jay Asher. (Penguin Books, 2007.) Clay Jensen receives a mysterious shoe box full of cassettes. The cassettes explain to Clay and 12 others the role they each played in their classmate Hannah Baker's suicide. The book is a portrait of the cruelties of teen life.

95. *The Prince and the Pauper.* Written by Mark Twain. (James R. Osgood & Co., 1881.) Set in the 16th century, the novel tells the story of two look-alike boys. Tom Canty, a street urchin, lives with his abusive father, and Prince Edward is the son of King Henry VIII. When the boys meet and switch clothing, the palace guards mistakenly toss the prince out into the street. The pauper declares he is not the prince of Wales, but the king and the court don't believe him.

96. *Stargirl.* Written by Jerry Spinelli. (Knopf, 2000.) *Stargirl* centers on a nonconforming and compassionate 10th-grade student in Arizona named Susan "Stargirl" Caraway. She offends the sensibilities of her high school when she cheers for not only her own team but also the opposing team. In addition, she angers everyone by comforting an injured player from the opposing team. Her boyfriend narrates the story.

97. *How I Live Now.* Written by Meg Rosoff. (Penguin Books, 2004.) At the outbreak of World War III, Daisy is sent to stay with her cousins in the English countryside. She falls in love with her cousin Edmond. An invading army occupies England, and soldiers take over their remote farm, sending the boys and girls to different locations.

98. *One Flew over the Cuckoo's Nest.* Written by Ken Kesey. (Viking Press, 1962.) When the indomitable Randle Patrick McMurphy arrives in a male psychiatric ward, he effectively takes control of it from the Big Nurse, who has dominated the ward through fear and intimidation. His rallying of the patients starts out as a game but turns into a grim struggle with disastrous consequences. A large Native American member of the ward whom McMurphy calls Chief narrates the story.

99. *Daughter of Smoke & Bone.* Written by Laini Taylor. (Little, Brown Books for Young Readers, 2011.) This novel is a fantasy about the chimaera and the seraph, a reimagining of the idea of angels and demons. Seventeen-year-old Prague art student Karou has been raised by chimaera, who have bodies that are part human and part animal. Blue-haired Karou leads a double life: part of the time she is an ordinary teenager, and part of the time she runs mysterious errands collecting teeth for Brimstone, the chimaera who raised her. She becomes romantically involved with a winged seraph named Akiva. Like others of his kind, he is fighting to destroy the chimaera world.

100. *Nation.* Written by Terry Pratchett. (HarperCollins, 2008.) When a tsunami wipes out an island and wrecks a British ship, Mau, a boy from the island, and Daphne, a girl from the ship, survive the catastrophe. These teenagers from very different cultures learn to work together.

CHAPTER 5

Adults (Ages 18+)

Fiction gives us a second chance that life denies us.

—Paul Theroux

1. Rabbit (series). Written by John Updike. *Rabbit, Run*; *Rabbit Redux*; *Rabbit Is Rich*; and *Rabbit at Rest*. (Knopf, 1960–1990.) These novels follow the life of one-time high-school basketball star Harry "Rabbit" Angstrom over several decades, from young adulthood, through paunchy middle age, to his retirement and death. In 2001, Updike wrote a novella sequel, *Rabbit Remembered*, which continues with some of the main characters.

2. *Bring Up the Bodies.* Written by Hilary Mantel. (Henry Holt, 2012.) This novel brings new energy to a familiar story of English history. It is the sequel to *Wolf Hall* and the second part of a planned trilogy about Thomas Cromwell, chief minister and henchman to King Henry VIII. Set in 16th-century England following Henry's controversial annulment from his first wife, Catherine, *Bring Up the Bodies* deals with the downfall of his second wife, the audacious Anne Boleyn. Because she fails to produce a male heir to the throne, the king wants to get rid of her to marry the younger Jane Seymour. Ruthless Cromwell does the king's bidding, orchestrating Anne's trial and execution for treason and adultery.

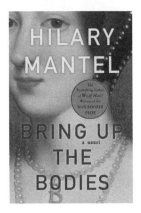

3. *This Is How You Lose Her.* Written by Junot Díaz. (Riverhead Books, 2012.) This is a collection of linked love stories, mostly about infidelity and relationships gone awry. At the heart of the collection is Díaz's alter ego Yunior, a macho, streetwise creative writing teacher and son of struggling immigrants from the Dominican Republic. Yunior is the same character who narrated parts of Díaz's novel *The Brief Wondrous Life of Oscar Wao* and *Drown*, his critically acclaimed collection of short stories. In *This Is How You Lose Her*, Yunior is perpetually chasing, abusing, losing, and missing women. He is likable, but is not a person you want to like. Yunior's popular, cancer-stricken brother Rafa is a recurring character in the stories and is an even bigger problem to women.

4. *Atonement.* Written by Ian McEwan. (Jonathan Cape, 2001.) At the heart of the novel is 13-year-old Briony Tallis's false accusation that Robbie Turner has raped her teenage cousin, which results in his imprisonment. Robbie and Celia, Briony's older sister, are lovers. After their lives are irrevocably changed by this tragic miscarriage of justice, Briony seeks atonement for what she has done.

5. *Lolita.* Written by Vladimir Nabokov. (Olympia Press, 1955.) Literature professor Humbert Humbert is an obsessive pedophile whose one true love is a 12-year-old girl name Lolita. The book is partly a commentary on American culture and partly a parody of its sexual perversions. Sexual scenes are not graphic in description, but the subject matter remains intensely controversial nonetheless.

6. *On the Road.* Written by Jack Kerouac. (Viking Press, 1957.) Drugs, alcohol, sex, Asian philosophy, freedom, and alienation from mainstream society are the defining elements of this road trip book about the Beats of the 1950s. Sal Paradise, the book's narrator, and Dean Moriarty are the central characters of a novel that presages the 1960s counterculture movement.

7. *The Corrections.* Written by Jonathan Franzen. (Farrar, Straus & Giroux, 2001.) This novel focuses on conflicts and issues within the Lambert family as they relate to the father's debilitating Parkinson's disease. Enid, his long-suffering wife; Gary, a banker; Denise, a chef; and Chip, a college professor who ends up working for a crime boss, all react in different ways. Things come to a head when Enid brings the family together for one last Christmas.

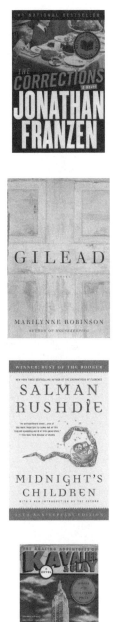

8. *Gilead.* Written by Marilynne Robinson. (Farrar, Straus & Giroux, 2004.) This novel is a fictional autobiography of the Reverend John Ames, a Congregationalist pastor in the town of Gilead, Iowa, who is dying of a heart condition. In the form of a letter to his young son, Ames tells his story, describing the tension between his father and grandfather, also Congregationalist ministers. Grandfather Ames was a fierce abolitionist who served in the Union army, while his son was an ardent pacifist.

9. *Midnight's Children.* Written by Salman Rushdie. (Jonathon Cape, 1981.) Saleem Sinai was born in a Bombay hospital at the stroke of midnight, at the moment of India's independence from Great Britain. Saleem, the narrator, is a poor Hindu who was switched at birth and raised as a rich Muslim, while Shiva, whom he was switched with, is raised in a Hindu tenement. Saleem is born with telepathic powers. He is destined to be an enemy of Shiva, who goes on to become an Indian war hero.

10. *The Amazing Adventures of Kavalier & Clay.* Written by Michael Chabon. (Random House, 2000.) Two Jewish cousins, Joe Kavalier and Sammy Klayman, make it big creating comic books. Klayman is a Brooklyn-born writer with a dream of creating comic book stories. Kavalier is a fine artist and refugee from Nazi-invaded Prague. Together they create the Escapist, a crime-fighting superhero.

11. *Cloud Atlas.* Written by David Mitchell. (Sceptre, 2004.) *Cloud Atlas* is a complex read. Six interlocking stories range from the 19th-century South Pacific to a distant, postapocalyptic future. The stories feature a clueless shipwrecked notary, a bisexual composer, a muckraking journalist, an imprisoned book publisher, a genetically engineered restaurant worker, and a Hawaiian goatherd.

12. *Invisible Man.* Written by Ralph Ellison. (Random House, 1952.) This novel recounts a black man's search for identity in a hostile world. An African American man who considers himself socially invisible tells his story in the first person.

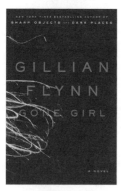

13. *Gone Girl.* Written by Gillian Flynn. (Crown Publishing Group, 2012.) In this thriller, Nick Dunne is suspected of killing his wife, Anne. The couple moves from New York to a small Missouri town after Nick is laid off from his job as a reporter. He opens a bar with the last of the money from his wife's trust fund, and their marriage goes progressively off course. On their fifth anniversary, Anne disappears. When Nick reveals that he has been having an affair, and the police find Anne's diary, Nick appears to be guilty, although no body has been found.

14. *Love in the Time of Cholera.* Written by Gabriel García Márquez. (Knopf, 1988.) Fermina Daza and would-be poet Florentino Ariza are enamored with each other until her father puts an end to their relationship. She instead marries Juvenal Urbino, a scientifically minded physician. After many years of marriage, Juvenal dies. Florentino goes to Fermina to declare that he still loves her.

15. *Possession.* Written by A. S. Byatt. (Chatto & Windus, 1990.) Two young modern-day scholars, Maud Bailey and Roland Michell, become obsessed with reconstructing the secret extramarital love affair between two Victorian poets. The relationship of Maud and Roland smolders on a parallel track.

16. *Ulysses.* Written by James Joyce. (Shakespeare & Co., 1922.) Irish writer James Joyce chronicles the passage of Leopold Bloom through Dublin during an ordinary day, June 16, 1904. The landmark stream-of-consciousness novel is divided into 18 chapters or episodes. The title of the book alludes to the hero of Homer's *Odyssey*, and there are many linkages between Joyce's novel and the epic poem.

17. *Billy Lynn's Long Halftime Walk.* Written by Ben Fountain. (Ecco, 2012.) This satirical novel follows 19-year-old Billy Lynn and the other surviving men of the Bravo Squad, soldiers who become sought-after heroes when Fox News captures their fierce battle with Iraqi insurgents on tape. Now the Bush administration has sent them on a nationwide tour to build support for the war, including spending Thanksgiving Day as guests of the Dallas Cowboys football team. Billy and the other soldiers are at the end of their "victory tour" and must return to Iraq. Surrounded by celebrities, wealthy admirers, and patriots, Billy deals with survivor's grief, finds love, and gains a new understanding of himself, his country, and what he has been fighting for.

18. *All the King's Men.* Written by Robert Penn Warren. (Harcourt, Brace, 1946.) Right-hand man Jack Burden tells the story of the rise and fall of Governor Willie Stark, a southern politician who begins with dreams of service to the common man and instead ends up a corrupt and ruthless political boss.

19. *The Handmaid's Tale.* Written by Margaret Atwood. (McClelland & Stewart, 1985.) In the futuristic Republic of Gilead, women are enslaved and valued according to their ability to reproduce. Women are not permitted to read, but they may listen to men read to them from the Bible. Homosexuals are sentenced to death. A woman named Offred, who functions as a handmaid or concubine, tells the story in the first person.

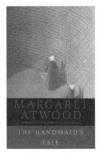

20. *Brideshead Revisited.* Written by Evelyn Waugh. (Chapman & Hall, 1945.) Charles Ryder narrates this story that centers on the deeply Roman Catholic Marchmain family. The youngest son, flamboyant Lord Sebastian Flyte, takes Charles to Brideshead, the family's palatial estate, where he introduces Charles to his sister Julia. Though Charles falls in love with Julia, they unwisely wed other people. They plan to divorce their spouses, but Julia changes her mind because to do so would be a sin.

21. *Housekeeping.* Written by Marilynne Robinson. (Farrar Straus Giroux, 1980.) After their mother commits suicide by plunging her car into a lake, Ruthie and Lucille Royce struggle with their loss and are raised by women family members in out-of-the-way Fingerbone, Idaho. For Ruthie, the narrator of the story, her deceased mother is a constant presence.

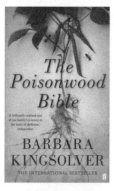

22. *The Poisonwood Bible.* Written by Barbra Kingsolver. (Harper Flamingo, 1998.) Baptist missionary Nathan Price moves his family from their comfortable home in Georgia to a remote village in the politically tumultuous Belgian Congo. The five women of the family, his wife Orleanna and their four daughters—Rachel, Leah, Adah, and Ruth May—each contribute to the story in alternating chapters. The family suffers great hardship when something terrible happens to one of the daughters. Nathan's culturally tone-deaf missionary work ultimately ends in failure.

23. *American Pastoral.* Written by Philip Roth. (Houghton Mifflin, 1997.) Nathan Zuckerman tells the story of Seymour "Swede" Levov, whose perfect life is turned upside down when his cherished daughter Merry commits an act of domestic terrorism. In protesting the Vietnam War, she plants a bomb in a post office that explodes and kills an innocent bystander. Merry goes into permanent hiding, and Swede is permanently separated from his pastoral life.

24. *White Teeth.* Written by Zadie Smith. (Hamish Hamilton, 2000.) Easygoing Archie Jones and devout Muslim Samad Iqbal are an unlikely pair who served together during World War II. Set in north London, the novel follows the trajectory of their friendship through marriage and parenthood.

25. *Bel Canto.* Written by Ann Patchett. (HarperCollins, 2001.) In an unnamed South American country, terrorists hold businessmen and politicians hostage in a house for several months. Somehow, romance grows in this unlikely setting in the form of a deep bond between singer Roxane Coss and business tycoon Katsumi Hosokawa, though they do not speak the same language. Mr. Hosokawa's gifted male assistant and a beautiful young terrorist woman conduct a secret love affair.

26. *Empire Falls.* Written by Richard Russo. (Knopf, 2001.) Miles Roby manages the Empire Grill in a small, dying blue-collar town in Maine. Miles is a decent man who dropped out of college to take care of his dying mother and lives with his teenage daughter above the diner. Though he left college with the expectation of staying maybe a year, he has made a life working for old Mrs. Whiting, who owns almost everything in town.

27. *Brave New World.* Written by Aldous Huxley. (Doubleday, 1932.) In this classic dystopian novel, individuality is sacrificed for physical pleasures and material comforts. The book begins with a hatchery tour that explains the society's rigid caste system. Embryos travel on a conveyer belt and are conditioned to belong to one of five castes: Alpha, Beta, Gamma, Delta, or Epsilon. The Alpha embryos are destined to become the leaders; each succeeding caste is conditioned to have lesser abilities.

28. *Love Medicine.* Written by Louise Erdrich. (Holt, Rinehart & Winston, 1984.) In the tradition of Native American storytelling, the novel adopts a conversational style, with a different person narrating each of the chapters. The book begins with a woman named June Morrissey, who freezes to death in a North Dakota snowstorm while trying to walk home to her reservation.

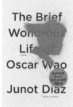

29. *The Brief Wondrous Life of Oscar Wao.* Written by Junot Díaz. (Riverhead, 2007.) The novel chronicles the life of Oscar de Leon, a fat Dominican boy growing up in New Jersey who hopes to become the next J. R. R. Tolkien. Oscar loves science and hopes to escape a curse that has haunted his family for generations.

30. *A Clockwork Orange.* Written by Anthony Burgess. (Heinemann, 1962.) In the not-too-distant future, Alex and his gang of teenagers go on nightly sprees of random violence and cruelty. When Alex is caught and sent to prison, he undergoes behavioral conditioning. While watching films of graphic violence, he receives injections that make him feel sick.

31. *Gone with the Wind.* Written by Margaret Mitchell. (Macmillan, 1936.) This novel is a sweeping account of a South ripped apart by the Civil War and the rupture of the slavery-supported plantation culture. At the center of the story is an epic romance between the fiery Scarlett O'Hara and roguish Rhett Butler.

32. *The Known World.* Written by Edward P. Jones. (Amistad Press, 2003.) Set in pre–Civil War Virginia, the novel deals with the uncomfortable reality of black slaves being owned by free black people, just as they were by whites. When black farmer and slave owner Henry Townsend dies, his plantation falls into chaos as his slaves begin to escape.

33. *The Yellow Birds.* Written by Kevin Powers. (Little, Brown & Company, 2012.) Two soldiers, 21-year-old Private Bartle and 18-year-old Private Murphy, struggle to stay alive during the brutal Iraq War. This novel of friendship begins when the two young men meet in boot camp, where Bartle pledges to Murphy's mother that he will keep her son safe. Bartle and Murphy encounter dangers and do things they never imagined. Murphy loses his grip on reality and is captured by Iraqi insurgents. Bartle, who narrates the book, reflects on how this happened and tries to deal with the aftermath.

34. *Middlesex.* Written by Jeffrey Eugenides. (Farrar, Straus & Giroux, 2002.) Protagonist Cal Stephanides is a man born with female characteristics. This novel follows the impact of a hermaphrodite gene that causes this condition on three generations of a Greek family, who are immigrants pursuing the American Dream.

35. *The Road.* Written by Cormac McCarthy. (Knopf, 2006.) A father and son travel across a grim postapocalyptic America years after a cataclysm destroyed most life and civilization. The boy's mother is not with them because she committed suicide. The pair cannot survive another cruel winter. They travel south in the hope of warmer weather, and life becomes treacherous as they encounter other humans who resort to cannibalism to survive.

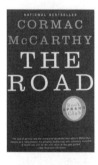

36. *On Beauty.* Written by Zadie Smith. (Penguin Press, 2005.) *On Beauty* is a snapshot of the politics of contemporary academic and family life. Howard Belsey is a white professor from England working at Boston College. He is married to an African American woman named Kiki, and the couple has two sons and a daughter and seems to be a liberal success story. However, their oldest son, Jerome, decided to embrace Christianity and conservatism and goes to work

for his father's right-wing academic rival, Monty Kipps. The book shapes up as a cultural war between Howard and Monty.

37. *The Remains of the Day.* Written by Kazuo Ishiguro. (Knopf, 1989.) This is a profile of Stevens, an old English butler, who reflects on and questions the life he has led in search of dignity and perfection. He concludes that his loyalty to the now-deceased Lord Darlington was misguided.

38. *The Sun Also Rises.* Written by Ernest Hemingway. (Scribners, 1926.) A group of American and British expatriates travel from Paris to the festival of San Fermín in Pamplona, Spain, to watch the running of the bulls. Jake Barnes, the protagonist, has suffered a war wound, which makes him impotent. He is in love with Lady Brett Ashley, a liberated Englishwoman.

39. *The Age of Innocence.* Written by Edith Wharton. (Appleton, 1920.) Newland Archer looks forward to marrying the seemingly passive and beautiful May Welland. The appearance of Countess Ellen Olenska, May's exotic and outspoken cousin, causes him to reconsider. He goes through with the marriage, but cannot get Ellen out of his mind.

40. *Years of Red Dust: Stories of Shanghai.* Written by Qiu Xiaolong. (St. Martin's Press, 2010.) This collection of 23 interrelated stories tells the fascinating tale of modern China—from the Communist Revolution, to the death of Mao, to the prodemocracy movement—from the perspective of the inhabitants of Red Dust Lane, a tiny Shanghai street. The stories show the different ways in which ordinary lives were shaped by larger events.

41. *As I Lay Dying.* Written by William Faulkner. (Random House, 1930.) This black comedy is about the death of Addie Bundren and her family's desire to honor her wish to be buried in the town of Jefferson, Mississippi. On the trip to Jefferson, the family encounters flooding. Because the bridges are washed out, they decide upon a river crossing. Their wagon overturns, the coffin is dumped into the water, and the mule team drowns.

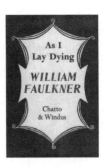

42. *Brick Lane.* Written by Monica Ali. (Scribner, 2003.) Eighteen-year-old Nazneen leaves her village in Bangladesh for an arranged marriage to a foolish man twice her age. They live in Brick Lane, a hub of London's Bangladeshi community, raising two daughters. Nazneen shakes off her domestic complacency when she has an affair with a younger man.

43. *Austerlitz.* Written by W. G. Sebald. (Random House, 2001.) An unnamed narrator tells the life story of Jacques Austerlitz, who arrived in Britain in 1939 as an infant refugee threatened by the Nazis. He is adopted and raised by a Welsh couple, and many years after their death, he goes in search of information about his past.

44. *The Bonfire of the Vanities.* Written by Tom Wolfe. (Farrar Straus Giroux, 1987.) Sherman McCoy is an arrogant but successful bond salesman married to a beautiful woman with a lovely daughter. They live in a penthouse apartment on the Upper East Side of New York. Sherman decides to have an affair with a woman named Maria, and when they seriously injure a black man in a hit-and-run accident, Maria leaves the country, and Sherman's world falls apart.

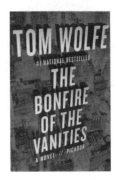

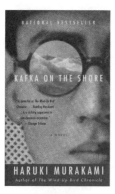

45. *Kafka on the Shore.* Written by Haruki Murakami. (Knopf, 2005.) Teenage Kafka Tamura runs away from home to escape an Oedipal curse and ends up in the town of Takamatsu. He spends his time in a library, imagining that the head librarian might be his mother. Meanwhile, an elderly man named Nakata is drawn to him. He cannot read or write, but he can speak to cats. Nakata's condition is the aftereffect of a strange World War II incident. The chapters of the novel alternate between Kafka and Nakata, and eventually their paths converge.

46. *Death Comes for the Archbishop.* Written by Willa Cather. (Knopf, 1927.) A Catholic bishop and a priest travel to recently acquired New Mexico Territory to establish a diocese. The devoted Frenchmen must contend with the well-entrenched Spanish-Mexican clergy they replace.

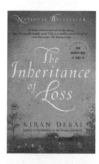

47. *The Inheritance of Loss.* Written by Kiran Desai. (Atlantic Monthly Press, 2005.) Biju is an illegal Indian immigrant with a miserable life who moves from one New York restaurant job to another, trying to stay out of the grasp of the Immigration and Naturalization Service. Sai is a girl living in the mountainous northeast corner of India with her grandfather Jemubhai, a retired judge, and his cook. The novel skillfully jumps back and forth between the worlds of Biju and Sai.

48. *Arcadia.* Written by Lauren Groff. (Voice, 2012.) The novel's protagonist, Bit Stone, is born on an upstate New York hippie commune named Arcadia, established in the 1960s by a few dozen idealists who wanted to live a simple and peaceful life as farmers. At first, the experimental community flourishes, but over the decades, its residents endure hardship and struggle to eke out even a poverty-level existence. When the commune eventually falls apart, Bit and his family make a new life in the outside world. Bit becomes a photography professor and marries the troubled daughter of Arcadia's spiritual leader. Now living in New York City, the soul of the now middle-aged Bit is still anchored to Arcadia.

49. *Ironweed.* Written by William Kennedy. (Viking Press, 1983.) Francis is a homeless alcoholic who is returning to Albany during the 1930s. Many years earlier, he deserted his family after accidentally dropping his infant son and causing his death. With his equally destitute companion, Helen, Francis sleeps wherever he can and eats at a mission. He considers visiting his long-lost family.

50. *The Kite Runner.* Written by Khaled Hosseini. (Riverhead Books, 2003.) In the tumultuous years of the Soviet invasion of Afghanistan and the rise of the Taliban, *The Kite Runner* focuses on the friendship between two boys: Amir, who is from a wealthy family, and Hassan, who is a servant to Amir's father. When Hassan refuses to give up Amir's kite, a bully rapes him, while Amir watches without intervening. Amir is consumed by guilt and avoids his close friend.

51. *The Maltese Falcon.* Written by Dashiell Hammett. (Knopf, 1930.) This action-packed detective story immortalizes the character of Sam Spade and launches the genre of the detached, hard-boiled detective with an eye for detail. The novel begins with the now iconic scene of a beautiful woman walking into the detective agency and asking Spade to follow a man.

52. *Wolf Hall.* Written by Hilary Mantel. (Henry Holt, 2009.) *Wolf Hall* is a fictionalized biography and the first installment of a trilogy, which covers the rapid rise to power of Thomas Cromwell in the court of Henry VIII. The novel is set in the period from 1500 to 1535. Against the wishes of the pope and Europe, Henry VIII decides to end his 20-year marriage to Catherine of Aragon and marry Anne Boleyn. The king needs a male heir to avoid the disaster of an English civil war. His wish is made possible through

the efforts of Thomas Cromwell, an astute politician and ruthless opportunist.

53. *The Name of the Rose.* Written by Umberto Eco. (Harcourt Brace Jovanovich, 1980.) The year is 1327. Brother William of Baskerville arrives at a Benedictine monastery in northern Italy to investigate allegations of heresy among the monks, and a series of murders overshadow his visit. The abbot asks him to investigate. Brother William uses his considerable intellectual powers to follow the clues and unravel the mystery.

54. *A Prayer for Owen Meany.* Written by John Irving. (Morrow, 1989.) Owen Meany is a small, odd, charismatic boy. He has a crush on his best friend's mother, Tabitha, and she likes him. One day at a Little League game, Owen hits a foul ball that strikes Tabitha on the head and kills her. Owen becomes the high-school valedictorian, goes on to college, gets a job escorting the bodies of dead soldiers back to their families, and dies in an airport saving the lives of Vietnam War orphans.

55. *Tree of Smoke.* Written by Denis Johnson. (Farrar, Straus & Giroux, 2007.) This novel is about Skip Sands, who joins the CIA in 1965 and works in psychological operations against the Viet Cong. The book traces the downfall of the main characters, who become crazed by the violence of combat.

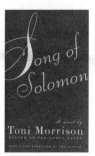

56. *Song of Solomon.* Written by Toni Morrison. (Knopf, 1977.) *Song of Solomon* follows the life of Macon Dead, a young African American male in search of his identity. His grandfather acquired the last name Dead from a Union soldier who mistakenly filled out his citizen documents. The family's actual name and its history are lost. Macon is nicknamed Milkman because his mother is seen nursing him well past infancy.

57. *To the Lighthouse.* Written by Virginia Woolf. (Hogarth Press, 1927.) *To the Lighthouse* tells the story of the Ramsay family and their visits to Scotland's Isle of Skye in the early 20th century. From the apparently minor postponement of a visit to a nearby lighthouse, Woolf constructs a novel that traces the complexities of family life. The book is introspective and follows the stream of consciousness of several characters.

58. *The Adventures of Augie March.* Written by Saul Bellow. (Viking Press, 1953.) In this coming-of-age novel, Augie is a poor boy who grows up in Chicago during the Great Depression. He leaves his home to find his way in a chaotic, alienating world.

59. *The Wind-Up Bird Chronicle.* Written by Haruki Murakami. (Knopf, 1997.) Toru Okada loses his job, his cat disappears, and his wife fails to return from work. When he searches for her and the cat, he encounters a strange cast of characters. A chain of events unfolds that makes Okada's seemingly ordinary life more complicated than it at first appears.

60. *Alias Grace.* Written by Margaret Atwood. (Nan A. Talese, 1996.) Set in mid-19th-century Canada and based on a true story, this is a psychological portrait of a seemingly mild-mannered servant girl sentenced to life in prison for the murder of her employer and his mistress. Her alleged coconspirator, a male servant in the household, was sentenced to death. But is she really guilty?

61. *Anna Karenina.* Written by Leo Tolstoy. (Thomas Y. Crowell, 1886.) In 19th-century upper-class Russia, Anna Karenina rejects her empty marriage and has an affair and a baby with handsome cavalry officer Count Vronsky. She begs her husband for a divorce and is shunned by society.

62. *Freedom.* Written by Jonathan Franzen. (Farrar, Straus & Giroux, 2010.) *Freedom* is a portrait of a midwestern family, an exploration of the soul of contemporary America, and a commentary on how the exercise of our freedom has tended to make us collectively more miserable. The central characters are Patty and Walter Berglund, progressive people who make compromises they never envisioned. Patty is an ex–college basketball star who becomes the perfect mother, wife, and suburbanite, but whose life goes wildly off track. Walter, an environmental lawyer, sells out to the coal industry. Joey, the son of the estranged couple, goes to work for a corrupt corporation profiteering from the Iraq War.

63. *Billy Bathgate.* Written by E. L. Doctorow. (Random House, 1989.) This novel is Billy Bathgate's first-person account of his transformation from errand boy to veritable son of mobster Dutch Schultz. The poor 15-year-old high-school dropout is in awe of flashy gangsters and their exciting world of money, sex, and violence.

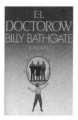

64. *Disgrace.* Written by J. M. Coetzee. (Viking Adult, 1999.) In postapartheid South Africa, David Lurie is a 52-year-old English professor who seems to lose everything. Disgraced when he seduces one of his students, he is fired from his teaching position. Lurie takes refuge on his daughter's farm and endures a violent attack by three teenagers in which he is assaulted and his daughter is raped and impregnated.

65. *The Blind Assassin.* Written by Margaret Atwood. (Nan A. Talese, 2001.) *The Blind Assassin* is a complex story-within-a-story centering on the recollections of Iris Chase and a science fiction novel written by her sister, Laura, who commits suicide by automobile.

66. *Cathedral.* Written by Raymond Carver. (Knopf, 1983.) *Cathedral* is a collection of twelve short stories, including a story for which the book is named. In "Cathedral," a blind man comes to a couple's home for a visit and the husband, who narrates the story, instinctively dislikes him. Strangely, at the end of the evening the husband and the blind man bond over a shared experience of what a cathedral looks like.

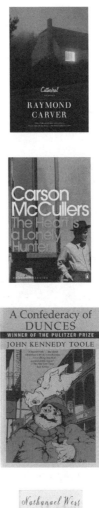

67. *The Heart Is a Lonely Hunter.* Written by Carson McCullers. (Houghton Mifflin, 1940.) A deaf-mute named John Singer and the people he encounters in a 1930s southern mill town drive the story. Each person, trying to escape his or her isolation, makes Singer his or her confidant. The book's heroine is a tomboyish girl named Mick Kelly who finds solace in her music.

68. *A Confederacy of Dunces.* Written by John Kennedy Toole. (Louisiana State University Press, 1980.) The book title comes from a Jonathan Swift quote: "When a true genius appears in the world, you may know him by this sign, that the dunces are all in confederacy against him." Ignatius J. Reilly is not a genius but an eccentric, pseudointellectual oddball who prefers medieval philosophy to the modern world. He cannot hold a job and is surrounded by strange characters.

69. *The Day of the Locust.* Written by Nathanael West. (Random House, 1939.) During the Great Depression, Tod Hackett works in Hollywood as a set designer. Through his eyes we see a broad group of odd B-grade outcasts who exist at the fringes of the movie industry, including a cocky dwarf, a fading vaudeville comic, and a repulsive child actor.

70. *A Flag for Sunrise.* Written by Robert Stone. (Knopf, 1981.) *A Flag for Sunrise* is a political thriller about Americans interfering in a small Central American country on the verge of a revolution, led by Marxist revolutionaries and a U.S.-backed dictator. The story follows a wide collection of characters, including a priest, a nun, an anthropologist, and a soldier of fortune.

71. *Dune.* Written by Frank Herbert. (Chilton Books, 1965.) Set on the desert planet Arrakis in the distant future, *Dune* is the story of young Duke Paul Atreides, the heir apparent to the planet. Arrakis is the only source of "spice" melange, the universe's most valuable substance, which grants psychic powers and enables interstellar travel. In an act of treachery, Atreides is cast out into the desert to die. Instead, he becomes the messianic leader of a desert army to reclaim what belongs to him and to his noble family. *Dune* is the first of five volumes.

72. *Howards End.* Written by E. M. Forster. (Edward Arnold, 1910.) *Howards End* revolves around three intertwined families representing three social classes in England. The Wilcoxes are rich capitalists, the Schlegel sisters are middle-class intellectuals, and the Basts are a struggling lower-middle-class couple.

73. *Life of Pi.* Written by Yann Martel. (Knopf, 2001.) Piscine Molitor "Pi" Patel is a teenage Indian boy whose passage to a new life aboard a ship full of zoo animals ends in a shipwreck. He must fend for himself on a life raft with an injured zebra, orangutan, hyena, and especially a Bengal tiger.

74. *The Human Stain.* Written by Philip Roth. (Houghton Mifflin, 2000.) Coleman Silk is a classics professor forced to resign because of an unfair accusation of racial prejudice. He has an affair with a woman half his age who works as a janitor at the college, which brings further condemnation.

75. *The Line of Beauty.* Written by Alan Hollinghurst. (Bloomsbury USA, 2004.) Gay Oxford postgraduate Nick Guest becomes a permanent houseguest in the home of the very wealthy Fedden family, who are in the inner orbit of Margaret Thatcher's Conservative Party. The heady atmosphere of sex, politics, and money transforms Nick's life.

76. *The Naked and the Dead.* Written by Norman Mailer. (Rinehart, 1948.) This gritty portrait of men at war is the story of a U.S. Army reconnaissance platoon on a Pacific island controlled by the Japanese during World War II. The novel depicts many conflicts within the army as it tries to drive out the Japanese. The story of combat is interspersed with background vignettes about the men.

77. *Lonesome Dove.* Written by Larry McMurtry. (Simon & Schuster, 1985.) A group of cowboys set out to make their fortune on a 2,000-mile cattle drive from the little town of Lonesome Dove, Texas, to Montana. The hazardous trip includes Indian attacks, lightning strikes, and impassable rivers. This epic Wild West novel is the first of four in a series.

78. *Angle of Repose.* Written by Wallace Stegner. (Doubleday, 1971.) Lyman Ward, a wheelchair-bound amputee with a failed marriage, decides to write about his grandmother, Susan Burling Ward. Married to a mining engineer, Susan and her husband travel to jobs in Colorado, California, and Mexico. The novel draws heavily on the actual letters and life of Mary Hallock Foote, an author and illustrator of American West stories.

79. *The Master.* Written by Colm Tóibín. (Scribner, 2004.) The book is a fictionalized biography of four years in the life of the self-effacing American novelist Henry James. It recreates his thoughts in a way that sheds new light on his aloof and lonely existence as a bachelor with an unresolved sexual identity. James comes across as approximating his own definition of an ideal writer, someone "on whom nothing is lost."

80. *The Lovely Bones.* Written by Alice Sebold. (Little, Brown, 2002.) Set in Norristown, Pennsylvania, *The Lovely Bones* is a novel of a teenage girl, Susie Salmon, who is raped and murdered by George Harvey, who lures her to an underground den in a cornfield, dismembers her body, and hides it in a sinkhole. She narrates the story from heaven. Susie's grief-stricken family members struggle to move on with their lives.

81. *Money: A Suicide Note.* Written by Martin Amis. (Viking, 1984.) This is a comedic portrait of a London advertising man, John Self, a hedonist who does everything to excess. In this story, Self is in New York shooting his first feature film, which will make him a lot of money.

82. *Old School.* Written by Tobias Wolff. (Knopf, 2003.) This novel is set in an elite prep school in 1960 where students write stories to compete for a private audience with great and famous writers. In order to get access to his hero, Ernest Hemingway, the book's narrator plagiarizes his story, an action that turns out to have profound consequences.

83. *The Moviegoer.* Written by Walker Percy. (Knopf, 1961.) At the start of the novel, Binx Bolling wakes up during Mardi Gras with the feeling that something more is needed in his life. Binx is a New Orleans stockbroker whose main activity is going to the movies because he finds more meaning there than in his actual life.

84. *A Passage to India.* Written by E. M. Forster. (Edward Arnold, 1924.) This novel focuses on the racial misunderstandings that shaped the interactions between the Indians and the English at the end of the British occupation of India. The book follows three English visitors to India, Miss Adela Quested, Mrs. Moore, and Cyril Fielding, and their friendship with Indian Dr. Aziz. Dr. Aziz is accused of raping Adela Quested.

85. *Mrs. Dalloway.* Written by Virginia Woolf. (Hogarth Press, 1925.) This day-in-the-life novel features Clarissa Dalloway, a high-society London socialite preparing to host a party that evening. Her mind travels back and forth between the current day in June 1923 and a variety of flashbacks. A visit by Peter Walsh reminds Clarissa of her momentous decision to marry the reserved Richard Dalloway instead of the more challenging Peter.

86. *Never Let Me Go.* Written by Kazuo Ishiguro. (Faber & Faber, 2005.) *Never Let Me Go* begins in an English boarding school for clones that are created to be organ donors. In this dystopian novel, Ruth, Tommy, and Kathy think they are special and accept the façade that they are objects of care and concern. As young adults, they are moved into cottages with nothing much to do. At the end of the novel, we learn that their lives are part of an experiment to decide if clones have souls.

87. *A Visit from the Goon Squad.* Written by Jennifer Egan. (Knopf Doubleday, 2010.) The novel is about people in the music business spanning 40 years. It focuses on Bennie Salazar, once a punk rocker and now a divorced, aging record producer, and on Sasha, his able and passionate assistant, who has a compulsion to steal. The book has a caste of loosely connected characters who tend toward self-destruction. Like a collection of short stories, Egan's novel moves the reader back and forth in time and place, and between styles and feelings.

88. *Portnoy's Complaint.* Written by Philip Roth. (Random House, 1969.) Alexander Portnoy speaks in a continuous monologue to his psychoanalyst in sexually explicit terms. This profane and funny masterpiece still generates controversy because of its depiction of obsessive masturbation and perceived anti-Semitism.

89. *Netherland.* Written by Joseph O'Neill. (Pantheon, 2008.) Hans van den Broek and his family are living in Lower Manhattan during the September 11 attacks. When his wife and son return to London, Hans feels lost. The Dutchman connects with other New York City immigrants and starts playing cricket at the Staten Island Cricket Club. Hans makes a friend in Chuck Ramkissoon, who is later found dead in the New York Canal.

90. *The Prime of Miss Jean Brodie.* Written by Muriel Spark. (Macmillan, 1961.) In Scotland during the 1930s, exemplary teacher Miss Brodie selects six 10-year-old-girls for special attention. She gives them a classical education, including an introduction to her politics. This elite set of girls later continues to have an almost cultlike attraction to Miss Brodie, although the one whom she considers her confidant eventually betrays her. Miss Brodie loses her job for encouraging fascism.

91. *Ragtime.* Written by E. L. Doctorow. (Random House, 1975.) Doctorow mixes famous people from history with his fictional characters in this picture of early 20th-century America, where anything goes. The lives of three families connect with those of well-known characters such as Harry Houdini, Sigmund Freud, Commodore Perry, Henry Ford, J. P. Morgan, and Emma Goldman.

92. *Schindler's List.* Written by Thomas Keneally. (Simon & Schuster, 1982.) Oskar Schindler, a flawed hero and industrialist, gambles everything to save 1,200 Jews from concentration camps by employing them in his factories. Following the war, his businesses fail, he separates from his wife, and he ends up living a meager existence.

93. *Rebecca.* Written by Daphne Du Maurier. (Doubleday, 1938.) A young bride is swept off her feet and brought by her handsome new husband to his isolated Manderley estate in England. At the manor house she is haunted by the memory of Rebecca, her husband's first wife. The housekeeper, Mrs. Danvers, is still loyal to the deceased Rebecca and intimidates the young woman, who is unnamed in the novel. The bride eventually learns that her husband killed Rebecca.

94. *The Satanic Verses.* Written by Salman Rushdie. (Viking, 1988.) Two Indian Muslim expatriates are trapped in a jet bound for Britain when it explodes over the English Channel. They fall into the ocean, are washed ashore, and then are miraculously transformed. Gibreel Farishta becomes an archangel and Saladin Chamcha becomes a devil.

95. *On Chesil Beach.* Written by Ian McEwan. (Nan A. Talese, 2007.) Edward and Florence are married and go to their wedding suite in a hotel on Chesil Beach to consummate their marriage. Both are virgins, and while Edward is eager, Florence feels nothing but fear and disgust.

96. *The Secret History.* Written by Donna Tartt. (Knopf, 1992.) This psychological thriller takes place at an elite New England college. When Richard Papen arrives at the school, he quickly become part of the inner circle of five gifted students who are all classical scholars. Untethered from normal morality, this group has already committed one murder and will commit another.

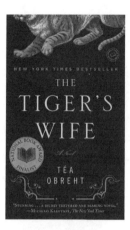

97. *The Tiger's Wife.* Written by Téa Obreht. (Random House, 2011.) A young doctor named Natalia works in a war-torn Balkan country besieged by secrets and superstitions. She learns that her ill grandfather died, supposedly on his way to meet her, alone and under suspicious circumstances in an isolated, ramshackle village. Natalia goes on a journey to investigate his death and follows the trail back to his early life. Recalling the stories her grandfather told her when she was growing up, she believes that her grandfather spent his final days searching for "the deathless man," who is linked to a World War II story from her grandfather's childhood involving an escaped tiger.

98. *The Sheltering Sky.* Written by Paul Bowles. (Lehmann, 1949.) Three young Americans—Kit and Port Moresby and George Tunner—travel to the Sahara Desert after World War II. After 10 years of marriage, Kit and Port have drifted apart, and Port hopes that this adventure will reinvigorate their relationship. The group does not anticipate the perils awaiting them in this alien environment.

99. *The March.* Written by E. L. Doctorow. (Random House, 2005.) *The March* is a retelling of Civil War history centered on glory-seeking General William Tecumseh's needlessly destructive march through the heart of the South. The host of characters includes freed slaves and soldiers on both sides of the war.

100. *Sophie's Choice.* Written by William Styron. (Random House, 1979.) The novel is narrated by Stingo, a young American writer from the South. He befriends Nathan Landau and his beautiful Sophie, a Polish survivor of the Nazi concentration camps. Sophie tells Stingo her terrible secret. When she arrived at Auschwitz, a doctor made her choose which of her two children would die immediately by gassing and which would remain alive in the concentration camp. Sophie chose to sacrifice her daughter and save her son. The crushing guilt ultimately leads to her suicide.

CHAPTER 6

Special Interests

I have always imagined that paradise will be a kind of library.

—Jorge Luis Borges

Adventures

PRESCHOOLERS

Curious George. Written and illustrated by H. A. and Margret Rey.
The Story about Ping. Written by Marjorie Flack. Illustrated by Kurt Wiese.
The Tale of Peter Rabbit. Written by Beatrix Potter.
Where the Wild Things Are. Written and illustrated by Maurice Sendak.

EARLY READERS

A Bear Called Paddington. Written by Michael Bond. Illustrated by Peggy Fortnum.
The Boxcar Children. Written by Gertrude Chandler Warner. Illustrated by L. Kate Deal.
Madeline. Written and illustrated by Ludwig Bemelmans.
My Father's Dragon. Written by Ruth Stiles Gannett. Illustrated by Ruth Chrisman Gannett.
Sylvester and the Magic Pebble. Written and illustrated by William Steig.

MIDDLE READERS

The Adventures of Tom Sawyer. Written by Mark Twain.

The Book of Three. Written by Lloyd Alexander.

Caddie Woodlawn. Written by Carol Ryrie Brink. Illustrated by Trina Schart Hyman.

Charlie and the Chocolate Factory. Written by Roald Dahl.

Homer Price. Written and illustrated by Robert McCloskey.

The Incredible Journey. Written by Sheila Burnford. Illustrated by Carl Burger.

James and the Giant Peach. Written by Roald Dahl. Illustrated by Nancy Ekholm Burkert.

Julie of the Wolves. Written by Jean Craighead George. Illustrated by John Schoenherr.

Mr. Popper's Penguins. Written by Richard and Florence Atwater. Illustrated by Robert Lawson.

Peter Pan. Written by J. M. Barrie. Illustrated by F. D. Bedford.

The Phantom Tollbooth. Written by Norton Juster. Illustrated by Jules Feiffer.

Pippi Longstocking. Written by Astrid Lindgren. Illustrated by Louis S. Glanzman.

Redwall. Written by Brian Jacques. Illustrated by Gary Chalk.

The Scorpio Races. Written by Maggie Stiefvater.

Stone Fox. Written by John Reynolds Gardiner. Illustrated by Marcia Sewall.

The Swiss Family Robinson. Written by Johann David Wyss.

Treasure Island. Written by Robert Louis Stevenson.

The Wind in the Willows. Written by Kenneth Grahame. Illustrated by Ernest H. Shepard.

The Wonderful Wizard of Oz. Written by L. Frank Baum. Illustrated by W. W. Denslow.

YOUNG ADULTS

The Adventures of Huckleberry Finn. Written by Mark Twain.

Blink & Caution. Written by Tim Wynne-Jones.

The Call of the Wild. Written by Jack London.

The Ear, the Eye, and the Arm. Written by Nancy Farmer.

Heart of Darkness. Written by Joseph Conrad.

The Hobbit. Written by J. R. R. Tolkien.

The Hunger Games (trilogy series). Written by Suzanne Collins.

The Lord of the Rings (trilogy series). Written by J. R. R. Tolkien.

The Merry Adventures of Robin Hood. Written by Howard Pyle.
Watership Down. Written by Richard Adams.

ADULTS

Life of Pi. Written by Yann Martel.
Lonesome Dove. Written by Larry McMurtry.
The March. Written by E. L. Doctorow.
The Sheltering Sky. Written by Paul Bowles.

Alphabet Books

PRESCHOOLERS

Chicka Chicka Boom Boom. Written by Bill Martin Jr. and John Archambault.
I Stink! Written by Kate McMullan. Illustrated by Jim McMullan.
Miss Bindergarten Gets Ready for Kindergarten. Written by Joseph Slate. Illustrated by Ashley Wolff.

EARLY READERS

Just in Case: A Trickster Tale and Spanish Alphabet Book. Written and illustrated by Yuji Morales.
Old Black Fly. Written by Jim Aylesworth. Illustrated by Stephen Gammell.

Animals

PRESCHOOLERS

Bark, George. Written and illustrated by Jules Feiffer.
Brown Bear, Brown Bear, What Do You See? Written by Bill Martin Jr.
Dear Zoo: A Lift-the-Flap Book. Written and illustrated by Rod Campbell.
Farmer Duck. Written by Martin Waddell. Illustrated by Helen Oxenbury
Goldilocks and the Three Bears. Retold and illustrated by James Marshall.
Good Night, Gorilla. Written and illustrated by Peggy Rathmann.

In the Tall, Tall Grass. Written and illustrated by Denise Fleming.
Is Your Mama a Llama? Written by Deborah Guarino.
Millions of Cats. Written and illustrated by Wanda Gág.
Oh, No! Written by Candace Fleming. Illustrated by Eric Rohmann.
Rosie's Walk. Written and illustrated by Pat Hutchins.
Seven Blind Mice. Written by Ed Young.
The Story of Ferdinand. Written by Munro Leaf.

EARLY READERS

Babe: The Gallant Pig. Written by Dick King-Smith. Illustrated by Mary Rayner.
Click, Clack, Moo: Cows That Type. Written by Doreen Cronin. Illustrated by
    Betsy Lewin.
Lyle, Lyle, Crocodile. Written and illustrated by Bernard Waber.
Martha Speaks. Written and illustrated by Susan Meddaugh.
Mr. Gumpy's Outing. Written and illustrated by John Burningham.
Olivia. Written and illustrated by Ian Falconer.
Over and Under the Snow. Written by Kate Messner. Illustrated by Christopher
    Silas Neal.
Where's Spot? Written and illustrated by Eric Hill.

MIDDLE READERS

Because of Winn-Dixie. Written by Kate DiCamillo.
Black Beauty. Written by Anna Sewell.
The Cricket in Times Square. Written by George Selden. Illustrated by Garth
    Williams.
The Incredible Journey. Written by Sheila Burnford. Illustrated by Carl Burger.
The Jungle Book. Written by Rudyard Kipling. Illustrated by John Lockwood
    Kipling.
Misty of Chincoteague. Written by Marguerite Henry. Illustrated by Wesley
    Dennis.
Mrs. Frisby and the Rats of NIMH. Written by Robert C. O'Brien. Illustrated by
    Zena Bernstein.
Mr. Popper's Penguins. Written by Richard and Florence Atwater. Illustrated by
    Robert Lawson.
Shiloh. Written by Phyllis Reynolds Naylor.
Stuart Little. Written by E. B. White. Illustrated by Garth Williams.
Where the Red Fern Grows. Written by Wilson Rawls.

YOUNG ADULTS

Animal Farm. Written by George Orwell.
Watership Down. Written by Richard Adams.
The Yearling. Written by Marjorie Kinnan Rawlings. Illustrated by N. C. Wyeth.

ADULTS

Life of Pi. Written by Yann Martel.

Bedtime

PRESCHOOLERS

Bedtime for Frances. Written by Russell Hoban. Illustrated by Garth Williams.
Five Little Monkeys Jumping on the Bed. Written and illustrated by Eileen Christelow.
Good Night, Gorilla. Written and illustrated by Peggy Rathmann.
Goodnight Moon. Written by Margaret Wise Brown. Illustrated by Clement Hurd.
Guess How Much I Love You. Written by Sam McBratney. Illustrated by Anita Jeram.
Harold and the Purple Crayon. Written and illustrated by Crockett Johnson.
How Do Dinosaurs Say Good Night? Written by Jane Yolen. Illustrated by Mark Teague.
Jesse Bear, What Will You Wear? Written by Nancy White Carlstrom. Illustrated by Bruce Degen.
Llama Llama Red Pajama. Written and illustrated by Anna Dewdney.
Nighttime Ninja. Written by Barbara DaCosta. Illustrated by Ed Young.
The Runaway Bunny. Written by Margaret Wise Brown. Illustrated by Clement Hurd.
Ten, Nine, Eight. Written and illustrated by Molly Bang.
Time for Bed. Written by Mem Fox. Illustrated by Jane Dyer.

EARLY READERS

Ira Sleeps Over. Written and illustrated by Bernard Waber.
Little Bear. Written by Else Holmelund Minarik.

The Napping House. Written by Audrey Wood. Illustrated by Don Wood.
Sleep Like a Tiger. Written by Mary Logue. Illustrated by Pamela Zagarenski.

Classics

PRESCHOOLERS

Blueberries for Sal. Written and illustrated by Robert McCloskey.
The Boxcar Children. Written by Gertrude Chandler Warner. Illustrated by L. Kate Deal.
The Carrot Seed. Written by Ruth Krauss. Illustrated by Crockett Johnson.
Curious George. Written and illustrated by H. A. and Margret Rey.
Frog and Toad Are Friends. Written and illustrated by Arnold Lobel.
Frog and Toad Together. Written and illustrated by Arnold Lobel.
Harry the Dirty Dog. Written by Gene Zion. Illustrated by Margaret Bloy.
Horton Hears a Who! Written and illustrated by Dr. Seuss.
The Lorax. Written and illustrated by Dr. Seuss.
Millions of Cats. Written and illustrated by Wanda Gág.
Pat the Bunny. Written and illustrated by Dorothy Kunhardt.
The Runaway Bunny. Written by Margaret Wise Brown. Illustrated by Clement Hurd.
The Story of Babar. Written and illustrated by Jean de Brunhoff.
The Story of Ferdinand. Written by Munro Leaf. Illustrated by Robert Lawson.
The Story about Ping. Written by Marjorie Flack. Illustrated by Kurt Wiese.
The Tale of Peter Rabbit. Written by Beatrix Potter.

EARLY READERS

Alexander and the Terrible, Horrible, No Good, Very Bad Day. Written by Judith Viorst. Illustrated by Ray Cruz.
Andy and the Lion. Written and illustrated by James Daugherty.
A Bear Called Paddington. Written by Michael Bond. Illustrated by Peggy Fortnum.
Caps for Sale. Written and illustrated by Esphyr Slobodkina.
The Cat in the Hat. Written and illustrated by Dr. Seuss.
Eloise. Written by Kay Thompson. Illustrated by Hilary Knight.
The Giving Tree. Written and illustrated by Shel Silverstein.
Green Eggs and Ham. Written and illustrated by Dr. Seuss.
Horton Hatches the Egg. Written and illustrated by Dr. Seuss.
How the Grinch Stole Christmas. Written and illustrated by Dr. Seuss.

The Hundred Dresses. Written by Eleanor Estes. Illustrated by Louis Slobbodkin.

The Little Engine That Could. Written by Watty Piper. Illustrated by George and Doris Hauman.

The Little House. Written and illustrated by Virginia Lee Burton.

Madeline. Written and illustrated by Ludwig Bemelmans.

Make Way for Ducklings. Written and illustrated by Robert McCloskey.

Mike Mulligan and His Steam Shovel. Written and illustrated by Virginia Lee Burton.

Stone Soup. Retold and illustrated by Marcia Brown.

The Velveteen Rabbit. Written by Margery Williams. Illustrated by William Nicholson.

MIDDLE READERS

The Adventures of Tom Sawyer. Written by Mark Twain.

Alice's Adventures in Wonderland. Written by Lewis Carroll. Illustrated by John Tenniel.

Anne of Green Gables. Written by L. M. Montgomery.

Black Beauty. Written by Anna Sewell.

Charlotte's Web. Written by E. B. White. Illustrated by Garth Williams.

Hatchet. Written by Gary Paulsen.

Heidi. Written by Johanna Spyri. Translated from German by Helen B. Dole.

Island of the Blue Dolphins. Written by Scott O'Dell.

The Jungle Book. Written by Rudyard Kipling. Illustrated by John Lockwood Kipling.

The Lion, the Witch, and the Wardrobe. Written by C. S. Lewis. Illustrated by Pauline Baynes.

Little House in the Big Woods. Written by Laura Ingalls Wilder. Illustrated by Garth Williams.

Little House on the Prairie. Written by Laura Ingalls Wilder. Illustrated by Garth Williams.

The Little Prince. Written and illustrated by Antoine de Saint-Exupéry.

Little Women. Written by Louisa May Alcott.

Mary Poppins. Written by P. L. Travers. Illustrated by Mary Shepard.

Peter Pan. Written by J. M. Barrie. Illustrated by F. D. Bedford.

Robinson Crusoe. Written by Daniel Defoe.

The Secret Garden. Written by Frances Hodgson Burnett. Illustrated by Tasha Tudor.

Stuart Little. Written by E. B. White. Illustrated by Garth Williams.

The Swiss Family Robinson. Written by Johann David Wyss.

Treasure Island. Written by Robert Louis Stevenson.

The Wind in the Willows. Written by Kenneth Grahame. Illustrated by Ernest H. Shepard.

Winnie-the-Pooh. Written by A. A. Milne. Illustrated by Ernest H. Shepard.

The Wonderful Wizard of Oz. Written by L. Frank Baum. Illustrated by W. W. Denslow.

YOUNG ADULTS

The Adventures of Huckleberry Finn. Written by Mark Twain.

Animal Farm. Written by George Orwell.

The Bell Jar. Written by Sylvia Plath.

Beloved. Written by Toni Morrison.

The Call of the Wild. Written by Jack London.

The Catcher in the Rye. Written by J. D. Salinger.

Catch-22. Written by Joseph Heller.

A Christmas Carol. Written by Charles Dickens.

The Color Purple. Written by Alice Walker.

Fahrenheit 451. Written by Ray Bradbury.

Frankenstein. Written by Mary Wollstonecraft Shelley.

The Giver. Written by Lois Lowry.

Go Tell It on the Mountain. Written by James A. Baldwin.

The Grapes of Wrath. Written by John Steinbeck.

The Great Gatsby. Written by F. Scott Fitzgerald.

Heart of Darkness. Written by Joseph Conrad.

The Hobbit. Written by J. R. R. Tolkien.

Jane Eyre. Written by Charlotte Brontë.

Kidnapped. Written by Robert Louis Stevenson.

Lord of the Flies. Written by William Golding.

The Lord of the Rings (trilogy series). Written by J. R. R. Tolkien.

The Merry Adventures of Robin Hood. Written by Howard Pyle.

The Moviegoer. Written by Walker Percy.

1984. Written by George Orwell.

One Flew over the Cuckoo's Nest. Written by Ken Kesey.

Pride and Prejudice. Written by Jane Austen.

The Prince and the Pauper. Written by Mark Twain.

The Scarlet Letter. Written by Nathaniel Hawthorne.

Slaughterhouse-Five. Written by Kurt Vonnegut.

The Sun Also Rises. Written by Ernest Hemingway.

The Sword in the Stone. Written by T. H. White.

To Kill a Mockingbird. Written by Harper Lee.
Twenty Thousand Leagues under the Sea. Written by Jules Verne.
Watership Down. Written by Richard Adams.

ADULTS

All the King's Men. Written by Robert Penn Warren.
Anna Karenina. Written by Leo Tolstoy.
As I Lay Dying. Written by William Faulkner.
Brave New World. Written by Aldous Huxley.
A Clockwork Orange. Written by Anthony Burgess.
A Confederacy of Dunces. Written by John Kennedy Toole.
The Day of the Locust. Written by Nathanael West.
Gone with the Wind. Written by Margaret Mitchell.
The Handmaid's Tale. Written by Margaret Atwood.
The Heart Is a Lonely Hunter. Written by Carson McCullers.
Invisible Man. Written by Ralph Ellison.
Lolita. Written by Vladimir Nabokov.
On the Road. Written by Jack Kerouac.
Portnoy's Complaint. Written by Philip Roth.
Rebecca. Written by Daphne Du Maurier.
The Sun Also Rises. Written by Ernest Hemingway.
Ulysses. Written by James Joyce.

Dystopia

MIDDLE READERS

Among the Hidden. Written by Margaret Peterson Haddix.

YOUNG ADULTS

Divergent. Written by Veronica Roth.
Fahrenheit 451. Written by Ray Bradbury.
Gathering Blue. Written by Lois Lowry.
The Giver. Written by Lois Lowry.
The Hunger Games (trilogy series). Written by Suzanne Collins.
1984. Written by George Orwell.
Son. Written by Lois Lowry.

ADULTS

Brave New World. Written by Aldous Huxley.
A Clockwork Orange. Written by Anthony Burgess.
The Handmaid's Tale. Written by Margaret Atwood.
Never Let Me Go. Written by Kazuo Ishiguro.
The Road. Written by Cormac McCarthy.

Fairy Tales, Fables, and Myths

PRESCHOOLERS

Goldilocks and the Three Bears. Retold and illustrated by James Marshall.
The Lion and the Mouse. Adapted and illustrated by Jerry Pinkney.
The Paper Bag Princess. Written by Robert N. Munsch. Illustrated by Michael Martchenko.
Seven Blind Mice. Written by Ed Young.
Tikki Tikki Tembo. Written by Arlene Mosel. Illustrated by Blair Lent.

EARLY READERS

Anansi and the Moss-Covered Rock. Written by Eric A. Kimmel. Illustrated by Janet Stevens.
Anansi the Spider: A Tale from the Ashanti. Written and illustrated by Gerald McDermott.
Andy and the Lion. Written and illustrated by James Daugherty.
Extra Yarn. Written by Mac Barnett. Illustrated by Jon Klassen.
John Henry. Written by Julius Lester. Illustrated by Jerry Pinkney.
Lon Po Po: A Red-Riding Hood Story from China. Translated and illustrated by Ed Young.
Mufaro's Beautiful Daughters: An African Tale. Written and illustrated by John Steptoe.
Rapunzel. Written by the Brothers Grimm. Retold and illustrated by Paul O. Zelinsky.
The Stinky Cheese Man and Other Fairly Stupid Tales. Written by Jon Scieszka. Illustrated by Lane Smith.
Strega Nona. Retold and illustrated by Tomie De Paola.
Swamp Angel. Written by Anne Isaacs. Illustrated by Paul O. Zelinsky.

The True Story of the Three Little Pigs. Written by Jon Scieszka. Illustrated by Lane Smith.

The Ugly Duckling, Written by Hans Christian Andersen. Adapted and illustrated by Jerry Pinkney.

MIDDLE READERS

The BFG. Written by Roald Dahl. Illustrated by Quentin Blake.

The Book of Three. Written by Lloyd Alexander.

D'Aulaires' Book of Greek Myths. Written and illustrated by Ingrid and Edgar Parin D'Aulaire.

Ella Enchanted. Written by Gail Carson Levine.

The Jungle Book. Written by Rudyard Kipling. Illustrated by John Lockwood Kipling.

The Whipping Boy. Written by Sid Fleischman. Illustrated by Peter Sís.

YOUNG ADULTS

American Born Chinese. Written by Gene Luen Yang.

The Dark Is Rising. Written by Susan Cooper.

The Merry Adventures of Robin Hood. Written by Howard Pyle.

The Sword in the Stone. Written by T. H. White. Illustrated by Robert Lawson.

A Wizard of Earthsea. Written by Ursula Le Guin. Illustrated by Ruth Robbins.

Families

PRESCHOOLERS

Come Along, Daisy! Written and illustrated by Jane Simmons.

In the Rain with Baby Duck. Written by Amy Hest. Illustrated by Jill Barton.

Knuffle Bunny Too: A Case of Mistaken Identity. Written and illustrated by Mo Willems.

"More More More," Said the Baby. Written and illustrated by Vera B. Williams.

No, David! Written and illustrated by David Shannon.

Pie in the Sky. Written and illustrated by Lois Ehlert.

The Relatives Came. Written by Cynthia Rylant. Illustrated by Stephen Gammell.

We're Going on a Bear Hunt. Written by Michael Rosen.

When Sophie Gets Angry—Really, Really Angry . . . Written and illustrated by Molly Garrett Bang.

EARLY READERS

Big Red Lollipop. Written by Rukhsana Khan. Illustrated by Sophie Blackall.
Blackout. Written and illustrated by John Rocco.
The Carrot Seed. Written by Ruth Krauss. Illustrated by Crockett Johnson.
A Chair for My Mother. Written and illustrated by Vera B. Williams.
The Gardener. Written by Sarah Stewart. Illustrated by David Small.
Grandfather's Journey. Written and illustrated by Allen Say.
Grandpa Green. Written and illustrated by Lane Smith.
The Hello, Goodbye Window. Written by Norton Juster. Illustrated by Chris Raschka.
Leo the Late Bloomer. Written by Robert Kraus. Illustrated by Jose Aruego.
Ling & Ting: Not Exactly the Same! Written by Grace Lin.
Little Bear. Written by Else Holmelund Minarik. Illustrated by Maurice Sendak.
Make Way for Ducklings. Written and illustrated by Robert McCloskey.
Owen. Written and illustrated by Kevin Henkes.
Owl Moon. Written by Jane Yolen. Illustrated by John Schoenherr.
Pecan Pie Baby. Written by Jacqueline Woodson. Illustrated by Sophie Blackall.
Tar Beach. Written and illustrated by Faith Ringgold.

MIDDLE READERS

Al Capone Does My Shirts. Written by Gennifer Choldenko.
All-of-a-Kind Family. Written by Sydney Taylor. Illustrated by Helen John.
Anastasia Krupnik. Written by Lois Lowry. Illustrated by Diane deGroat.
Because of Winn-Dixie. Written by Kate DiCamillo.
The Borrowers. Written by Mary Norton. Illustrated by Beth and Joe Krush.
Bud, Not Buddy. Written by Christopher Paul Curtis.
Dear Mr. Henshaw. Written by Beverly Cleary. Illustrated by Paul O. Zelinsky.
The Great Gilly Hopkins. Written by Katherine Paterson.
Heidi. Written by Johanna Spyri. Translated from German by Helen B. Dole.
Little House in the Big Woods. Written by Laura Ingalls Wilder. Illustrated by Garth Williams.
Little House on the Prairie. Written by Laura Ingalls Wilder. Illustrated by Garth Williams.

Little Women. Written by Louisa May Alcott.
A Long Way from Chicago. Written by Richard Peck.
Out of the Dust. Written by Karen Hesse.
The Phantom Tollbooth. Written by Norton Juster. Illustrated by Jules Feiffer.
Sarah, Plain and Tall. Written by Patricia MacLachlan.
Shiloh. Written by Phyllis Reynolds Naylor.
Sounder. Written by William H. Armstrong. Illustrated by James Barkley.
Tales of a Fourth Grade Nothing. Written by Judy Blume. Illustrated by Roy Doty.
Turtle in Paradise. Written by Jennifer L. Holm.
Where the Red Fern Grows. Written by Wilson Rawls.

YOUNG ADULTS

The Curious Incident of the Dog in the Night-Time. Written by Mark Haddon.
The First Part Last. Written by Angela Johnson.
Homecoming. Written by Cynthia Voigt.
Jacob Have I Loved. Written by Katherine Paterson.
M. C. Higgins the Great. Written by Virginia Hamilton.
Monster Calls: Inspired by an Idea from Siobhan Dowd. Written by Patrick Ness.
    Illustrated by Jim Kay.
One-Eyed Cat. Written by Paula Fox.
Pride and Prejudice. Written by Jane Austen.
Roll of Thunder, Hear My Cry. Written by Mildred Taylor.
Shabanu, Daughter of the Wind. Written by Suzanne Fisher Staples.
Sweet Whispers, Brother Rush. Written by Virginia Hamilton.
Walk Two Moons. Written by Sharon Creech.
The Yearling. Written by Marjorie Kinnan Rawlings.

ADULTS

The Corrections. Written by Jonathan Franzen.
Empire Falls. Written by Richard Russo.
Freedom. Written by Jonathan Franzen.
Gilead. Written by Marilynne Robinson.
Housekeeping. Written by Marilynne Robinson.
Howards End. Written by E. M. Forster.
The Line of Beauty. Written by Alan Hollinghurst.
The Lovely Bones. Written by Alice Sebold.

The Master. Written by Colm Tóibín.
Middlesex. Written by Jeffrey Eugenides.
On Beauty. Written by Zadie Smith.
The Poisonwood Bible. Written by Barbra Kingsolver.
To the Lighthouse. Written by Virginia Woolf.

Fantasy

PRESCHOOLERS

Abuela. Written by Arthur Dorros. Illustrated by Elisa Kleven.
Corduroy. Written and illustrated by Don Freeman.
Harold and the Purple Crayon. Written and illustrated by Crockett Johnson.
Horton Hears a Who! Written and illustrated by Dr. Seuss.
The Snowman. Illustrated by Raymond Briggs.
The Tiger's Wife. Written by Téa Obreht.
Where the Wild Things Are. Written and illustrated by Maurice Sendak.

EARLY READERS

Flotsam. Illustrated by David Wiesner.
Jumanji. Written and illustrated by Chris Van Allsburg.
Matilda. Written by Roald Dahl. Illustrated by Quentin Blake.
My Father's Dragon. Written by Ruth Stiles Gannett. Illustrated by Ruth Chrisman Gannett.
Sector 7. Written and illustrated by David Wiesner.
Tuesday. Written and illustrated by David Wiesner.

MIDDLE READERS

Alice's Adventures in Wonderland. Written by Lewis Carroll. Illustrated by John Tenniel.
The Borrowers. Written by Mary Norton. Illustrated by Beth and Joe Krush.
Bridge to Terabithia. Written by Katherine Paterson. Illustrated by Donna Diamond.
Charlie and the Chocolate Factory. Written by Roald Dahl.
Ella Enchanted. Written by Gail Carson Levine.
Harry Potter (series). Written by J. K. Rowling.

The Indian in the Cupboard. Written by Lynne Reid Banks. Illustrated by Brock Cole.

James and the Giant Peach. Written by Roald Dahl. Illustrated by Nancy Ekholm Burkert.

The Lion, the Witch, and the Wardrobe. Written by C. S. Lewis. Illustrated by Pauline Baynes.

The Little Prince. Written and illustrated by Antoine de Saint-Exupéry.

Peter Pan. Written by J. M. Barrie. Illustrated by F. D. Bedford.

The Phantom Tollbooth. Written by Norton Juster. Illustrated by Jules Feiffer.

Tuck Everlasting. Written by Natalie Babbitt.

The Wonderful Wizard of Oz. Written by L. Frank Baum. Illustrated by W. W. Denslow.

A Wrinkle in Time. Written by Madeleine L'Engle.

YOUNG ADULTS

Animal Farm. Written by George Orwell.

The Changeover: A Supernatural Romance. Written by Margaret Mahy.

Chime. Written by Franny Billingsley.

The Dark Is Rising. Written by Susan Cooper.

Daughter of Smoke & Bone. Written by Laini Taylor.

The Devil's Arithmetic. Written by Jane Yolen.

The Ear, the Eye, and the Arm. Written by Nancy Farmer.

Eragon. Written by Christopher Paolini.

The Golden Compass. Written by Philip Pullman.

Gossamer. Written by Lois Lowry.

The Hobbit. Written by J. R. R. Tolkien.

The Lord of the Rings (trilogy series). Written by J. R. R. Tolkien.

Monster Calls: Inspired by an Idea from Siobhan Dowd. Written by Patrick Ness. Illustrated by Jim Kay.

The Scorpio Races. Written by Maggie Stiefvater.

A Wizard of Earthsea. Written by Ursula Le Guin. Illustrated by Ruth Robbins.

ADULTS

Cloud Atlas. Written by David Mitchell.

Kafka on the Shore. Written by Haruki Murakami.

Midnight's Children. Written by Salman Rushdie.

The Satanic Verses. Written by Salman Rushdie.

Friendship

PRESCHOOLERS

City Dog, Country Frog. Written by Mo Willems. Illustrated by Jon J. Muth.

If You Give a Mouse a Cookie. Written by Laura Joffe Numeroff. Illustrated by Felicia Bond.

My Friend Rabbit. Written and illustrated by Eric Rohmann.

The Snowman. Illustrated by Raymond Briggs.

Timothy Goes to School. Written and illustrated by Rosemary Wells.

EARLY READERS

Frog and Toad Are Friends. Written and illustrated by Arnold Lobel.

Frog and Toad Together. Written and illustrated by Arnold Lobel.

George and Martha. Written and illustrated by James Marshall.

Mr. Rabbit and the Lovely Present. Written by Charlotte Zolotow. Illustrated by Maurice Sendak.

A Sick Day for Amos McGee. Written by Philip C. Stead. Illustrated by Erin E. Stead.

Will I Have a Friend? Written by Miriam Cohen. Illustrated by Lillian Hoban.

MIDDLE READERS

Among the Hidden. Written by Margaret Peterson Haddix.

Are You There God? It's Me, Margaret. Written by Judy Blume.

The Black Stallion. Written by Walter Farley.

Bridge to Terabithia. Written by Katherine Paterson. Illustrated by Donna Diamond.

Charlotte's Web. Written by E. B. White. Illustrated by Garth Williams.

The Cricket in Times Square. Written by George Selden. Illustrated by Garth Williams.

The Egypt Game. Written by Zilpha Keatley Snyder. Illustrated by Alton Raible.

Heidi. Written by Johanna Spyri. Translated from German by Helen B. Dole.

Holes. Written by Louis Sachar.

The Secret Garden. Written by Frances Hodgson Burnett. Illustrated by Tasha Tudor.

Stuart Little. Written by E. B. White. Illustrated by Garth Williams.

YOUNG ADULTS

The Cay. Written by Theodore Taylor.
Code Name Verity. Written by Elizabeth Wein.
Hoops. Written by Walter Dean Myers.
The Moves Make the Man. Written by Bruce Brooks.
The Outsiders. Written by S. E. Hinton.
The Pigman. Written by Paul Zindel.
A Prayer for Owen Meany. Written by John Irving.
Skellig. Written by David Almond.
The Yellow Birds. Written by Kevin Powers.

ADULTS

The Amazing Adventures of Kavalier & Clay. Written by Michael Chabon.
Cathedral. Written by Raymond Carver.
The Kite Runner. Written by Khaled Hosseini.
The Line of Beauty. Written by Alan Hollinghurst.
The Master. Written by Colm Tóibín.
Netherland. Written by Joseph O'Neill.
On the Road. Written by Jack Kerouac.
A Passage to India. Written by E. M. Forster.
The Remains of the Day. Written by Kazuo Ishiguro.
A Visit from the Goon Squad. Written by Jennifer Egan.
White Teeth. Written by Zadie Smith.

Historical Fiction

EARLY READERS

The Gardener. Written by Sarah Stewart. Illustrated by David Small.
Ox-Cart Man. Written by Donald Hall. Illustrated by Barbara Cooney.

MIDDLE READERS

Caddie Woodlawn. Written by Carol Ryrie Brink. Illustrated by Trina Schart Hyman.

Crispin: The Cross of Lead. Written by Avi.
Dead End in Norvelt. Written by Jack Gantos.
The Invention of Hugo Cabret. Written and illustrated by Brian Selznick.
Island of the Blue Dolphins. Written by Scott O'Dell.
Johnny Tremain. Written by Esther Forbes.
A Long Way from Chicago. Written by Richard Peck.
Number the Stars. Written by Lois Lowry.
One Crazy Summer. Written by Rita Williams-Garcia.

YOUNG ADULTS

Across Five Aprils. Written by Irene Hunt. Illustrated by Albert John Pucci.
The Astonishing Life of Octavian Nothing, Traitor to the Nation. Volume 1, *The Pox Party.* M. T. Anderson.
Beloved. Written by Toni Morrison.
Between Shades of Gray. Written by Ruta Sepetys
The Book Thief. Written by Markus Zusak.
Catherine, Called Birdy. Written by Karen Cushman.
A Christmas Carol. Written by Charles Dickens.
Code Name Verity. Written by Elizabeth Wein.
The Devil's Arithmetic. Written by Jane Yolen.
Go Tell It on the Mountain. Written by James A. Baldwin.
The Midwife's Apprentice. Written by Karen Cushman.
My Brother Sam Is Dead. Written by James Lincoln Collier and Christopher Collier.
The Prince and the Pauper. Written by Mark Twain.
Roll of Thunder, Hear My Cry. Written by Mildred Taylor.
The Scarlet Letter. Written by Nathaniel Hawthorne.
The Slave Dancer. Written by Paula Fox.
The True Confessions of Charlotte Doyle. Written by Avi.
The Witch of Blackbird Pond. Written by Elizabeth George Speare.

ADULTS

Alias Grace. Written by Margaret Atwood.
Angle of Repose. Written by Wallace Stegner.
Austerlitz. Written by W. G. Sebald.
The Bonfire of the Vanities. Written by Tom Wolfe.
Bring Up the Bodies. Written by Hilary Mantel.
Death Comes for the Archbishop. Written by Willa Cather.

Ironweed. Written by William Kennedy.
The Known World. Written by Edward P. Jones.
The March. Written by E. L. Doctorow.
The Name of the Rose. Written by Umberto Eco
On the Road. Written by Jack Kerouac.
Ragtime. Written by E. L. Doctorow.
Schindler's List. Written by Thomas Keneally.
Sophie's Choice. Written by William Styron.
Wolf Hall. Written by Hilary Mantel.

Humor

PRESCHOOLERS

Bark, George. Written and illustrated by Jules Feiffer.
Don't Let the Pigeon Drive the Bus! Written and illustrated by Mo Willems.
Duck on a Bike. Written and illustrated by David Shannon.
Go, Dog. Go! Written and illustrated by P. D. Eastman.
King Bidgood's in the Bathtub. Written by Audrey Wood. Illustrated by Don Wood.
Not a Box. Written and illustrated by Antoinette Portis.
Shark vs. Train. Written by Chris Barton. Illustrated by Tom Lichtenheld.
Sheep in a Jeep. Written by Nancy Shaw. Illustrated by Margot Apple.
Where's Spot? Written and illustrated by Eric Hill.
Where's Walrus? Written and illustrated by Stephen Savage.

EARLY READERS

Amelia Bedelia. Written by Peggy Parish. Illustrated by Fritz Siebel.
Animals Should Definitely Not Wear Clothing. Written by Judi Barrett. Illustrated by Ronald Barrett.
Caps for Sale. Written and illustrated by Esphyr Slobodkina.
Click, Clack, Moo: Cows That Type. Written by Doreen Cronin. Illustrated by Betsy Lewin.
Cloudy with a Chance of Meatballs. Written by Judi Barrett. Illustrated by Ronald Barrett.
Crictor. Written and illustrated by Tomi Ungerer.
The Day Jimmy's Boa Ate the Wash. Written by Trinka Hakes Noble. Illustrated by Steven Kellogg.
Martha Speaks. Written and illustrated by Susan Meddaugh.

Officer Buckle and Gloria. Written and illustrated by Peggy Rathmann.

The Stinky Cheese Man and Other Fairly Stupid Tales. Written by Jon Scieszka. Illustrated by Lane Smith.

There Was an Old Lady Who Swallowed a Fly. Written and illustrated by Simms Taback.

This Is Not My Hat. Written and illustrated by Jon Klassen.

The True Story of the Three Little Pigs. Written by Jon Scieszka. Illustrated by Lane Smith.

Tuesday. Written and illustrated by David Wiesner.

MIDDLE READERS

Ramona the Pest. Written by Beverly Cleary. Illustrated by Louis Darling.

Ramona Quimby, Age Eight. Written by Beverly Cleary. Illustrated by Jacqueline Rogers.

Where the Sidewalk Ends. Written and illustrated by Shel Silverstein.

Winnie-the-Pooh. Written by A. A. Milne.

YOUNG ADULTS

The Hitchhiker's Guide to the Galaxy. Written by Douglas Adams.

ADULTS

Money: A Suicide Note. Written by Martin Amis.

Literary Fiction

MIDDLE READERS

Anne of Green Gables. Written by L. M. Montgomery.

Charlotte's Web. Written by E. B. White.

YOUNG ADULTS

The Adventures of Huckleberry Finn. Written by Mark Twain.

Beloved. Written by Toni Morrison.

The Catcher in the Rye. Written by J. D. Salinger.
The Color Purple. Written by Alice Walker.
The Giver. Written by Lois Lowry.
The Grapes of Wrath. Written by John Steinbeck.
The Great Gatsby. Written by F. Scott Fitzgerald.
Lord of the Flies. Written by William Golding.
One Flew over the Cuckoo's Nest. Written by Ken Kesey.
Pride and Prejudice. Written by Jane Austen.
To Kill a Mockingbird. Written by Harper Lee.

ADULTS

The Adventures of Augie March. Written by Saul Bellow.
American Pastoral. Written by Philip Roth.
Arcadia. Written by Lauren Groff.
As I Lay Dying. Written by William Faulkner.
Atonement. Written by Ian McEwan.
Billy Bathgate. Written by E. L. Doctorow.
The Blind Assassin. Written by Margaret Atwood.
The Brief Wondrous Life of Oscar Wao. Written by Junot Díaz.
Bring Up the Bodies. Written by Hilary Mantel.
Cloud Atlas. Written by David Mitchell.
The Corrections. Written by Jonathan Franzen.
Disgrace. Written by J. M. Coetzee.
Empire Falls. Written by Richard Russo.
Freedom. Written by Jonathan Franzen.
Gilead. Written by Marilynne Robinson.
Housekeeping. Written by Marilynne Robinson.
Howards End. Written by E. M. Forster.
The Human Stain. Written by Philip Roth.
The Inheritance of Loss. Written by Kiran Desai.
Invisible Man. Written by Ralph Ellison.
Kafka on the Shore. Written by Haruki Murakami.
Lolita. Written by Vladimir Nabokov.
Midnight's Children. Written by Salman Rushdie.
Mrs. Dalloway. Written by Virginia Woolf.
On the Road. Written by Jack Kerouac.
Rabbit (series). Written by John Updike.
Song of Solomon. Written by Toni Morrison.
The Sun Also Rises. Written by Ernest Hemingway.

This Is How You Lose Her. Written by Junot Díaz.
To the Lighthouse. Written by Virginia Woolf.
Ulysses. Written by James Joyce.
Wolf Hall. Written by Hilary Mantel.

Love

PRESCHOOLERS

Guess How Much I Love You. Written by Sam McBratney. Illustrated by Anita Jeram.
Have You Seen My Duckling? Written and illustrated by Nancy Tafuri.
The Kissing Hand. Written by Audrey Penn. Illustrated by Nancy M. Leak.
Koala Lou. Written by Mem Fox.
Mama, Do You Love Me? Written by Barbara M. Joosse. Illustrated by Barbara Lavallee.
"More More More," Said the Baby. Written and illustrated by Vera B. Williams.

EARLY READERS

Rapunzel. Written by the Brothers Grimm. Retold and illustrated by Paul O. Zelinsky.
The Velveteen Rabbit. Written by Margery Williams. Illustrated by William Nicholson.

MIDDLE READERS

Sarah, Plain and Tall. Written by Patricia MacLachlan.
The Summer of the Swans. Written by Betsy Byars. Illustrated by Ted Coconis.

YOUNG ADULTS

Aristotle and Dante Discover the Secrets of the Universe. Written by Benjamin Alire Sáenz.
Brick Lane. Written by Monica Ali.
The Changeover: A Supernatural Romance. Written by Margaret Mahy.
Chime. Written by Franny Billingsley.
Daughter of Smoke & Bone. Written by Laini Taylor.

The Fault in Our Stars. Written by John Green.
The Great Gatsby. Written by F. Scott Fitzgerald.
The Hunger Games (trilogy series). Written by Suzanne Collins.
The Scorpio Races. Written by Maggie Stiefvater.
Son. Written by Lois Lowry.
Weetzie Bat. Written by Francesca Lia Block.
The Yearling. Written by Marjorie Kinnan Rawlings.

ADULTS

The Age of Innocence. Written by Edith Wharton.
Anna Karenina. Written by Leo Tolstoy.
Atonement. Written by Ian McEwan.
Bel Canto. Written by Ann Patchett.
Brick Lane. Written by Monica Ali.
Brideshead Revisited. Written by Evelyn Waugh.
Gone with the Wind. Written by Margaret Mitchell.
Lolita. Written by Vladimir Nabokov.
Love in the Time of Cholera. Written by Gabriel García Márquez.
Love Medicine. Written by Louise Erdrich.
On Chesil Beach. Written by Ian McEwan.
Possession. Written by A. S. Byatt.
Rebecca. Written by Daphne Du Maurier.
The Road. Written by Cormac McCarthy.
This Is How You Lose Her. Written by Junot Díaz.

Multicultural

PRESCHOOLERS

Abuela. Written by Arthur Dorros. Illustrated by Elisa Kleven.
Fiesta Babies. Written by Carmen Tafolla. Illustrated by Amy Córdova.
The Snowy Day. Written and illustrated by Ezra Jack Keats.

EARLY READERS

Amazing Grace. Written by Mary Hoffman. Illustrated by Caroline Binch.
Chato's Kitchen. Written by Gary Soto. Illustrated by Susan Guevara.
John Henry. Written by Julius Lester. Illustrated by Jerry Pinkney.

Mirandy and Brother Wind. Written by Patricia C. McKissack. Illustrated by Jerry Pinkney.

Mufaro's Beautiful Daughters: An African Tale. Written and illustrated by John Steptoe.

Tar Beach. Written and illustrated by Faith Ringgold.

MIDDLE READERS

All-of-a-Kind Family. Written by Sydney Taylor. Illustrated by Helen John.

Bud, Not Buddy. Written by Christopher Paul Curtis.

Esperanza Rising. Written by Pam Muñoz Ryan.

Grandfather's Journey. Written and illustrated by Allen Say.

Maniac Magee. Written by Jerry Spinelli.

The People Could Fly: American Black Folktales. Written by Virginia Hamilton. Illustrated by Leo and Diane Dillon.

The Watsons Go to Birmingham—1963. Written by Christopher Paul Curtis.

YOUNG ADULTS

The Absolutely True Diary of a Part-Time Indian. Written by Sherman Alexie.

American Born Chinese. Written by Gene Luen Yang.

Aristotle and Dante Discover the Secrets of the Universe. Written by Benjamin Alire Sáenz.

Beloved. Written by Toni Morrison.

The Color Purple. Written by Alice Walker.

Dragonwings. Written by Laurence Yep.

The First Part Last. Written by Angela Johnson.

Go Tell It on the Mountain. Written by James A. Baldwin.

The Joy Luck Club. Written by Amy Tan.

M. C. Higgins the Great. Written by Virginia Hamilton.

Monster. Written by Walter Dean Myers.

No Crystal Stair: A Documentary Novel of the Life and Work of Lewis Michaux, Harlem Bookseller. Written by Vaunda Micheaux Nelson.

Roll of Thunder, Hear My Cry. Written by Mildred Taylor.

Shabanu, Daughter of the Wind. Written by Suzanne Fisher Staples.

ADULTS

Brick Lane. Written by Monica Ali.

The Brief Wondrous Life of Oscar Wao. Written by Junot Díaz.

The Inheritance of Loss. Written by Kiran Desai.
Invisible Man. Written by Ralph Ellison.
The Kite Runner. Written by Khaled Hosseini.
The Known World. Written by Edward P. Jones.
Love Medicine. Written by Louise Erdrich.
Middlesex. Written by Jeffrey Eugenides.
The Poisonwood Bible. Written by Barbra Kingsolver.
Song of Solomon. Written by Toni Morrison.
This Is How You Lose Her. Written by Junot Díaz.
Years of Red Dust: Stories of Shanghai. Written by Qiu Xiaolong.

Mystery

MIDDLE READERS

Bunnicula: A Rabbit Tale of Mystery. Written by Deborah Howe and James Howe. Illustrated by Alan Daniel.
The Egypt Game. Written by Zilpha Keatley Snyder. Illustrated by Alton Raible.
From the Mixed-Up Files of Mrs. Basil E. Frankweiler. Written and illustrated by E. L. Konigsburg.
Harriet the Spy. Written and illustrated by Louise Fitzhugh.
Splendors and Glooms. Written by Laura Amy Schlitz.
When You Reach Me. Written by Rebecca Stead.
Wonderstruck. Written and illustrated by Brian Selznick.

YOUNG ADULTS

Blink & Caution. Written by Tim Wynne-Jones.
The Curious Incident of the Dog in the Night-Time. Written by Mark Haddon.
The Westing Game. Written by Ellen Raskin.

ADULTS

Gone Girl. Written by Gillian Flynn.
The Maltese Falcon. Written by Dashiell Hammett.
The Name of the Rose. Written by Umberto Eco.
The Secret History. Written by Donna Tartt.
The Tiger's Wife. Written by Téa Obreht.
The Wind-Up Bird Chronicle. Written by Haruki Murakami.

Perseverance

PRESCHOOLERS

Angelina Ballerina. Written by Katharine Holabird. Illustrated by Helen Craig.
Don't Let the Pigeon Drive the Bus! Written and illustrated by Mo Willems.

EARLY READERS

Amazing Grace. Written by Mary Hoffman. Illustrated by Caroline Binch.
The Carrot Seed. Written by Ruth Krauss. Illustrated by Crockett Johnson.
Green Eggs and Ham. Written and illustrated by Dr. Seuss.
Horton Hatches the Egg. Written and illustrated by Dr. Seuss.
John Henry. Written by Julius Lester. Illustrated by Jerry Pinkney.
The Little Engine That Could. Written by Watty Piper. Illustrated by George
    and Doris Hauman.
Mirandy and Brother Wind. Written by Patricia C. McKissack. Illustrated by
    Jerry Pinkney.
Whistle for Willie. Written and illustrated by Ezra Jack Keats.

MIDDLE READERS

Okay for Now. Written by Gary D. Schmidt.

YOUNG ADULTS

Between Shades of Gray. Written by Ruta Sepetys.
*No Crystal Stair: A Documentary Novel of the Life and Work of Lewis Michaux,
    Harlem Bookseller.* Written by Vaunda Micheaux Nelson.

Picture Books

PRESCHOOLERS

City Dog, Country Frog. Written by Mo Willems. Illustrated by Jon J. Muth.
Color Zoo. Written and illustrated by Lois Ehlert.
Corduroy. Written and illustrated by Don Freeman.
Doctor De Soto. Written and illustrated by William Steig.

Ella Sarah Gets Dressed. Written and illustrated by Margaret Chodos-Irvine.

Freight Train. Written and illustrated by Donald Crews.

Go Away, Big Green Monster. Written and illustrated by Ed Emberley.

Good Night, Gorilla. Written and illustrated by Peggy Rathmann.

Happy Birthday, Moon. Written and illustrated by Frank Asch.

In the Night Kitchen. Written and illustrated by Maurice Sendak

Kitten's First Full Moon. Written and illustrated by Kevin Henkes.

Knuffle Bunny: A Cautionary Tale. Written and illustrated by Mo Willems.

The Lion and the Mouse. Adapted and illustrated by Jerry Pinkney.

Mouse Paint. Written and illustrated by Ellen Stoll Walsh.

Mr. Gumpy's Outing. Written and illustrated by John Burningham.

My Friend Rabbit. Written and illustrated by Eric Rohmann.

Oh, No! Written by Candace Fleming. Illustrated by Eric Rohmann.

One Fine Day. Written and illustrated by Nonny Hogrogian.

Owl Babies. Written and illustrated by Martin Waddell.

The Quiet Book. Written by Deborah Underwood. Illustrated by Renata Liwska.

The Rainbow Fish. Written and illustrated by Marcus Pfister.

The Relatives Came. Written by Cynthia Rylant. Illustrated by Stephen Gammell.

Snow. Written and illustrated by Uri Shulevitz.

The Snowman. Illustrated by Raymond Briggs.

The Snowy Day. Written and illustrated by Ezra Jack Keats.

Swimmy. Written and illustrated by Leo Lionni.

There Was an Old Lady Who Swallowed a Fly. Written and illustrated by Simms Taback.

Tikki Tikki Tembo. Written by Arlene Mosel. Illustrated by Blair Lent.

The Ugly Duckling, Written by Hans Christian Andersen. Adapted and illustrated by Jerry Pinkney.

The Very Hungry Caterpillar. Written and illustrated by Eric Carle.

EARLY READERS

Are You My Mother? Written and illustrated by P. D. Eastman.

Click, Clack, Moo: Cows That Type. Written by Doreen Cronin. Illustrated by Betsy Lewin.

Clifford the Big Red Dog. Written and illustrated by Norman Bridwell.

The Doorbell Rang. Written and illustrated by Pat Hutchins.

Flotsam. Illustrated by David Wiesner.

Frederick. Written and illustrated by Leo Lionni.

The Hello, Goodbye Window. Written by Norton Juster. Illustrated by Chris Raschka.

Henry and Mudge. Written by Cynthia Rylant. Illustrated by Suçie Stevenson.
How to Heal a Broken Wing. Written and illustrated by Bob Graham.
Joseph Had a Little Overcoat. Written and illustrated by Simms Taback.
Jumanji. Written and illustrated by Chris Van Allsburg.
Lilly's Purple Plastic Purse. Written and illustrated by Kevin Henkes.
Little Bear. Written by Else Holmelund Minarik. Illustrated by Maurice Sendak.
Lon Po Po: A Red-Riding Hood Story from China. Translated and illustrated by
    Ed Young.
Lyle, Lyle, Crocodile. Written and illustrated by Bernard Waber.
Madeline. Written and illustrated by Ludwig Bemelmans.
Make Way for Ducklings. Written and illustrated by Robert McCloskey.
Mirandy and Brother Wind. Written by Patricia C. McKissack. Illustrated by
    Jerry Pinkney.
Miss Rumphius. Written and illustrated by Barbara Cooney.
Officer Buckle and Gloria. Written and illustrated by Peggy Rathmann.
Olivia. Written and illustrated by Ian Falconer.
Owl Moon. Written by Jane Yolen. Illustrated by John Schoenherr.
The Polar Express. Written and illustrated by Chris Van Allsburg.
Sector 7. Written and illustrated by David Wiesner.
Stellaluna. Written and illustrated by Janell Cannon.
Stone Soup. Retold and illustrated by Marcia Brown.
Sylvester and the Magic Pebble. Written and illustrated by William Steig.
Tuesday. Written and illustrated by David Wiesner.

MIDDLE READERS

The Arrival. Illustrated by Shaun Tan.
The Dreamer. Written by Pam Muñoz Ryan. Illustrated by Peter Sís.
The Invention of Hugo Cabret. Written and illustrated by Brian Selznick.

YOUNG ADULTS

American Born Chinese. Written by Gene Luen Yang.

Read-Aloud Books

PRESCHOOLERS

Chicka Chicka Boom Boom. Written by Bill Martin Jr. and John Archambault.
    Illustrated by Lois Ehlert.

Chicken Soup with Rice: A Book of Months. Written and illustrated by Maurice Sendak.

Froggy Gets Dressed. Written by Jonathan London. Illustrated by Frank Remkiewicz.

How Do Dinosaurs Say Good Night? Written by Jane Yolen. Illustrated by Mark Teague.

I Must Have Bobo! Written and illustrated by Eileen Rosenthal.

The Little Mouse, the Red Ripe Strawberry, and the Big Hungry Bear. Written by Audrey Wood. Illustrated by Don Wood.

The Lorax. Written and illustrated by Dr. Seuss.

Oh, No! Written by Candace Fleming. Illustrated by Eric Rohmann.

Press Here. Written and illustrated by Hervé Tullet.

EARLY READERS

Alexander and the Terrible, Horrible, No Good, Very Bad Day. Written by Judith Viorst. Illustrated by Ray Cruz.

Bread and Jam for Frances. Written by Russell Hoban. Illustrated by Lillian Hoban.

Caps for Sale. Written and illustrated by Esphyr Slobodkina.

The Cat in the Hat. Written and illustrated by Dr. Seuss.

A Couple of Boys Have the Best Week Ever. Written and illustrated by Marla Frazee.

Eloise. Written by Kay Thompson. Illustrated by Hilary Knight.

Green Eggs and Ham. Written and illustrated by Dr. Seuss.

The Hundred Dresses. Written by Eleanor Estes. Illustrated by Louis Slobbodkin.

Ira Sleeps Over. Written and illustrated by Bernard Waber.

Miss Rumphius. Written and illustrated by Barbara Cooney.

The Mitten. Written and illustrated by Jan Brett.

MIDDLE READERS

The Borrowers. Written by Mary Norton. Illustrated by Beth and Joe Krush.

Bridge to Terabithia. Written by Katherine Paterson. Illustrated by Donna Diamond.

The Great Gilly Hopkins. Written by Katherine Paterson.

Pippi Longstocking. Written by Astrid Lindgren. Illustrated by Louis S. Glanzman.

The Secret Garden. Written by Frances Hodgson Burnett. Illustrated by Tasha Tudor.

The Whipping Boy. Written by Sid Fleischman. Illustrated by Peter Sís.

Recent Fiction

PRESCHOOLERS

City Dog, Country Frog. Written by Mo Willems. Illustrated by Jon J. Muth.
Fiesta Babies. Written by Carmen Tafolla. Illustrated by Amy Córdova.
I Must Have Bobo! Written and illustrated by Eileen Rosenthal.
Nighttime Ninja. Written by Barbara DaCosta. Illustrated by Ed Young.
Oh, No! Written by Candace Fleming. Illustrated by Eric Rohmann.
Pirates Don't Take Baths. Written and illustrated by John Segal.
Pocketful of Posies: A Treasury of Nursery Rhymes. Compiled and illustrated by Salley Mavor.
Press Here. Written and illustrated by Hervé Tullet.
The Quiet Book. Written by Deborah Underwood. Illustrated by Renata Liwska.
Shark vs. Train. Written by Chris Barton. Illustrated by Tom Lichtenheld.
Ten Little Caterpillars. Written by Bill Martin Jr. Illustrated by Lois Ehlert.
Where's Walrus? Written and illustrated by Stephen Savage.

EARLY READERS

Big Red Lollipop. Written by Rukhsana Khan. Illustrated by Sophie Blackall.
Blackout. Written and illustrated by John Rocco.
Extra Yarn. Written by Mac Barnett. Illustrated by Jon Klassen.
Grandpa Green. Written and illustrated by Lane Smith.
Ling & Ting: Not Exactly the Same! Written by Grace Lin.
Over and Under the Snow. Written by Kate Messner. Illustrated by Christopher Silas Neal.
Pecan Pie Baby. Written by Jacqueline Woodson. Illustrated by Sophie Blackall.
A Sick Day for Amos McGee. Written by Philip C. Stead. Illustrated by Erin E. Stead.
Sleep Like a Tiger. Written by Mary Logue. Illustrated by Pamela Zagarenski.
This Is Not My Hat. Written and illustrated by Jon Klassen.

MIDDLE READERS

Dead End in Norvelt. Written by Jack Gantos.
The Dreamer. Written by Pam Muñoz Ryan.

Inside Out and Back Again. Written by Thanhha Lai.
Ninth Ward. Written by Jewell Parker Rhodes.
Okay for Now. Written by Gary D. Schmidt.
One Crazy Summer. Written by Rita Williams-Garcia.
Splendors and Glooms. Written by Laura Amy Schlitz.
Turtle in Paradise. Written by Jennifer L. Holm.
Wonder. Written by R. J. Palacio.
Wonderstruck. Written and illustrated by Brian Selznick.

YOUNG ADULTS

Aristotle and Dante Discover the Secrets of the Universe. Written by Benjamin
    Alire Sáenz.
Between Shades of Gray. Written by Ruta Sepetys.
Blink & Caution. Written by Tim Wynne-Jones.
Chime. Written by Franny Billingsley.
Code Name Verity. Written by Elizabeth Wein.
Daughter of Smoke & Bone. Written by Laini Taylor.
Divergent. Written by Veronica Roth.
The Fault in Our Stars. Written by John Green.
The Hunger Games (trilogy series). Written by Suzanne Collins.
Monster Calls: Inspired by an Idea from Siobhan Dowd. Written by Patrick Ness.
    Illustrated by Jim Kay.
Never Fall Down. Written by Patricia McCormick.
*No Crystal Stair: A Documentary Novel of the Life and Work of Lewis Michaux,
    Harlem Bookseller.* Written by Vaunda Micheaux Nelson.
Son. Written by Lois Lowry.

ADULTS

Arcadia. Written by Lauren Groff.
Bring Up the Bodies. Written by Hilary Mantel.
Freedom. Written by Jonathan Franzen.
Gone Girl. Written by Gillian Flynn.
This Is How You Lose Her. Written by Junot Díaz.
The Tiger's Wife. Written by Téa Obreht.
A Visit from the Goon Squad. Written by Jennifer Egan.

Years of Red Dust: Stories of Shanghai. Written by Qiu Xiaolong.
The Yellow Birds. Written by Kevin Powers.

Rhyme and Verse

PRESCHOOLERS

Brown Bear, Brown Bear, What Do You See? Written by Bill Martin Jr. and illustrated by Eric Carle.

Chicka Chicka Boom Boom. Written by Bill Martin Jr. and John Archambault. Illustrated by Lois Ehlert.

Chicken Soup with Rice: A Book of Months. Written and illustrated by Maurice Sendak.

Fiesta Babies. Written by Carmen Tafolla. Illustrated by Amy Córdova.

How Do Dinosaurs Say Good Night? Written by Jane Yolen. Illustrated by Mark Teague.

In the Tall, Tall Grass. Written and illustrated by Denise Fleming.

Is Your Mama a Llama? Written by Deborah Guarino. Illustrated by Steven Kellogg.

Jamberry. Written and illustrated by Bruce Degen.

Jesse Bear, What Will You Wear? Written by Nancy White Carlstrom. Illustrated by Bruce Degen.

Llama Llama Red Pajama. Written and illustrated by Anna Dewdney.

Pocketful of Posies: A Treasury of Nursery Rhymes. Compiled and illustrated by Salley Mavor.

Sheep in a Jeep. Written by Nancy Shaw. Illustrated by Margot Apple.

Ten Little Caterpillars. Written by Bill Martin Jr. Illustrated by Lois Ehlert.

Time for Bed. Written by Mem Fox. Illustrated by Jane Dyer.

EARLY READERS

Old Black Fly. Written by Jim Aylesworth. Illustrated by Stephen Gammell.

MIDDLE READERS

Inside Out and Back Again. Written by Thanhha Lai.
Where the Sidewalk Ends. Written and illustrated by Shel Silverstein.

School Life

PRESCHOOLERS

Knuffle Bunny Too: A Case of Mistaken Identity. Written and illustrated by Mo Willems.

Miss Bindergarten Gets Ready for Kindergarten. Written by Joseph Slate. Illustrated by Ashley Wolff.

Off to School, Baby Duck! Written by Amy Hest. Illustrated by Jill Barton.

Timothy Goes to School. Written and illustrated by Rosemary Wells.

EARLY READERS

Chrysanthemum. Written and illustrated by Kevin Henkes.

Crictor. Written and illustrated by Tomi Ungerer.

Lilly's Purple Plastic Purse. Written and illustrated by Kevin Henkes.

Miss Nelson Is Missing! Written by Harry Allard. Illustrated by James Marshall.

Owen. Written and illustrated by Kevin Henkes.

Will I Have a Friend? Written by Miriam Cohen. Illustrated by Lillian Hoban.

MIDDLE READERS

Dear Mr. Henshaw. Written by Beverly Cleary. Illustrated by Paul O. Zelinsky.

Frindle. Written by Andrew Clements. Illustrated by Brian Selznick.

Harriet the Spy. Written and illustrated by Louise Fitzhugh.

Hoot. Written by Carl Hiaasen.

Inside Out and Back Again. Written by Thanhha Lai.

Nothing but the Truth. Written by Avi.

Ramona the Pest. Written by Beverly Cleary. Illustrated by Louis Darling.

Ramona Quimby, Age Eight. Written by Beverly Cleary. Illustrated by Jacqueline Rogers.

Wonder. Written by R. J. Palacio.

YOUNG ADULTS

The Absolutely True Diary of a Part-Time Indian. Written by Sherman Alexie. Illustrated by Ellen Forney.

American Born Chinese. Written by Gene Luen Yang.

The Chocolate War. Written by Robert Cormier.
Hoops. Written by Walter Dean Myers.
The Moves Make the Man. Written by Bruce Brooks.
Stargirl. Written by Jerry Spinelli.
Thirteen Reasons Why. Written by Jay Asher.

ADULTS

Old School. Written by Tobias Wolff.
The Prime of Miss Jean Brodie. Written by Muriel Spark.
The Secret History. Written by Donna Tartt.

Science Fiction

MIDDLE READERS

Mrs. Frisby and the Rats of NIMH. Written by Robert C. O'Brien. Illustrated by
    Zena Bernstein.
When You Reach Me. Written by Rebecca Stead.
A Wrinkle in Time. Written by Madeleine L'Engle.

YOUNG ADULTS

The Ear, the Eye, and the Arm. Written by Nancy Farmer.
Ender's Game. Written by Orson Scott Card.
Eva. Written by Peter Dickinson.
Frankenstein. Written by Mary Wollstonecraft Shelley.
The Golden Compass. Written by Philip Pullman.
The Hitchhiker's Guide to the Galaxy. Written by Douglas Adams.
The House of the Scorpion. Written by Nancy Farmer.
1984. Written by George Orwell.
Slaughterhouse-Five. Written by Kurt Vonnegut.
Twenty Thousand Leagues under the Sea. Written by Jules Verne.
Z for Zachariah. Written by Robert O'Brien.

ADULTS

Brave New World. Written by Aldous Huxley.
Dune. Written by Frank Herbert.

Survival

MIDDLE READERS

Abel's Island. Written by William Steig.
The Black Stallion. Written by Walter Farley.
Hatchet. Written by Gary Paulsen.
Island of the Blue Dolphins. Written by Scott O'Dell.
Julie of the Wolves. Written by Jean Craighead George. Illustrated by John
    Schoenherr.
My Side of the Mountain. Written and illustrated by Jean Craighead George.
Ninth Ward. Written by Jewell Parker Rhodes.
Robinson Crusoe. Written by Daniel Defoe.
The Swiss Family Robinson. Written by Johann David Wyss.

YOUNG ADULTS

Between Shades of Gray. Written by Ruta Sepetys.
The Cay. Written by Theodore Taylor.
Lord of the Flies. Written by William Golding.
Nation. Written by Terry Pratchett.
Never Fall Down. Written by Patricia McCormick.

ADULTS

Life of Pi. Written by Yann Martel.

War

YOUNG ADULTS

Across Five Aprils. Written by Irene Hunt. Illustrated by Albert John Pucci.
Before We Were Free. Written by Julia Alvarez.
Between Shades of Gray. Written by Ruta Sepetys.
Catch-22. Written by Joseph Heller.
Code Name Verity. Written by Elizabeth Wein.
Fallen Angels. Written by Walter Dean Myers.
How I Live Now. Written by Meg Rosoff.

My Brother Sam Is Dead. Written by James Lincoln Collier and Christopher Collier.
Never Fall Down. Written by Patricia McCormick.
Slaughterhouse-Five. Written by Kurt Vonnegut.

ADULTS

Billy Lynn's Long Halftime Walk. Written by Ben Fountain.
A Flag for Sunrise. Written by Robert Stone.
The Naked and the Dead. Written by Norman Mailer.
Tree of Smoke. Written by Denis Johnson.
Years of Red Dust: Stories of Shanghai. Written by Qiu Xiaolong.
The Yellow Birds. Written by Kevin Powers.

CHAPTER 7

27 Writers You Should Know

> We do not write because we want to; we write because we have to.
>
> —Somerset Maugham

With millions of books published, for an author to have one book qualify for listing in *A Lifetime of Fiction* is an impressive achievement. But to have several books singled out by such an important cross section of literary, educational, and journalistic experts is extraordinary: we naturally want to know more about this respected group of authors and illustrators. What follow are 27 biographical sketches, a sketch of each person whose works appear three or more times on the reading lists. Listed alphabetically by author and illustrator, each sketch begins with the works cited in *A Lifetime of Fiction*.

Courtesy of and copyright Jean Malek. Reprinted with permission of the author.

MARGARET ATWOOD (B. 1939)

The Handmaid's Tale (1985)
Alias Grace (1996)
The Blind Assassin (2001)

Margaret Atwood is one of Canada's greatest living novelists. She spent much of her childhood living in the wilderness of northern Quebec with her mother, a nutritionist, and her father, an entomologist. The second of three children, Atwood became a voracious reader, but did not go to school full-time until the eighth grade. She studied at the University of

Toronto, received a master's degree at Radcliffe College, and became a lecturer in English literature. Atwood received the Arthur C. Clarke award for *The Handmaid's Tale* and the Man Booker Prize for *The Blind Assassin*, which *Time* magazine included on its list of the 100 best English-language novels. Atwood has been published in more than 40 languages and has produced more than 50 volumes of poetry, children's literature, fiction, and nonfiction. The perils of science and the role of women are recurring themes in her work. Some of Atwood's other noteworthy books include *The Edible Woman* (1969), *Cat's Eye* (1988), *The Robber Bride* (1994), and the dystopian trilogy *Oryx and Crake* (2003), *The Year of the Flood* (2009), and *MaddAddam* (2013).

AVI (B. 1937)

The True Confessions of Charlotte Doyle (1990)
Nothing but the Truth (1992)
Crispin: The Cross of Lead (2002)

Courtesy of Scholastic, Inc.

Edward Irving Wortis, pen name "Avi," is an acclaimed author who has written in many genres but is best known for his historical fiction. He was raised in Brooklyn and has a twin sister who named him Avi. His parents—mother a social worker and father a psychiatrist—read to him nightly and took him to the library often. In school, he struggled with a writing and learning disability, which he eventually overcame thanks to the work of a tutor. His first professional attempt at writing was as a playwright, and he turned to writing children's literature after the birth of his son. A frequent visitor to schools, Avi often asks to speak to learning-disabled students and advises all students to reach their own conclusions and write what they honestly feel. Avi has written over 70 books for children and young adults. Avi received the Scott O'Dell Historical Fiction Award for *The Fighting Ground* (1984), Newbery Honors for *The True Confessions of Charlotte Doyle* and *Nothing but the Truth*, and the Newberry Medal for *Crispin: The Cross of Lead*. The sequels are *Crispin: At the Edge of the World* (2006) and *Crispin: The End of Time* (2010).

BEVERLY CLEARY (B. 1916)

Ramona the Pest (1968)
Ramona Quimby, Age Eight (1981)
Dear Mr. Henshaw (1983)

Courtesy of Alan McEwan.

Beverly Cleary credits the early influence of librarians for her love of reading and her decision to write children's books. She spent her early years on a farm in Oregon and attended college at the University of California at Berkeley. While working as a librarian, Cleary realized there was a need for more stories and characters with whom children could relate. She has written over 30 books for children and young adults. Cleary earned a Newbery Honor for *Ramona Quimby, Age Eight* and was given the Newbery Medal for *Dear Mr. Henshaw*. She has received the Laura Ingalls Wilder Award and the National Medal of Art and was named a Living Legend by the Library of Congress for her contributions to children's literature. Her Ramona books were adapted into a 10-part television series. *Ramona and Her Mother* (1979) earned her the National Book Award. Some of Cleary's other books include *Petey's Bedtime Story* (1993), *Ramona's World* (1999), and *My Own Two Feet* (1995), a memoir.

Copyright Roald Dahl, Nominee Ltd., courtesy of the Roald Dahl Museum and Story Centre.

ROALD DAHL (1916–1990)

James and the Giant Peach (1961)
Charlie and the Chocolate Factory (1964)
The BFG (1982)
Matilda (1988)

Roald Dahl was a British writer known for his macabre children's stories and for his stories about children who are mistreated by adults. The six-feet-six-inch author started writing as a young boy by keeping a secret diary that he hid at the top of a tree. Dahl was a World War II pilot with the Royal Air Force who crash-landed his plane in the Libyan Desert, where he suffered spinal injuries and a fractured skull. In

1953 he married Academy Award–winning American actress Patricia Neal. Dahl wrote nine collections of short stories, several screenplays and television scripts, and 19 children's books. Dahl adapted *Charlie and the Chocolate Factory* for the big screen under the title *Willy Wonka and the Chocolate Factory*. He was given the Edgar Allen Poe Award from the Mystery Writers of America for his short stories. Dahl won the Federation of Children's Book Groups Award for *James and the Giant Peach* and *The BFG* and the Whitbread Award for *The Witches* (1983). *Matilda* has been made into a Broadway musical and was once voted the Nation's Favorite Children's Book in a British Broadcast Company Bookworm Poll. Two of Dahl's other notable children's books are *Fantastic Mr. Fox* (1970) and *Danny, the Champion of the World* (1975).

E. L. DOCTOROW (B. 1931)

Ragtime (1975)
Billy Bathgate (1989)
The March (2005)

Courtesy of Francesca Magnani and E. L. Doctorow.

Named after Edgar Allan Poe, Edgar Lawrence Doctorow is one of America's most accomplished novelists, best known for his historical fiction, fiction about the American working class, and political activism. His mother, a pianist, and his father, a music shop owner, raised him in Brooklyn. After attending college and being drafted into the army, Doctorow worked as a kind of literary talent scout for Columbia Pictures. His job was to read novels and evaluate them for their potential as movies, an experience he would later apply to his work. While working as an editor at New American Library, he published his first novel, *Welcome to Hard Times* (1960). While editor in chief at Dial Press, he published *The Book of Daniel* (1971), nominated for the National Book Award. *Billy Bathgate* earned the National Book Critics Circle Award and the PEN/Faulkner Award and was the runner-up for the Pulitzer Prize. For *Ragtime*, he received the National Book Critics Circle Award, and the novel was made into both a film and a musical. For *The March*, Doctorow received the PEN/Faulkner Award and the Pulitzer Prize. Doctorow belongs to the American Academy of Arts and Sciences and the American Philosophical Society and has taught at many colleges and universities. Some of his other novels are *World's Fair* (1985), *The Waterworks* (1994), and *Homer & Langley* (2009).

LOIS EHLERT (B. 1934)

Color Zoo (1989)
Pie in the Sky (2004)
Chicka Chicka Boom Boom (illustrator only; 1989)
Ten Little Caterpillars (illustrator only; 2011)

Lois Ehlert is a Wisconsin writer and graphic artist known for her distinctive collage approach to illustration. Her images celebrate the beauty of the natural world and in the common objects people find every day. Ehlert's mother was a seamstress and her father was a woodworker, and she used discarded pieces of lumber and fabric for creative projects. Her usual method is to cut out pieces of cloth and paper, paste them onto a flat surface, and then photograph them for her books. She won a Caldecott Honor for *Color Zoo*; the Boston Globe–Horn Book Award for *Chicka Chicka Boom Boom*, which was also named an American Library Association Notable Children's Book; the Publishers Weekly Best Book of the Year recognition for *Snowballs* (1995); and the Booklist Editors' Choice for *Cuckoo/Cucú: A Mexican Folktale/Un cuento folklórico mexicano* (1997). Some of Ehlert's other notable books are *Growing Vegetable Soup* (1987), *Planting a Rainbow* (1988), *Eating the Alphabet: Fruits and Vegetables from A to Z* (1989), and *Waiting for Wings* (2000).

VIRGINIA HAMILTON (1936–2002)

M. C. Higgins the Great (1974)
Sweet Whispers, Brother Rush (1982)
The People Could Fly: American Black Folktales (1985)

Virginia Hamilton is the first African American author ever to receive the Newbery Medal, awarded to her for *M. C. Higgins the Great*. The book also earned her a National Book Award and Boston Globe–Horn Book Award. The youngest of five children, Hamilton grew up in Ohio, where her family has lived ever since her grandfather arrived there via the Underground Railroad. Pursuing her goal of becoming a writer, she moved to New York City and worked odd jobs such as a museum receptionist, nightclub singer, and cost accountant. For *Sweet Whispers, Brother Rush*, Hamilton won the Coretta Scott King Award, the Boston Globe–Horn Book Award, a Newbery Honor, and the American Book Award. For *The People Could Fly*, Hamilton received the School Library Journal Best Book of the Year Award, Booklist's Editor's Choice recognition and New York Times Best Illustrated Book acknowledgment. Hamilton wrote 41 books in her lifetime and was the first author of children's books to ever win a MacArthur Fellowship. Some of her most recent books are *Time Pieces: The Book of Times* (2001), *Bruh Rabbit and the Tar Baby Girl* (2003), and *Wee Winnie Witch's Skinny: An Original African American Scare Tale* (2004).

KEVIN HENKES (B. 1960)

Chrysanthemum (1991)
Owen (1993)
Lilly's Purple Plastic Purse (1996)
Kitten's First Full Moon (2004)

Kevin Henkes is one of the foremost creators of picture books, and is particularly known for books that feature mouse characters. Henkes created his first picture book while he was enrolled at the University of Wisconsin School of Education's Cooperative Children's Book Center. Henkes has published 32 picture books and 11 novels. *Chrysanthemum* was recognized as an outstanding book by the American Library Association and the *School Library Journal*. Henkes won a Newbery Honor Award for *Olive's Ocean* (2005), the Caldecott Honor Award for *Owen*, and the Caldecott Medal for *Kitten's First Full Moon*. In 2013, the Catholic Library Association gave him the Regina Medal for his contribution to children's literature. His most famous book is *Lilly's Purple Plastic Purse*, recognized by ALA as both a notable book and a Booklist Editor's Choice. His other works include *Lilly's Big Day* (2006), *Little White Rabbit* (2011), *Junonia* (2011), *Penny and Her Song* (2012), and *The Year of Billy Miller* (2013).

Courtesy of Lois Lowry and MattMcKeePhoto.com.

LOIS LOWRY (B. 1937)

Anastasia Krupnik (1979)
Number the Stars (1989)
The Giver (1994)
Gathering Blue (2000)
Gossamer (2006)
Son (2012)

Lois Lowry is one of America's great writers of middle- and young-adult fiction. Her writing ranges from the good-natured Anastasia novels to the deadly serious *Number the Stars* and *The Giver*, both of which earned the Newbery Medal. The daughter of a career army officer, Lowry has lived all over the world. She was born in Hawaii, went to elementary school in Carlisle, Pennsylvania, and then moved to Tokyo. Lowry's first book, *A Summer to Die* (1977), a fictionalized retelling of the death of her sister, received the Children's Literature Award from the International Reading Association. She has written over 30 children's books, including a quartet of books: *The Giver* (1993), *Gathering Blue* (2000), *Messenger* (2004), and *Son* (2012). Lowry received the Parents' Choice Award for *Anastasia Krupnik* and the American Library Association Notable Book designation for *Autumn Street* (1980). For *Rabble Starkey* (1987), she received the Boston Globe–Horn Book Award and the Golden Kite Award. Three of her recent books are *The Birthday Ball* (2010), *Bless This Mouse* (2011), and *Like the Willow Tree* (2011).

BILL MARTIN JR. (1916–2004)

Brown Bear, Brown Bear, What Do You See? (1967)
Chicka Chicka Boom Boom (1989)
Ten Little Caterpillars (2011)

Courtesy of Dr. Michael Sampson.

Bill Martin Jr., the author of over 300 books, was born and raised in Hiawatha, Kansas, the state that later established a children's picture-book award in his honor. In 1945, Martin self-published his first book, *The Little Squeegy Bug* (2001), for his artist brother to illustrate while recovering from World War II wounds. The book eventually sold many copies after Eleanor Roosevelt praised it in one of her newspaper columns. Martin said there were no books in his home and that he always had great difficulty reading, yet he went on to earn a doctorate in early childhood education from Northwestern University. Over the course of his career he worked as a teacher, school principal, textbook editor, and writer. A library at Texas A&M University is named in Martin's honor. Martin described *Brown Bear, Brown Bear, What Do You See?* as a watershed moment because it marked his recognition of the importance of writing stories with rhyme and pattern. *Brown Bear, Brown Bear, What Do You See?* and *Chicka Chicka Boom Boom* both appear on the *School Library Journal*'s top-100 picture-book list. *Chicka Chicka 1, 2, 3!* (2004), coauthored with Michael Sampson, was designated book of the year by *Parenting* magazine. Two more of Martin's most recognized books are *Polar Bear, Polar Bear, What Do You Hear?* (1991) and *Panda Bear, Panda Bear, What Do You See?* (2003).

ROBERT MCCLOSKEY (1914–2003)

Make Way for Ducklings (1941)
Homer Price (1943)
Blueberries for Sal (1948)

Courtesy of Jane
McCloskey.

Robert McCloskey wrote and illustrated eight books, two of which, *Make Way for Ducklings* and *Time of Wonder*, won the Caldecott Medal. Two others, *Blueberries for Sal* (1948) and *One Morning in Maine* (1952), were Caldecott Honor books. Until he started making drawings in high school, McCloskey thought his niche would be playing the piano or another musical instrument or inventing something electrical or mechanical. Several of McCloskey's picture books show the coast of Maine, where he lived most of his adult life. To recognize McCloskey's contribution to children's literature, there are bronze statues of mallard ducks located near Boston Public Garden, the site of his most famous book, *Make Way for Ducklings*, and the Commonwealth of Massachusetts has designated this classic as its official state book. Replicas of the ducks are also on display in a park in Moscow, Russia, where First Lady Barbara Bush presented them to Raisa M. Gorbachev during a summit meeting in 1991. McCloskey's other books as author and illustrator are *Lentil* (1940), *Centerburg Tales: More Adventures of Homer Price* (1951), and *Dow, Deep-Water Man* (1963). He worked as an illustrator on 10 other books.

Reprinted by permission of
Miriam Altshuler Agency
on behalf of Walter Dean
Myers.

WALTER DEAN MYERS (B. 1937)

Hoops (1981)
Fallen Angels (1988)
Monster (1999)

Walter Dean Myers is a prolific writer best known for his powerful books about young African Americans. His tumultuous Harlem upbringing included being raised by foster parents, suffering from speech impairment, and dropping out of high school to join the army. Myers has written over 50 books, both fiction and nonfiction. He is a five-time recipient of the Coretta Scott King Award. Both *Hoops* and *Fallen Angels* were selected as ALA Best Books for Young Adults, and *Monster* earned him the Michael L. Printz Award. *Somewhere in the Darkness* (1993) earned a Newbery Honor and *Malcolm X: By Any Means Necessary* (1994) was named an ALA Best Book for Young Adults. The American Library Association and *School Library Journal* have honored him with a Lifetime Achievement Award. In 2012, the Library of Congress designated Myers an ambassador for young people's literature. His recent works include *The Cruisers* (2011), *We Were Heroes: The Journal of Scott Pendleton Collins, a World War II Soldier* (2012), and *A Star Is Born* (2012).

KATHERINE PATERSON (B. 1932)

Bridge to Terabithia (1977)
The Great Gilly Hopkins (1978)
Jacob Have I Loved (1980)

Katherine Paterson was born in China, the child of missionaries. She became a missionary herself and married a minister. Paterson originally had a problem reading and writing English because her first language was Chinese. She has written more than 30 books, including 16 novels for children and young people. She has won the Newbery Medal for both *Bridge to Terabithia* and *Jacob Have I Loved*. She has twice won the National Book Award, for *The Master Puppeteer* (1975) and *The Great Gilly Hopkins*. In recognition for her body of work, Paterson received the Hans Christian Anderson Award. She was given the Laura Ingalls Wilder Medal by the American Library Association in 2013. Her recent novels include *The Same Stuff as Stars* (2002), *Bread and Roses, Too* (2006), and *The Day of the Pelican* (2009).

Courtesy of Samantha Loomis Paterson.

JERRY PINKNEY (B. 1939)

Mirandy and Brother Wind (1988)
John Henry (1994)
The Ugly Duckling (1999)
The Lion and the Mouse (2009)

Courtesy of Thomas Kristich and the Penguin Group.

Jerry Pinkney is one of America's great illustrators of children's books. He grew up in Philadelphia and studied at the Philadelphia College of Art. Pinkney's artistic ability was first noticed when, as a child, he drew on the backs of wallpaper that his father, a wallpaper hanger, brought home from work. As a child Pinkney struggled with dyslexia but had a rare gift for drawing. When he was a high-school student, he worked at a newsstand and sketched people on the street. He decided to pursue drawing as a career when a professional cartoonist noticed his work and encouraged him. Pinkney has won five Caldecott Honor Medals, a Caldecott Medal, and his work has been included in the New York Times Best Illustrated Books list five times. He has received five Coretta Scott King Awards and four Coretta Scott King Honor Awards. Besides illustrating children's books, Pinkney is an artist who has exhibited around the world. Both the city of Philadelphia and the Commonwealth of Pennsylvania officially declared June 26, 2013, to be Jerry Pinkney Day. He has illustrated over 100 books. Two of Pinkney's most recent children's books are *Puss in Boots* (2012) and *Twinkle, Twinkle Little Star* (2011).

PHILIP ROTH (B. 1933)

Portnoy's Complaint (1969)
American Pastoral (1997)
The Human Stain (2000)

Courtesy of Robert Wiener, New Jersey Jewish News.

Philip Roth is one of America's most respected and decorated novelists, best known for his challenging and sometimes controversial explorations of Jewish identity. He was born and raised in Newark, New Jersey, attended Bucknell University and the University of Chicago, and taught for many years at the University of Pennsylvania. *Portnoy's Complaint*, the comedic, sexually explicit book that made Roth famous, was included on both the Modern Library's and *Time* magazine's lists of the 100 best English-language novels. Roth has won PEN/Faulkner Awards for *Operation Shylock* (1993) and *The Human Stain*

(2000), and a Pulitzer Prize for *American Pastoral* (1997). Two of his books, *Goodbye Columbus* (1960) and *Sabbath's Theater* (1995), have won the National Book Award, while *My Life as a Man* (1975) and *The Ghost Writer* (1980) were finalists. Two of his books, *The Counterlife* (1987) and *Patrimony* (1992), have won the National Book Critic's Circle Award, while two others, *The Professor of Desire* (1978) and *The Anatomy Lesson* (1984), were finalists. Having devoted his entire adult life to reading, writing, and teaching about novels, Roth now claims that he has retired from fiction. His last novel was *Nemeses* (2010).

J. K. ROWLING (1965)

Harry Potter and the Sorcerer's Stone (1998)
Harry Potter and the Chamber of Secrets (1999)
Harry Potter and the Prisoner of Azkaban (1999)
Harry Potter and the Goblet of Fire (2000)
Harry Potter and the Order of the Phoenix (2003)
Harry Potter and the Half-Blood Prince (2005)
Harry Potter and the Deathly Hallows (2007)

Courtesy of Mulholland Books.

Joanne "Jo" Rowling, pen name J. K. Rowling, the best-selling novelist in history, has also earned critical acclaim. Her awards and honors include Publishers Weekly Best Book, Newsweek Best Book, Hugo Award, British Book Awards Author of the Year and Lifetime Achievement Award, Order of the British Empire, James Joyce Award, and the Hans Christian Andersen Award. Four hundred million copies of the Harry Potter series have sold throughout the world. Rowling's life is a rags-to-riches tale. After her marriage ended in divorce, Rowling and her daughter moved to Edinburgh, Scotland, and were forced to go on welfare. Rowling used this time to write her first Harry Potter book. After her seven *Harry Potter* novels, movie deals, and merchandising, she became the world's first billionaire author. Rowling's latest novels are written for adults. They are *The Casual Vacancy* (2012) and *The Cuckoo's Calling* (2013), the later book published under the pseudonym Robert Galbraith.

MAURICE SENDAK (1928–2012)

Chicken Soup with Rice: A Book of Months (1962)
Where the Wild Things Are (1963)
In the Night Kitchen (1970)
Little Bear (illustrator only; 1957)
Mr. Rabbit and the Lovely Present (illustrator only; 1962)

Maurice Sendak is often considered the most important creator of children's picture books in the 20th century. In Sendak's world, children's books were not always safe, bright, and predictable. His best-known book, the Caldecott Medal–winning *Where the Wild Things Are*, has fanged monsters and changed what was permitted in children's illustration. Sendak observed that he was brought up in a world threatened by illness, the Depression, World War II, and the Holocaust, in which many of his relatives died. Growing up as a gay boy, Sendak often felt marginalized because he was unable to openly acknowledge his sexual orientation with his family. One of Sendak's recurring themes is that children should be respected enough to be told the truth. He has received many awards, including the Hans Christian Andersen Award for Illustration, the Laura Ingalls Wilder Award, the National Medal of the Arts, and the National Book Award. Twenty-two of his books have made it to the *New York Times* yearly summation of best illustrated books. His most recent titles are *Bumble-Ardy* (2011) and *My Brother's Book* (2013).

Courtesy Dr. Seuss Enterprises.

DR. SEUSS (1904–1991)

Horton Hatches the Egg (1940)
Horton Hears a Who (1954)
How the Grinch Stole Christmas (1957)
The Cat in the Hat (1957)
Green Eggs and Ham (1960)
The Lorax (1971)

Theodor Seuss Geisel, pen name Dr. Seuss, is one of the towering figures in the history of children's literature. He grew up in Springfield, Massachusetts, where his father was a curator of a small zoo. Dr. Seuss wrote whimsical books that often include important social messages. *The Lorax* espouses environmentalism, and *How the Grinch Stole Christmas* criticizes the excessive consumerism and materialism of Christmas. In recognition of his body of work, he was awarded a Pulitzer Prize. He also received two Academy Awards, two Emmy Awards, a Peabody Award, and the Laura Ingalls Wilder Medal. Seuss won Caldecott Honors for two of his lesser-known books, *McElligot's Pool* (1947) and *Bartholomew and the Oobleck* (1949). The National Education Association has designated Dr. Seuss's birthday, March 2, as National Read across America Day, an annual observance. Dr. Seuss never actually earned a doctorate, but his alma mater, Dartmouth College, awarded him an honorary one. Dr. Seuss, who authored 48 books in his long career, is known for his madcap animal characters and silly book titles, such as *Yertle the Turtle and Other Stories* (1958), *One Fish, Two Fish, Red Fish, Blue Fish* (1960), *Fox in Socks* (1965), *Mr. Brown Can Moo! Can You?* (1970), and *Oh, the Places You'll Go!* (1990).

WILLIAM STEIG (1907–2003)

Sylvester and the Magic Pebble (1969)
Abel's Island (1976)
Doctor De Soto (1982)

William Steig was a longtime cartoonist for *The New Yorker* magazine and wrote 25 children's books. Dubbed the King of Cartoons in a *Newsweek* profile, he is the creator of *Shrek!* (1990), the picture book about a young ogre, which inspired the movie series. Steig was born and raised in New York City, where his father was a house painter and his mother was a seamstress. When Steig's father couldn't find work during the Depression, Steig supported the family by selling cartoons to *The New Yorker* and other magazines. In his long career, he produced 1,600 drawings and 117 covers for *The New Yorker*. Steig received the Caldecott Medal for *Sylvester and the Magic Pebble*, a Caldecott Honor for *The Amazing Bone* (1976), and Newbery Honors for both *Abel's Island* and *Doctor De Soto*. His most recent books include *Made for Each Other* (2000), *Wizzil* (2000), *A Gift from Zeus* (2001), and *When Everybody Wore a Hat* (2003).

J. R. R. TOLKIEN (1892–1973)

The Hobbit (1937)
The Fellowship of the Ring (1954)
The Two Towers (1954)
The Return of the King (1955)

John Ronald Reuel Tolkien was a writer and Oxford scholar who was an expert in medieval literature, ancient legends, and languages. He was born in South Africa, and in his childhood, before moving to England, he was bitten by a baboon spider and a snake. After the death of his mother and father, a Roman Catholic priest raised him. Tolkien fought in World War I and served in a regiment that suffered heavy casualties, an experience that deeply affected him. His first job after the war was to work on the *Oxford English Dictionary*. Tolkien originally wrote *The Hobbit* for his own children. *The Hobbit* and *The Lord of the Rings* create an elaborate fantasy world known as Middle-earth, populated by hobbits, dwarves, elves, men, wizards, and goblin-like Orcs, locked in a struggle between good and evil. The trilogy has at different times been voted the most beloved books, in Britain and Australia. The *Silmarillion* (1977), a narrative describing the universe within which *The Hobbit* and *The Lord of the Rings* take place, was published posthumously and was edited by Tolkien's son, Christopher.

Courtesy of the Mark Twain House & Museum, Hartford, CT.

MARK TWAIN (1835–1910)

The Adventures of Tom Sawyer (1876)
The Prince and the Pauper (1881)
The Adventures of Huckleberry Finn (1885)

Considered one of the great humorists and founders of the American literary tradition, Mark Twain was born Samuel Langhorne Clemens and grew up in Hannibal, Missouri, a port town on the Mississippi River, the setting for *The Adventures of Tom Sawyer* and *The Adventures of Huckleberry Finn*. Twain worked as a printer, prospector, and riverboat captain before turning to writing. At the outbreak of the Civil War, Twain briefly joined the Confederate army, but he eventually became an ardent supporter of the abolition of slavery, as well as women's suffrage and labor unions. Twain was a popular public speaker known for his humor. He wrote *A Connecticut Yankee in*

King Arthur's Court (1889), *Pudd'nhead Wilson* (1894), *Personal Recollections of Joan of Arc* (1896), and *The Mysterious Stranger* (1916), published six years after his death. His legacy lives on in many ways, including the Mark Twain Award, given annually for an outstanding children's book, and the Mark Twain Prize for American Humor, awarded each year by the John F. Kennedy Center for the Performing Arts.

JOHN UPDIKE (1932–2009)

Rabbit, Run (1960)
Rabbit Redux (1971)
Rabbit Is Rich (1981)
Rabbit at Rest (1990)

Courtesy of Dr. James Plath, Illinois Wesleyan University.

John Updike is one of America's most renowned fiction writers, twice featured on the cover of *Time* magazine. He grew up in Shillington, Pennsylvania, about 60 miles northwest of Philadelphia. He was first in his class at Shillington High School and graduated summa cum laude from Harvard, where he edited the *Harvard Lampoon*. Before he became a regular contributor to *The New Yorker*, he planned to be a cartoonist. Starting in 1954, he wrote hundreds of short stories, reviews, and poems for the literary magazine. Updike published more than 20 novels and more than a dozen collections of short stories. *Time* magazine ranked *Rabbit, Run* as one of its 100 all-time greatest novels. *Rabbit Is Rich* and *Rabbit at Rest* each received the Pulitzer Prize. Updike is one of the only authors to win the Pulitzer Prize more than once. His awards include the Guggenheim Fellowship, O Henry Award, PEN/Faulkner Award for Fiction, American Academy of Arts and Letters Gold Medal for Fiction, National Book Award for Fiction, National Book Critics Circle Award for Fiction, National Book Critics Circle Award for Criticism, Common Wealth Award of Distinguished Service, and Medal of Distinguished Contribution to American Letters. In addition to his famous tetralogy, Updike's other noteworthy fiction includes *The Centaur* (1963), *Couples* (1968), *The Witches of Eastwick* (1984), *Terrorist* (2006), and *John Updike: The Collected Stories* (2013).

DAVID WIESNER (B. 1956)

Tuesday (1997)
Sector 7 (1999)
Flotsam (2006)

Courtesy of Peggy Morsch.

Known for his wordless stories, David Wiesner is one of America's leading illustrators of children's books, consistently conveying the notion that there is something utterly fantastic in everyday life. He lives near Philadelphia and grew up in suburban New Jersey. As a child he was a gifted artist and attended the Rhode Island School of Design. Wiesner's engaging, cinematic style seems to make the reader responsible for telling the story. He usually spends years creating new books, making numerous revisions and even creating three-dimensional models to add more realism to his illustrations. Wiesner won the Caldecott Medal, the most prestigious award for children's illustration, for *Tuesday* (1997), *The Three Pigs* (2001), and *Flotsam* (2006), making him only the second person in the history of the award to win three times. *Free Fall* (1988) and *Sector 7* (1999) earned Caldecott Honors. His other picture books include *Hurricane* (1990), *June 29, 1999* (1992), *Night of the Gargoyles* (1994), *The Loathsome Dragon* (2005), *Art & Max* (2010), and *Mr. Wuffles!* (2013). He has also partnered with 17 different authors to illustrate their books.

Courtesy of Marty Umans and Disney Publishing Worldwide.

MO WILLEMS (B. 1968)

Don't Let the Pigeon Drive the Bus! (2003)
Knuffle Bunny: A Cautionary Tale (2004)
Knuffle Bunny Too: A Case of Mistaken Identity (2007)

Mo Willems is known for his unique sense of humor. He grew up in New Orleans, moved to New York, studied at the Tisch School of the Arts, and formed an improv troupe. After graduating from Tisch, Willems went on a backpacking trip around the world, visiting more than 30 countries. At the conclusion of every day of his 12-month journey, he sketched one thing that stood out in his mind. The result was *You*

Can Never Find a Rickshaw When It Monsoons: The World on One Cartoon a Day (2006). Upon his return, he got a writing job on *Sesame Street*, for which he eventually won six Emmy Awards. He has worked as a stand-up comic and has created two animated television shows. Some of his greatest work has been in writing children's books. He earned Caldecott Honors for three books: *Don't Let the Pigeon Drive the Bus!*, *Knuffle Bunny: A Cautionary Tale*, and *Knuffle Bunny Too: A Case of Mistaken Identity*. Willems won Geisel Awards for *Are You Ready to Play Outside?* (2008) and *There Is a Bird on Your Head* (2007). He received Geisel Honors for *I Broke My Trunk* (2011) and *We Are in a Book!* (2010). His recent work includes *I'm a Frog* (2013) and *The Pigeon Needs a Bath!* (2014).

AUDREY AND DON WOOD (B. 1948 AND 1945)

The Napping House (1984)
The Little Mouse, the Red Ripe Strawberry, and the Big Hungry Bear (1984)
King Bidgood's in the Bathtub (1985)

Courtesy of Houghton Mifflin Harcourt.

Audrey Wood's first memories are of the Ringling Brothers Circus in Florida, where she lived while her father, an art student, painted circus murals. She remembers being bounced on the knee of the tallest man in the world and being babysat by little people who lived in a trailer next door. Don Wood grew up on a farm in California. By age 12 he was working 16-hour shifts. One summer, as a teenager, he worked the family farm 26 hours straight. Audrey and Don met in Berkeley and they began collaborating on children's books after being married seven years. Don has illustrated 20 of Audrey's books. *King Bidgood's in the Bathtub* earned the Caldecott Medal. *The Napping House* won the Society of Children's Book Writers and Illustrators' Golden Kite Best Picture Illustration Award and was an ALA Notable Children's Book. Three of their other notable books are *Heckedy Peg* (1987), *Piggies* (1991), and *The Birthday Queen* (2013).

JANE YOLEN (B. 1939)

Owl Moon (1987)
The Devil's Arithmetic (1988)
How Do Dinosaurs Say Good Night? (2000)

Jane Yolen has written over 300 books and thousands of poems and short stories for preschool through adulthood, with themes ranging from the Holocaust, to folklore, to disability. She was born in New York City and spent much of her childhood there. Yolen attended Smith College, where she studied journalism and poetry. She was once president of the Science Fiction Writers of America and has served for over 25 years on the board of directors for the Society of Children's Book Writers and Illustrators. She was the first woman ever invited to give the Andrew Lang Lecture at Scotland's University of St. Andrews. For her body of children's writing, the Catholic Library Association awarded her its Regina Medal. *The Emperor and the Kite* (1967) was a Caldecott Honor book and *Owl Moon* won a Caldecott Medal. *The Devil's Arithmetic* was a Nebula Award finalist and received the Jewish Book Council Award. *The Seeing Stick* (1977) and *How Do Dinosaurs Say Good Night?* (2000) both earned the Christopher Medal. Yolen's recent works include *The Hostage Prince* (2013), *The Emily Sonnets: The Life of Emily Dickinson* (2013), and *Wee Rhymes* (2013).

Courtesy of Jason Stemple, 2011.

PAUL O. ZELINSKY (B. 1953)

Illustration of *Dear Mr. Henshaw* (1983)
Illustration of *Swamp Angel* (1994)
Retelling and illustration of *Rapunzel* (1997)

Paul O. Zelinsky is a master illustrator known for his ability to harmonize his art to the text. Zelinsky grew up in Illinois, where his mother was a medical illustrator and his father was a math professor. When Zelinsky attended Yale College, he had the good fortune to enroll in a course being cotaught by Maurice Sendak, which led to a career in children's books. Ze-

Courtesy of Paul O. Zelinsky.

linsky received the Caldecott Medal for his illustration and retelling of the classic story of *Rapunzel*. He earned Caldecott Honors for three of his books: *Hansel and Gretel* (1984), *Rumpelstiltskin* (1987), and *Swamp Angel*. Zelinsky illustrated *The Lion and the Stoat* (1984), *Knick-Knack Paddywhack!* (2002), and *The Maid and the Mouse and the Odd-Shaped House* (1981). He has teamed up with some of the best children's authors to illustrate an additional 25 books. Most recently, Zelinsky illustrated *Z Is for Moose* (2012) and *Earwig and the Witch* (2012). His most popular book is *The Wheels on the Bus* (1990).

APPENDIX 1

Preschool Booklist

1. *The Very Hungry Caterpillar.* Written and illustrated by Eric Carle.
2. *City Dog, Country Frog.* Written by Mo Willems. Illustrated by Jon J. Muth.
3. *Goodnight Moon.* Written by Margaret Wise Brown. Illustrated by Clement Hurd.
4. *Where the Wild Things Are.* Written and illustrated by Maurice Sendak.
5. *The Snowy Day.* Written and illustrated by Ezra Jack Keats.
6. *The Quiet Book.* Written by Deborah Underwood. Illustrated by Renata Liwska.
7. *Brown Bear, Brown Bear, What Do You See?* Written by Bill Martin Jr. Illustrated by Eric Carle.
8. *The Lion and the Mouse.* Adapted and illustrated by Jerry Pinkney.
9. *Chicka Chicka Boom Boom.* Written by Bill Martin Jr. and John Archambault. Illustrated by Lois Ehlert.
10. *The Tale of Peter Rabbit.* Written by Beatrix Potter.
11. *Corduroy.* Written and illustrated by Don Freeman.
12. *Curious George.* Written and illustrated by H. A. and Margret Rey.
13. *If You Give a Mouse a Cookie.* Written by Laura Joffe Numeroff. Illustrated by Felicia Bond.
14. *Millions of Cats.* Written and illustrated by Wanda Gág.
15. *Freight Train.* Written and illustrated by Donald Crews.
16. *The Story of Ferdinand.* Written by Munro Leaf. Illustrated by Robert Lawson.
17. *Swimmy.* Written and illustrated by Leo Lionni.
18. *Harold and the Purple Crayon.* Written and illustrated by Crockett Johnson.
19. *Bark, George.* Written and illustrated by Jules Feiffer.
20. *Guess How Much I Love You.* Written by Sam McBratney. Illustrated by Anita Jeram.

21. *The Story of Babar.* Written and illustrated by Jean de Brunhoff.
22. *Blueberries for Sal.* Written and illustrated by Robert McCloskey.
23. *Oh, No!* Written by Candace Fleming. Illustrated by Eric Rohmann.
24. *Doctor De Soto.* Written and illustrated by William Steig.
25. *Kitten's First Full Moon.* Written and illustrated by Kevin Henkes.
26. *No, David!* Written and illustrated by David Shannon.
27. *Where's Spot?* Written and illustrated by Eric Hill.
28. *Don't Let the Pigeon Drive the Bus.* Written and illustrated by Mo Willems.
29. *Harry the Dirty Dog.* Written by Gene Zion. Illustrated by Margaret Bloy Graham.
30. *How Do Dinosaurs Say Good Night?* Written by Jane Yolen. Illustrated by Mark Teague.
31. *The Runaway Bunny.* Written by Margaret Wise Brown. Illustrated by Clement Hurd.
32. *The Snowman.* Illustrated by Raymond Briggs.
33. *Go Away, Big Green Monster.* Written and illustrated by Ed Emberley.
34. *Happy Birthday, Moon.* Written and illustrated by Frank Asch.
35. *The Kissing Hand.* Written by Audrey Penn. Illustrated by Nancy M. Leak.
36. *Mouse Paint.* Written and illustrated by Ellen Stoll Walsh.
37. *Sheep in a Jeep.* Written by Nancy Shaw. Illustrated by Margot Apple.
38. *Not a Box.* Written and illustrated by Antoinette Portis.
39. *Seven Blind Mice.* Written by Ed Young.
40. *Pocketful of Posies: A Treasury of Nursery Rhymes.* Compiled and illustrated by Salley Mavor.
41. *The Story about Ping.* Written by Marjorie Flack. Illustrated by Kurt Wiese.
42. *Ten, Nine, Eight.* Written and illustrated by Molly Bang.
43. *Tikki Tikki Tembo.* Written by Arlene Mosel. Illustrated by Blair Lent.
44. *We're Going on a Bear Hunt.* Written by Michael Rosen. Illustrated by Helen Oxenbury.
45. *"More More More" Said the Baby.* Written and illustrated by Vera B. Williams.
46. *Bedtime for Frances.* Written by Russell Hoban. Illustrated by Garth Williams.
47. *Good Night Gorilla.* Written and illustrated by Peggy Rathmann.
48. *Is Your Mama a Llama?* Written by Deborah Guarino. Illustrated by Steven Kellogg.
49. *Shark vs. Train.* Written by Chris Barton. Illustrated by Tom Lichtenheld.
50. *King Bidgood's in the Bathtub.* Written by Audrey Wood. Illustrated by Don Wood.
51. *Mama, Do You Love Me?* Written by Barbara M. Joosse. Illustrated by Barbara Lavallee.

52. *The Rainbow Fish.* Written and illustrated by Marcus Pfister.
53. *Rosie's Walk.* Written and illustrated by Pat Hutchins.
54. *Come Along, Daisy!* Written and illustrated by Jane Simmons.
55. *Ella Sarah Gets Dressed.* Written and illustrated by Margaret Chodos-Irvine.
56. *Dear Zoo: A Lift-the-Flap Book.* Written and illustrated by Rod Campbell.
57. *Five Little Monkeys Jumping on the Bed.* Written and illustrated by Eileen Christelow.
58. *Froggy Gets Dressed.* Written by Jonathan London. Illustrated by Frank Remkiewicz.
59. *Jamberry.* Written and illustrated by Bruce Degen.
60. *Koala Lou.* Written by Mem Fox. Illustrated by Pamela Lofts.
61. *The Little Mouse, the Red Ripe Strawberry, and the Big Hungry Bear.* Written by Audrey Wood. Illustrated by Don Wood.
62. *Knuffle Bunny: A Cautionary Tale.* Written and illustrated by Mo Willems.
63. *Miss Bindergarten Gets Ready for Kindergarten.* Written by Joseph Slate. Illustrated by Ashley Wolff.
64. *The Relatives Came.* Written by Cynthia Rylant. Illustrated by Stephen Gammell.
65. *Timothy Goes to School.* Written and illustrated by Rosemary Wells.
66. *When Sophie Gets Angry—Really, Really Angry . . .* Written and illustrated by Molly Garrett Bang.
67. *Time for Bed.* Written by Mem Fox. Illustrated by Jane Dyer.
68. *Where's Walrus?* Written and illustrated by Stephen Savage.
69. *Duck on a Bike.* Written and illustrated by David Shannon.
70. *Go, Dog. Go!* Written and illustrated by P. D. Eastman.
71. *Have You Seen My Duckling?* Written and illustrated by Nancy Tafuri.
72. *Abuela.* Written by Arthur Dorros. Illustrated by Elisa Kleven.
73. *I Must Have Bobo!* Written and Illustrated by Eileen Rosenthal.
74. *I Stink!* Written by Kate McMullan. Illustrated by Jim McMullan.
75. *The Paper Bag Princess.* Written by Robert N. Munsch. Illustrated by Michael Martchenko.
76. *Snow.* Written and illustrated by Uri Shulevitz.
77. *Angelina Ballerina.* Written by Katharine Holabird. Illustrated by Helen Craig.
78. *Chicken Soup with Rice: A Book of Months.* Written and illustrated by Maurice Sendak.
79. *Pirates Don't Take Baths.* Written and illustrated by John Segal.
80. *Color Zoo.* Written and illustrated by Lois Ehlert
81. *Farmer Duck.* Written by Martin Waddell. Illustrated by Helen Oxenbury
82. *In the Rain with Baby Duck.* Written by Amy Hest. Illustrated by Jill Barton.
83. *Goldilocks and the Three Bears.* Retold and illustrated by James Marshall.

84. *Horton Hears a Who!* Written and illustrated by Dr. Seuss.
85. *In the Night Kitchen.* Written and illustrated by Maurice Sendak.
86. *Jesse Bear, What Will You Wear?* Written by Nancy White Carlstrom. Illustrated by Bruce Degen.
87. *Ten Little Caterpillars.* Written by Bill Martin Jr. Illustrated by Lois Ehlert.
88. *In the Tall, Tall Grass.* Written and illustrated by Denise Fleming.
89. *Nighttime Ninja.* Written by Barbara DaCosta. Illustrated by Ed Young.
90. *Knuffle Bunny Too: A Case of Mistaken Identity.* Written and illustrated by Mo Willems.
91. *Llama Llama Red Pajama.* Written and illustrated by Anna Dewdney.
92. *Off to School, Baby Duck!* Written by Amy Hest. Illustrated by Jill Barton.
93. *The Lorax.* Written and illustrated by Dr. Seuss.
94. *Pat the Bunny.* Written and illustrated by Dorothy Kunhardt
95. *My Friend Rabbit.* Written and illustrated by Eric Rohmann.
96. *One Fine Day.* Written and illustrated by Nonny Hogrogian.
97. *Owl Babies.* Written and illustrated by Martin Waddell.
98. *Press Here.* Written and illustrated by Hervé Tullet.
99. *Fiesta Babies.* Written by Carmen Tafolla. Illustrated by Amy Córdova.
100. *Pie in the Sky.* Written and illustrated by Lois Ehlert.

APPENDIX 2

Early-Reader Booklist

1. *Madeline*. Written and illustrated by Ludwig Bemelmans.
2. *Sleep Like a Tiger*. Written by Mary Logue. Illustrated by Pamela Zagarenski.
3. *Make Way for Ducklings*. Written and illustrated by Robert McCloskey.
4. *Caps for Sale*. Written and illustrated by Esphyr Slobodkina.
5. *A Chair for My Mother*. Written and illustrated by Vera B. Williams.
6. *The Napping House*. Written by Audrey Wood. Illustrated by Don Wood.
7. *The Polar Express*. Written and illustrated by Chris Van Allsburg.
8. *Over and Under the Snow*. Written by Kate Messner. Illustrated by Christopher Silas Neal.
9. *Alexander and the Terrible, Horrible, No Good, Very Bad Day*. Written by Judith Viorst. Illustrated by Ray Cruz.
10. *The Little Engine That Could*. Written by Watty Piper. Illustrated by George and Doris Hauman.
11. *Mike Mulligan and His Steam Shovel*. Written and illustrated by Virginia Lee Burton.
12. *Frog and Toad Are Friends*. Written and illustrated by Arnold Lobel.
13. *Owl Moon*. Written by Jane Yolen. Illustrated by John Schoenherr.
14. *Strega Nona*. Retold and Illustrated by Tomie dePaola.
15. *Sylvester and the Magic Pebble*. Written and illustrated by William Steig.
16. *George and Martha*. Written and illustrated by James Marshall.
17. *Jumanji*. Written and illustrated by Chris Van Allsburg.
18. *This Is Not My Hat*. Written and illustrated by Jon Klassen.
19. *Miss Nelson Is Missing!* Written by Harry Allard. Illustrated by James Marshall.
20. *Olivia*. Written and illustrated by Ian Falconer.
21. *The Mitten*. Written and illustrated by Jan Brett.

22. *The Cat in the Hat.* Written and illustrated by Dr. Seuss.
23. *Lilly's Purple Plastic Purse.* Written and illustrated by Kevin Henkes.
24. *Click, Clack, Moo: Cows That Type.* Written by Doreen Cronin. Illustrated by Betsy Lewin.
25. *The Little House.* Written and illustrated by Virginia Lee Burton.
26. *Mufaro's Beautiful Daughters: An African Tale.* Written and illustrated by John Steptoe.
27. *The True Story of the Three Little Pigs.* Written by Jon Scieszka. Illustrated by Lane Smith.
28. *Amelia Bedelia.* Written by Peggy Parish. Illustrated by Fritz Seibel.
29. *The Carrot Seed.* Written by Ruth Krauss. Illustrated by Crockett Johnson.
30. *Are You My Mother?* Written and illustrated by P. D. Eastman.
31. *How to Heal a Broken Wing.* Written and illustrated by Bob Graham.
32. *Cloudy with a Chance of Meatballs.* Written by Judi Barrett. Illustrated by Ronald Barrett.
33. *Little Bear.* Written by Else Holmelund Minarik. Illustrated by Maurice Sendak.
34. *Officer Buckle and Gloria.* Written and illustrated by Peggy Rathmann.
35. *Stone Soup.* Retold and illustrated by Marcia Brown.
36. *Chrysanthemum.* Written and illustrated by Kevin Henkes.
37. *Miss Rumphius.* Written and illustrated by Barbara Cooney.
38. *Leo the Late Bloomer.* Written by Robert Kraus. Illustrated by Jose Aruego.
39. *Martha Speaks.* Written and illustrated by Susan Meddaugh.
40. *Owen.* Written and illustrated by Kevin Henkes.
41. *Mr. Gumpy's Outing.* Written and illustrated by John Burningham.
42. *Stellaluna.* Written and illustrated by Janell Cannon.
43. *Amazing Grace.* Written by Mary Hoffman. Illustrated by Caroline Binch.
44. *Horton Hatches the Egg.* Written and illustrated by Dr. Seuss.
45. *Bread and Jam for Frances.* Written by Russell Hoban. Illustrated by Lillian Hoban.
46. *The Giving Tree.* Written and illustrated by Shel Silverstein.
47. *Big Red Lollipop.* Written by Rukhsana Khan. Illustrated by Sophie Blackall.
48. *There Was an Old Lady Who Swallowed a Fly.* Written and illustrated by Simms Taback.
49. *The Ugly Duckling.* Written by Hans Christian Andersen. Adapted and illustrated by Jerry Pinkney.
50. *Babe: The Gallant Pig.* Written by Dick King-Smith. Illustrated by Mary Rayner.
51. *Lon Po Po: A Red-Riding Hood Story from China.* Translated and illustrated by Ed Young.

52. *The Day Jimmy's Boa Ate the Wash.* Written by Trinka Hakes Noble. Illustrated by Steven Kellogg.
53. *Green Eggs and Ham.* Written and illustrated by Dr. Seuss.
54. *Blackout.* Written and illustrated by John Rocco.
55. *Joseph Had a Little Overcoat.* Written and illustrated by Simms Taback.
56. *Lyle, Lyle, Crocodile.* Written and illustrated by Bernard Waber.
57. *My Father's Dragon.* Written by Ruth Stiles Gannett. Illustrated by Ruth Chrisman Gannett.
58. *Tar Beach.* Written and illustrated by Faith Ringgold.
59. *The Boxcar Children.* Written by Gertrude Chandler Warner. Illustrated by L. Kate Deal.
60. *The Velveteen Rabbit.* Written by Margery Williams. Illustrated by William Nicholson.
61. *Clifford the Big Red Dog.* Written and illustrated by Norman Bridwell.
62. *Eloise.* Written by Kay Thompson. Illustrated by Hilary Knight.
63. *The Hundred Dresses.* Written by Eleanor Estes. Illustrated by Louis Slobodkin.
64. *Extra Yarn.* Written by Mac Barnett. Illustrated by Jon Klassen.
65. *Ira Sleeps Over.* Written and illustrated by Bernard Waber.
66. *Old Black Fly.* Written by Jim Aylesworth. Illustrated by Stephen Gammell.
67. *Rapunzel.* Written by the Brothers Grimm. Retold and illustrated by Paul O. Zelinsky.
68. *Ox-Cart Man.* Written by Donald Hall. Illustrated by Barbara Cooney.
69. *The Stinky Cheese Man and Other Fairly Stupid Tales.* Written by Jon Scieszka. Illustrated by Lane Smith.
70. *Andy and the Lion.* Written and illustrated by James Daugherty.
71. *Frederick.* Written and illustrated by Leo Lionni.
72. *A Couple of Boys Have the Best Week Ever.* Written and illustrated by Marla Frazee.
73. *The Doorbell Rang.* Written and illustrated by Pat Hutchins.
74. *The Gardener.* Written by Sarah Stewart. Illustrated by David Small.
75. *The Hello, Goodbye Window.* Written by Norton Juster. Illustrated by Chris Raschka.
76. *Mr. Rabbit and the Lovely Present.* Written by Charlotte Zolotow. Illustrated by Maurice Sendak.
77. *How the Grinch Stole Christmas.* Written and illustrated by Dr. Seuss.
78. *Sick Day for Amos McGee.* Written by Philip C. Stead. Illustrated by Erin E. Stead.
79. *John Henry.* Written by Julius Lester. Illustrated by Jerry Pinkney.
80. *Swamp Angel.* Written by Anne Isaacs. Illustrated by Paul O. Zelinsky.

81. *Tuesday.* Written and illustrated by David Wiesner.
82. *Whistle for Willie.* Written and illustrated by Ezra Jack Keats.
83. *Anansi and the Moss-Covered Rock.* Written by Eric A. Kimmel. Illustrated by Janet Stevens.
84. *Will I Have a Friend?* Written by Miriam Cohen. Illustrated by Lillian Hoban.
85. *Pecan Pie Baby.* Written by Jacqueline Woodson. Illustrated by Sophie Blackall.
86. *Anansi the Spider: A Tale from the Ashanti.* Written and illustrated by Gerald McDermott.
87. *Grandpa Green.* Written and illustrated by Lane Smith.
88. *Animals Should Definitely Not Wear Clothing.* Written by Judi Barrett. Illustrated by Ronald Barrett.
89. *A Bear Called Paddington.* Written by Michael Bond. Illustrated by Peggy Fortnum.
90. *Chato's Kitchen.* Written by Gary Soto. Illustrated by Susan Guevara.
91. *Flotsam.* Illustrated by David Wiesner.
92. *Crictor.* Written and illustrated by Tomi Ungerer.
93. *Frog and Toad Together.* Written and illustrated by Arnold Lobel.
94. *Grandfather's Journey.* Written and illustrated by Allen Say.
95. *Henry and Mudge.* Written by Cynthia Rylant. Illustrated by Suçie Stevenson.
96. *Matilda.* Written by Roald Dahl. Illustrated by Quentin Blake.
97. *Just In Case: A Trickster Tale and Spanish Alphabet Book.* Written and illustrated by Yuyi Morales.
98. *Sector 7.* Written and illustrated by David Wiesner.
99. *Mirandy and Brother Wind.* Written by Patricia C. McKissack. Illustrated by Jerry Pinkney.
100. *Ling & Ting: Not Exactly the Same!* Written and illustrated by Grace Lin.

Middle-Reader Booklist

1. Harry Potter (series). *Harry Potter and the Sorcerer's Stone, Harry Potter and the Chamber of Secrets, Harry Potter and the Prisoner of Azkaban, Harry Potter and the Goblet of Fire, Harry Potter and the Order of the Phoenix, Harry Potter and the Half-Blood Prince, Harry Potter and the Deathly Hallows.* Written by J. K. Rowling.
2. *Charlotte's Web.* Written by E. B. White. Illustrated by Garth Williams.
3. *Hatchet.* Written by Gary Paulsen.
4. *One Crazy Summer.* Written by Rita Williams-Garcia.
5. *Wonderstruck.* Written and illustrated by Brian Selznick.
6. *Holes.* Written by Louis Sachar.
7. *Island of the Blue Dolphins.* Written by Scott O'Dell.
8. *Mrs. Frisby and the Rats of NIMH.* Written by Robert C. O'Brien. Illustrated by Zena Bernstein.
9. *A Wrinkle in Time.* Written by Madeleine L'Engle.
10. *Maniac Magee.* Written by Jerry Spinelli.
11. *Tuck Everlasting.* Written by Natalie Babbitt.
12. *Anne of Green Gables.* Written by L. M. Montgomery.
13. *Wonder.* Written by R. J. Palacio.
14. *Bridge to Terabithia.* Written by Katherine Paterson. Illustrated by Donna Diamond.
15. *The Phantom Tollbooth.* Written by Norton Juster. Illustrated by Jules Feiffer.
16. *Shiloh.* Written by Phyllis Reynolds Naylor.
17. *Little Women.* Written by Louisa May Alcott.
18. *Sarah, Plain and Tall.* Written by Patricia MacLachlan.
19. *Treasure Island.* Written by Robert Louis Stevenson.
20. *Ella Enchanted.* Written by Gail Carson Levine.

21. *From the Mixed-Up Files of Mrs. Basil E. Frankweiler.* Written and illustrated by E. L. Konigsburg.
22. *The Great Gilly Hopkins.* Written by Katherine Paterson.
23. *When You Reach Me.* Written by Rebecca Stead.
24. *Harriet the Spy.* Written and illustrated by Louise Fitzhugh.
25. *The Lion, the Witch, and the Wardrobe.* Written by C. S. Lewis. Illustrated by Pauline Baynes.
26. *The Secret Garden.* Written by Frances Hodgson Burnett. Illustrated by Tasha Tudor.
27. *Johnny Tremain.* Written by Esther Forbes.
28. *Where the Red Fern Grows.* Written by Wilson Rawls.
29. *Alice's Adventures in Wonderland.* Written by Lewis Carroll. Illustrated by John Tenniel.
30. *The Book of Three.* Written by Lloyd Alexander.
31. *Julie of the Wolves.* Written by Jean Craighead George. Illustrated by John Schoenherr.
32. *Number the Stars.* Written by Lois Lowry.
33. *The Wind in the Willows.* Written by Kenneth Grahame. Illustrated by Ernest H. Shepard.
34. *Black Beauty.* Written by Anna Sewell.
35. *The Adventures of Tom Sawyer.* Written by Mark Twain.
36. *The Borrowers.* Written by Mary Norton. Illustrated by Beth and Joe Krush.
37. *Charlie and the Chocolate Factory.* Written by Roald Dahl. Illustrated by Joseph Schindelman.
38. *Because of Winn-Dixie.* Written by Kate DiCamillo.
39. *The Cricket in Times Square.* Written by George Selden. Illustrated by Garth Williams.
40. *The Incredible Journey.* Written by Sheila Burnford. Illustrated by Carl Burger.
41. *The Jungle Book.* Written by Rudyard Kipling. Illustrated by John Lockwood Kipling.
42. *Okay for Now.* Written by Gary D. Schmidt.
43. *Mr. Popper's Penguins.* Written by Richard and Florence Atwater. Illustrated by Robert Lawson.
44. *Redwall.* Written by Brian Jacques. Illustrated by Gary Chalk.
45. *The People Could Fly: American Black Folktales.* Written by Virginia Hamilton. Illustrated by Leo and Diane Dillon.
46. *Robinson Crusoe.* Written by Daniel Defoe.
47. *Stuart Little.* Written by E. B. White. Illustrated by Garth Williams.
48. *The Whipping Boy.* Written by Sid Fleischman. Illustrated by Peter Sís.
49. *Winnie-the-Pooh.* Written by A. A. Milne. Illustrated by Ernest H. Shepard.

50. *The BFG*. Written by Roald Dahl. Illustrated by Quentin Blake.
51. *Anastasia Krupnik*. Written by Lois Lowry. Illustrated by Diane deGroat.
52. *The Wonderful Wizard of Oz*. Written by L. Frank Baum. Illustrated by W. W. Denslow.
53. *Are You There God? It's Me, Margaret*. Written by Judy Blume.
54. *Bud, Not Buddy*. Written by Christopher Paul Curtis.
55. *Bunnicula: A Rabbit-Tale of Mystery*. Written by Deborah Howe and James Howe. Illustrated by Alan Daniel.
56. *Dear Mr. Henshaw*. Written by Beverly Cleary. Illustrated by Paul O. Zelinsky.
57. *The Egypt Game*. Written by Zilpha Keatley Snyder. Illustrated by Alton Raible.
58. *Heidi*. Written by Johanna Spyri. Translated from German by Helen B. Dole.
59. *Splendors and Glooms*. Written by Laura Amy Schlitz.
60. *The Indian in the Cupboard*. Written by Lynne Reid Banks. Illustrated by Brock Cole.
61. *Little House in the Big Woods*. Written by Laura Ingalls Wilder. Illustrated by Garth Williams.
62. *Out of the Dust*. Written by Karen Hesse.
63. *Inside Out and Back Again*. Written by Thanhha Lai.
64. *Tales of a Fourth Grade Nothing*. Written by Judy Blume. Illustrated by Roy Doty.
65. *My Side of the Mountain*. Written and illustrated by Jean Craighead George.
66. *The Watsons Go to Birmingham—1963*. Written by Christopher Paul Curtis.
67. *Little House on the Prairie*. Written by Laura Ingalls Wilder. Illustrated by Garth Williams.
68. *Misty of Chincoteague*. Written by Marguerite Henry. Illustrated by Wesley Dennis.
69. *Ramona Quimby, Age Eight*. Written by Beverly Cleary. Illustrated by Jacqueline Rogers.
70. *Pippi Longstocking*. Written by Astrid Lindgren. Illustrated by Louis S. Glanzman.
71. *Stone Fox*. Written by John Reynolds Gardiner. Illustrated by Marcia Sewall.
72. *Where the Sidewalk Ends*. Written and illustrated by Shel Silverstein.
73. *Sounder*. Written by William H. Armstrong. Illustrated by James Barkley.
74. *D'Aulaires' Book of Greek Myths*. Written and illustrated by Ingrid and Edgar Parin D'Aulaire.
75. *Turtle in Paradise*. Written by Jennifer L. Holm.
76. *Esperanza Rising*. Written by Pam Muñoz Ryan.
77. *Frindle*. Written by Andrew Clements. Illustrated by Brian Selznick.

78. *Homer Price.* Written and illustrated by Robert McCloskey.
79. *Ninth Ward.* Written by Jewell Parker Rhodes.
80. *The Little Prince.* Written and illustrated by Antoine de Saint-Exupéry.
81. *Hoot.* Written by Carl Hiaasen.
82. *The Invention of Hugo Cabret.* Written and illustrated by Brian Selznick.
83. *James and the Giant Peach.* Written by Roald Dahl. Illustrated by Nancy Ekholm Burkert.
84. *Peter Pan.* Written by J. M. Barrie. Illustrated by F. D. Bedford.
85. *A Long Way from Chicago.* Written by Richard Peck.
86. *Mary Poppins.* Written by P. L. Travers. Illustrated by Mary Shepard.
87. *Crispin: The Cross of Lead.* Written by Avi.
88. *The Summer of the Swans.* Written by Betsy Byars. Illustrated by Ted Coconis.
89. *Ramona the Pest.* Written by Beverly Cleary. Illustrated by Louis Darling.
90. *The Dreamer.* Written by Pam Muñoz Ryan.
91. *The Swiss Family Robinson.* Written by Johann David Wyss.
92. *Abel's Island.* Written by William Steig.
93. *Dead End in Norvelt.* Written by Jack Gantos.
94. *Al Capone Does My Shirts.* Written by Gennifer Choldenko.
95. *The Black Stallion.* Written by Walter Farley.
96. *Among the Hidden.* Written by Margaret Peterson Haddix.
97. *Caddie Woodlawn.* Written by Carol Ryrie Brink. Illustrated by Trina Schart Hyman.
98. *The Arrival.* Illustrated by Shaun Tan.
99. *Nothing but the Truth.* Written by Avi.
100. *All-of-a-Kind Family.* Written by Sydney Taylor. Illustrated by Helen John.

APPENDIX 4

Young-Adult Booklist

1. *The Giver*. Written by Lois Lowry.
2. *Code Name Verity*. Written by Elizabeth Wein.
3. *The Hobbit*. Written by J. R. R. Tolkien.
4. *Roll of Thunder, Hear My Cry*. Written by Mildred Taylor.
5. The Lord of the Rings (trilogy). *The Fellowship of the Ring, The Two Towers, The Return of the King*. Written by J. R. R. Tolkien.
6. *Pride and Prejudice*. Written by Jane Austen.
7. *Monster Calls: Inspired by an Idea from Siobhan Dowd*. Written by Patrick Ness. Illustrated by Jim Kay.
8. *The Call of the Wild*. Written by Jack London.
9. *The Chocolate War*. Written by Robert Cormier.
10. *Skellig*. Written by David Almond.
11. *To Kill a Mockingbird*. Written by Harper Lee.
12. *The Fault in Our Stars*. Written by John Green.
13. *Walk Two Moons*. Written by Sharon Creech.
14. *The Witch of Blackbird Pond*. Written by Elizabeth George Speare.
15. *Son*. Written by Lois Lowry.
16. *The Outsiders*. Written by S. E. Hinton.
17. *A Wizard of Earthsea*. Written by Ursula Le Guin. Illustrated by Ruth Robbins.
18. *The Catcher in the Rye*. Written by J. D. Salinger.
19. *Between Shades of Gray*. Written by Ruta Sepetys.
20. *Catherine, Called Birdy*. Written by Karen Cushman.
21. *Lord of the Flies*. Written by William Golding.
22. *The True Confessions of Charlotte Doyle*. Written by Avi.
23. *The Westing Game*. Written by Ellen Raskin.
24. *The Bell Jar*. Written by Sylvia Plath.
25. *Fallen Angels*. Written by Walter Dean Myers.

26. *The House of the Scorpion.* Written by Nancy Farmer.
27. *The Moves Make the Man.* Written by Bruce Brooks.
28. *The Absolutely True Diary of a Part-Time Indian.* Written by Sherman Alexie. Illustrated by Ellen Forney.
29. *M. C. Higgins the Great.* Written by Virginia Hamilton.
30. *The Dark Is Rising.* Written by Susan Cooper.
31. *Jacob Have I Loved.* Written by Katherine Paterson.
32. *Eva.* Written by Peter Dickinson.
33. *The Joy Luck Club.* Written by Amy Tan.
34. *My Brother Sam Is Dead.* Written by James Lincoln Collier and Christopher Collier.
35. *Chime.* Written by Franny Billingsley.
36. *The Adventures of Huckleberry Finn.* Written by Mark Twain.
37. *The Color Purple.* Written by Alice Walker.
38. *Animal Farm.* Written by George Orwell.
39. *The Astonishing Life of Octavian Nothing, Traitor to the Nation.* Volume 1, *The Pox Party.* Written by M. T. Anderson.
40. *The Book Thief.* Written by Markus Zusak.
41. *Aristotle and Dante Discover the Secrets of the Universe.* Written by Benjamin Alire Sáenz.
42. *The Ear, the Eye, and the Arm.* Written by Nancy Farmer.
43. *Fahrenheit 451.* Written by Ray Bradbury.
44. *The Golden Compass.* Written by Philip Pullman.
45. *Frankenstein.* Written by Mary Wollstonecraft Shelley.
46. *The Grapes of Wrath.* Written by John Steinbeck.
47. *Kidnapped.* Written by Robert Louis Stevenson.
48. *The Great Gatsby.* Written by F. Scott Fitzgerald.
49. *Homecoming.* Written by Cynthia Voigt.
50. *Jane Eyre.* Written by Charlotte Brontë.
51. *Divergent.* Written by Veronica Roth.
52. *The Midwife's Apprentice.* Written by Karen Cushman.
53. The Hunger Games (trilogy series). *The Hunger Games, Catching Fire,* and *Mockingjay.* Written by Suzanne Collins.
54. *Shabanu: Daughter of the Wind.* Written by Suzanne Fisher Staples.
55. *One-Eyed Cat.* Written by Paula Fox.
56. *Slaughterhouse-Five.* Written by Kurt Vonnegut.
57. *Monster.* Written by Walter Dean Myers.
58. *The Slave Dancer.* Written by Paula Fox. Illustrated by Eros Keith.
59. *Weetzie Bat.* Written by Francesca Lia Block.
60. *The Sword in the Stone.* Written by T. H. White. Illustrated by Robert Lawson.
61. *Twenty Thousand Leagues under the Sea.* Written by Jules Verne.

62. *Watership Down*. Written by Richard Adams.
63. *The Scorpio Races*. Written by Maggie Stiefvater.
64. *The Yearling*. Written by Marjorie Kinnan Rawlings. Illustrated by N. C. Wyeth.
65. *Blink & Caution*. Written by Tim Wynne-Jones.
66. *Z for Zachariah*. Written by Robert O'Brien.
67. *1984*. Written by George Orwell.
68. *Across Five Aprils*. Written by Irene Hunt. Illustrated by Albert John Pucci.
69. *Catch-22*. Written by Joseph Heller.
70. *American Born Chinese*. Written by Gene Luen Yang.
71. *Before We Were Free*. Written by Julia Alvarez.
72. *The Devil's Arithmetic*. Written by Jane Yolen.
73. *Beloved*. Written by Toni Morrison.
74. *The Cay*. Written by Theodore Taylor.
75. *The Changeover: A Supernatural Romance*. Written by Margaret Mahy.
76. *A Christmas Carol*. Written by Charles Dickens.
77. *Never Fall Down*. Written by Patricia McCormick.
78. *The Curious Incident of the Dog in the Night-Time*. Written by Mark Haddon.
79. *Dragonwings*. Written by Laurence Yep.
80. *Ender's Game*. Written by Orson Scott Card.
81. *Gathering Blue*. Written by Lois Lowry.
82. *Eragon*. Written by Christopher Paolini.
83. *The First Part Last*. Written by Angela Johnson.
84. *Heart of Darkness*. Written by Joseph Conrad.
85. *Go Tell It on the Mountain*. Written by James A. Baldwin.
86. *Gossamer*. Written by Lois Lowry.
87. *Sweet Whispers, Brother Rush*. Written by Virginia Hamilton.
88. *The Merry Adventures of Robin Hood*. Written by Howard Pyle.
89. *The Hitchhiker's Guide to the Galaxy*. Written by Douglas Adams.
90. *The Scarlet Letter*. Written by Nathaniel Hawthorne.
91. *Hoops*. Written by Walter Dean Myers.
92. *No Crystal Stair: A Documentary Novel of the Life and Work of Lewis Michaux, Harlem Bookseller*. Written by Vaunda Micheaux Nelson.
93. *The Pigman*. Written by Paul Zindel.
94. *Thirteen Reasons Why*. Written by Jay Asher.
95. *The Prince and the Pauper*. Written by Mark Twain.
96. *Stargirl*. Written by Jerry Spinelli.
97. *How I Live Now*. Written by Meg Rosoff.
98. *One Flew over the Cuckoo's Nest*. Written by Ken Kesey.
99. *Daughter of Smoke & Bone*. Written by Laini Taylor.
100. *Nation*. Written by Terry Pratchett.

APPENDIX 5

Adult Booklist

1. Rabbit (series). *Rabbit, Run; Rabbit Redux; Rabbit Is Rich;* and *Rabbit at Rest.* Written by John Updike.
2. *Bring Up the Bodies.* Written by Hilary Mantel.
3. *This Is How You Lose Her.* Written by Junot Díaz.
4. *Atonement.* Written by Ian McEwan.
5. *Lolita.* Written by Vladimir Nabokov.
6. *On the Road.* Written by Jack Kerouac.
7. *The Corrections.* Written by Jonathan Franzen.
8. *Gilead.* Written by Marilynne Robinson.
9. *Midnight's Children.* Written by Salman Rushdie.
10. *The Amazing Adventures of Kavalier & Clay.* Written by Michael Chabon.
11. *Cloud Atlas.* Written by David Mitchell.
12. *Invisible Man.* Written by Ralph Ellison.
13. *Gone Girl.* Written by Gillian Flynn.
14. *Love in the Time of Cholera.* Written by Gabriel García Márquez.
15. *Possession.* Written by A. S. Byatt.
16. *Ulysses.* Written by James Joyce.
17. *Billy Lynn's Long Halftime Walk.* Written by Ben Fountain.
18. *All the King's Men.* Written by Robert Penn Warren.
19. *The Handmaid's Tale.* Written by Margaret Atwood.
20. *Brideshead Revisited.* Written by Evelyn Waugh.
21. *Housekeeping.* Written by Marilynne Robinson.
22. *The Poisonwood Bible.* Written by Barbra Kingsolver.
23. *American Pastoral.* Written by Philip Roth.
24. *White Teeth.* Written by Zadie Smith.
25. *Bel Canto.* Written by Ann Patchett.
26. *Empire Falls.* Written by Richard Russo.

27. *Brave New World*. Written by Aldous Huxley.
28. *Love Medicine*. Written by Louise Erdrich.
29. *The Brief Wondrous Life of Oscar Wao*. Written by Junot Díaz.
30. *A Clockwork Orange*. Written by Anthony Burgess.
31. *Gone with the Wind*. Written by Margaret Mitchell.
32. *The Known World*. Written by Edward P. Jones.
33. *The Yellow Birds*. Written by Kevin Powers.
34. *Middlesex*. Written by Jeffrey Eugenides.
35. *The Road*. Written by Cormac McCarthy.
36. *On Beauty*. Written by Zadie Smith.
37. *The Remains of the Day*. Written by Kazuo Ishiguro.
38. *The Sun Also Rises*. Written by Ernest Hemingway.
39. *The Age of Innocence*. Written by Edith Wharton.
40. *Years of Red Dust: Stories of Shanghai*. Written by Qiu Xiaolong.
41. *As I Lay Dying*. Written by William Faulkner.
42. *Brick Lane*. Written by Monica Ali.
43. *Austerlitz*. Written by W. G. Sebald.
44. *The Bonfire of the Vanities*. Written by Tom Wolfe.
45. *Kafka on the Shore*. Written by Haruki Murakami.
46. *Death Comes for the Archbishop*. Written by Willa Cather.
47. *The Inheritance of Loss*. Written by Kiran Desai.
48. *Arcadia*. Written by Lauren Groff.
49. *Ironweed*. Written by William Kennedy.
50. *The Kite Runner*. Written by Khaled Hosseini.
51. *The Maltese Falcon*. Written by Dashiell Hammett.
52. *Wolf Hall*. Written by Hilary Mantel.
53. *The Name of the Rose*. Written by Umberto Eco.
54. *A Prayer for Owen Meany*. Written by John Irving.
55. *Tree of Smoke*. Written by Denis Johnson.
56. *Song of Solomon*. Written by Toni Morrison.
57. *To the Lighthouse*. Written by Virginia Woolf.
58. *The Adventures of Augie March*. Written by Saul Bellow.
59. *The Wind-Up Bird Chronicle*. Written by Haruki Murakami.
60. *Alias Grace*. Written by Margaret Atwood.
61. *Anna Karenina*. Written by Leo Tolstoy.
62. *Freedom*. Written by Jonathan Franzen.
63. *Billy Bathgate*. Written by E. L. Doctorow.
64. *Disgrace*. Written by J. M. Coetzee.
65. *The Blind Assassin*. Written by Margaret Atwood.
66. *Cathedral*. Written by Raymond Carver.
67. *The Heart Is a Lonely Hunter*. Written by Carson McCullers.

68. *A Confederacy of Dunces*. Written by John Kennedy Toole.
69. *The Day of the Locust*. Written by Nathanael West.
70. *A Flag for Sunrise*. Written by Robert Stone.
71. *Dune*. Written by Frank Herbert.
72. *Howards End*. Written by E. M. Forster.
73. *Life of Pi*. Written by Yann Martel.
74. *The Human Stain*. Written by Philip Roth.
75. *The Line of Beauty*. Written by Alan Hollinghurst.
76. *The Naked and the Dead*. Written by Norman Mailer.
77. *Lonesome Dove*. Written by Larry McMurtry.
78. *Angle of Repose*. Written by Wallace Stegner.
79. *The Master*. Written by Colm Tóibín.
80. *The Lovely Bones*. Written by Alice Sebold.
81. *Money: A Suicide Note*. Written by Martin Amis.
82. *Old School*. Written by Tobias Wolff.
83. *The Moviegoer*. Written by Walker Percy.
84. *A Passage to India*. Written by E. M. Forster.
85. *Mrs. Dalloway*. Written by Virginia Woolf.
86. *Never Let Me Go*. Written by Kazuo Ishiguro.
87. *A Visit from the Goon Squad*. Written by Jennifer Egan.
88. *Portnoy's Complaint*. Written by Philip Roth.
89. *Netherland*. Written by Joseph O'Neill.
90. *The Prime of Miss Jean Brodie*. Written by Muriel Spark.
91. *Ragtime*. Written by E. L. Doctorow.
92. *Schindler's List*. Written by Thomas Keneally.
93. *Rebecca*. Written by Daphne Du Maurier.
94. *The Satanic Verses*. Written by Salman Rushdie.
95. *On Chesil Beach*. Written by Ian McEwan.
96. *The Secret History*. Written by Donna Tartt.
97. *The Tiger's Wife*. Written by Téa Obreht.
98. *The Sheltering Sky*. Written by Paul Bowles.
99. *The March*. Written by E. L. Doctorow.
100. *Sophie's Choice*. Written by William Styron.

Bibliography

A Lifetime of Fiction: The 500 Most Recommended Reads for Ages 2 to 102 is a composite of the most reliable and influential English-language book awards, references, web guides, and reading lists from leading magazines, newspapers, consumer and parenting organizations, schools, and libraries. Award winner and finalist information was gathered from the date of inception of the award to the most recent material available. In cases where best-book lists encompassed multiple years, the web address of the most recent year was used.

The bibliography is organized into seven sections. The Book Awards and Best-Book Lists sections contain additional annotations. Section 7 lists the additional reading sources mentioned in the 27 biographical sketches in chapter 7. The seven sections are

Book Awards—Preschool through Young Adult
Best-Book Lists—Preschool through Young Adult
Library and School Reading Lists—Preschool through Young Adult
Book Awards—Adult
Best-Book Lists—Adult
Library and School Reading Lists—Adult
Additional Reading (Chapter 7)

Book Awards—Preschool through Young Adult

"Alex Awards." Young Adult Library Services Association, American Library Association. Accessed March 22, 2013. http://www.ala.org/yalsa/booklists/alex/.

The association gives awards each year to recognize books written for adults with special appeal to young adults. Award information was collected for the years 1998 through 2013.

"Amelia Frances Howard-Gibbon Illustrator's Award." Canadian Library Association. Accessed March 22, 2013. http://www.cla.ca/AM/Template.cfm?Section=Amelia_ Frances_Howard_Gibbon_Illustrator_s_Award.
This medal is awarded each year for the best-illustrated children's book published in Canada for children up to age 12. Award information was collected for the years 1971 through 2012.

"Américas Award for Children's and Young Adult Literature." Consortium of Latin American Studies Programs. Accessed July 23, 2013. http://www4.uwm.edu/clacs/aa/.
The award is presented in recognition of distinguished U.S. works published in English or Spanish that engagingly portray Latin America, the Caribbean, or Latinos in the United States. Award information was collected for the years 1993 through 2013.

"Australian Children's Book of the Year Award." Children's Book Council of Australia. Accessed July 23, 2013. http://cbca.org.au/awards.htm.
Each year the council presents awards for outstanding books in the categories of early childhood, younger readers, older readers, and picture books. Award information was collected for the years 1946 through 2013.

"Boston Globe–Horn Book Awards." Accessed July 23, 2013. http://www.hbook.com/ boston-globe-horn-book-awards/.
These annual awards recognize and reward excellence in literature for children and young adults. Award information was collected for the years 1967 through 2013.

"Caldecott Awards." Association for Library Service to Children, American Library Association. Accessed March 23, 2013. http://www.ala.org/alsc/awardsgrants/bookmedia/ caldecottmedal/caldecottmedal.
The Randolph Caldecott Medal is generally considered the pinnacle of achievement for illustration of children's books in the United States. The annual award goes to the artist of the most distinguished picture book for children. Award information was collected for the years 1938 through 2013.

"Canadian Library Association Book of the Year for Children." Canadian Library Association. Accessed March 23, 2013. http://www.cla.ca/AM/Template.cfm?Section=Book_ of_the_Year_for_Children_Award.
The association awards a medal annually to the Canadian author of the best children's book published in Canada. Award information was collected for the years 1947 through 2012.

"Canadian Library Association Young Adult Book Award." Accessed March 23, 2013. http://www.cla.ca/AM/Template.cfm?Section=Young_Adult_Canadian_Book_ Award&Template=/CM/HTMLDisplay.cfm&ContentID=14242.
This annual award recognizes an author of an outstanding English-language Canadian fiction book for teens between the ages of 13 and 18. Award information was collected for the years 1981 through 2012.

"Carnegie Medal." Chartered Institute of Library and Information Professionals. Accessed March 28, 2013. http://www.carnegiegreenaway.org.uk/carnegie/.
  The Carnegie Medal is awarded annually to the writer of an outstanding United Kingdom book for children and young people. Award information was collected for the years 1936 through 2012.

"Charlotte Zolotow Award." Cooperative Children's Book Center of the School of Education, University of Wisconsin, Madison. Accessed March 29, 2013. http://www .education.wisc.edu/ccbc/books/zolotow.asp.
  The center presents an annual award for outstanding text in picture books published in the United States. Award information was collected for the years 1998 through 2013.

"Children's Crown Award." Texas Christian Schools Association. Accessed July 23, 2013. http://www.childrenscrownaward.org/home.htm.
  The awards recognize wholesome and uplifting mainstream books. Award information was collected for the years 2000 through 2013.

"Christopher Award." Christopher Foundation. Accessed April 4, 2013. http://www .christophers.org/page.aspx?pid=217.
  The organization presents annual awards for books affirming spiritual values. Award information was collected for the years 2002 through 2013.

"Coretta Scott King Awards." American Library Association. Accessed July 23, 2013. http://www.ala.org/emiert/cskbookawards.
  This annual award is given to African American authors and illustrators who demonstrate an appreciation of African American culture and universal human values through children and young-adult books. Award information was collected for the years 1970 through 2013.

"Geisel Award." Association for Library Service to Children, American Library Association. Accessed April 4, 2013. http://www.ala.org/alsc/awardsgrants/bookmedia/ geiselaward.
  The annual (Theodor Seuss) Geisel Award honors the year's most distinguished American book for beginning readers. Award information was collected for the years 2006 through 2013.

"Golden Kite Awards." Society of Children's Book Writers and Illustrators. Accessed July 23, 2013. http://www.scbwi.org/Pages.aspx/Golden-Kite-Award.
  Established to recognize excellence in children's literature, the annual Golden Kite Awards are the only children's literary awards judged by a jury of peers. Award information was collected for the years 1974 through 2013.

"Michael L. Printz Award for Excellence in Young Adult Literature." Young Adult Library Services Association, American Library Association. Accessed July 23, 2013. http://www.ala.org/yalsa/printz.
  This annual award recognizes works of literary excellence written for a teenage audience. Award information was collected for the years 2000 through 2013.

"National Book Award for Young People's Literature." National Book Foundation. Accessed July 23, 2013. http://www.nationalbook.org/nbawinners_category.html#.Ue_G8RbvyRs.

The National Book Foundation presents annual awards to recognize outstanding merit in children's literature. The foundation gave out book awards for children's literature from 1969 through 1983 and from 1996 to the present.

"National Parenting Publication Awards." Accessed April 9, 2013. http://www.nappaawards.com/index.php/award-winners1/.

This organization evaluates parent resources and children's products, selecting those that are the most attractive, safe, educational, and age appropriate. Award information was collected for the years 2010 through 2012.

"Newbery Awards." Association for Library Service to Children, American Library Association. Accessed March 23, 2013. http://www.ala.org/alsc/awardsgrants/bookmedia/newberymedal/newberymedal.

The annual Newbery Medal is America's most distinguished and widely recognized award for excellence in children's literature. Award information was collected for the years 1922 through 2013.

"Pura Belpré Award." Association for Library Service to Children, American Library Association. Accessed March 24, 2013. http://www.ala.org/alsc/awardsgrants/bookmedia/belpremedal.

The award is presented to a Latino/Latina writer and illustrator whose work best portrays the Latino cultural experience in an outstanding work of literature for children and youth. The prize was given every two years from 1996 through 2008 and has been awarded annually from 2009 through 2013.

"Schneider Family Book Award." American Library Association. Accessed April 4, 2013. http://www.ala.org/news/mediapresscenter/presskits/youthmediaawards/schneiderfamilybookaward.

The award honors an author or illustrator of a book that best expresses the disability experience of children and adolescents. Award information was collected for 2012, the first year the award was given.

"Scott O'Dell Award for Historical Fiction." O'Dell Committee. Accessed April 4, 2013. http://www.scottodell.com/pages/ScottO'DellAwardforHistoricalFiction.aspx.

This annual award goes to a meritorious book in order to encourage authors to focus on history. Award information was collected for the years 1984 through 2013.

"Stonewall Book Award–Mike Morgan and Larry Romans Children's & Young Adult Literature Award." Gay, Lesbian, Bisexual, and Transgender Round Table, American Library Association. Accessed March 24, 2013. http://www.ala.org/awardsgrants/stonewall-book-awards-mike-morgan-larry-romans-children's-young-adult-literature-award.

The annual awards are presented to English-language books that have exceptional merit relating to the gay/lesbian/bisexual/transgendered experience. Award information was collected for the years 2010 through 2013.

"Tomas Rivera Mexican-American Children's Book Award." College of Education, Texas State University at San Marcos. Accessed April 3, 2013. http://www.education .txstate.edu/c-p/Tomas-Rivera-Book-Award-Project-Link.html.

The university annually recognizes the most distinguished book for children and young adults about Mexican Americans. Award information was collected for the years 1996 through 2012.

Best-Book Lists—Preschool through Young Adult

"100 Best Books for Teens." Last modified October 2, 2002. http://archive.ala.org/yalsa/ booklists/bestofbest2000.html.

During the American Library Association's 2000 best-of-the-best preconference, librarians for young adults picked the 100 books they considered to be the best. The scope of their selection was the ALA's Best Books for Young Adults lists published from 1966 to 2000.

"100 Best Children's Books of All Time." Parenthood.com. Accessed April 17, 2013. http://www.parenthood.com/article-topics/the_100_best_childrens_books.html/ full-view.

This list represents the views of parents, readers, and children's literature experts on books expected to stand the test of time.

"100 Greatest Books for Kids." *USA Today.* Accessed April 7, 2013. http://www.usa today.com/life/books/news/story/2012-02-14/100-greatest-books-for-kids/53095042 /1?loc=interstitialskip.

The newspaper's list of best books was ranked by *Scholastic Parent & Child* magazine.

"101 Great Books Recommended for College-Bound Readers." The College Board. Accessed March 24, 2013. http://www.stut-hs.eu.dodea.edu/site/media/documents/101 GreatBooksRecommendedforCollege.pdf.

The College Board is made up of more than 5,700 schools, colleges, universities, and other educational organizations.

"All-Time Best Books for Preschoolers." Parents.com. Accessed April 17, 2013. http:// www.parents.com/fun/entertainment/books/the-all-time-best-books-for-preschoolers/ #page=1.

Parents.com is the online home of *Parents, American Baby,* and *Family Circle* magazines.

"Amelia Bloomer Project." Feminist Task Force of the American Library Association's Social Responsibilities Round Table. Accessed March 26, 2013. http://ameliabloomer .wordpress.com.

Task force committees create annual booklists of the best feminist books for young readers up to age 18. Booklists were collected for the years 2002 through 2013.

Barr, Catherine. *Best Books for Children: Preschool through Grade 6; Supplement to the 9th Edition*. New York: Libraries Unlimited, 2013.

This supplement is intended for librarians who want to stay abreast of school curriculum trends and children's interests.

"Best 25 Books of 25 Years: Infant to Age 9." Parents' Choice Foundation. Accessed April 17, 2013. http://www.parents-choice.org/article.cfm?art_id=395.

The Parents' Choice "Best 25 of 25" Book Committee is comprised of parents, teachers, librarians, and critics.

"Best Books: Our Recommendations for Families." Common Sense Media. Accessed March 19, 2013. http://www.commonsensemedia.org/lists/book.

This not-for-profit organization provides reliable information regarding children's media and technology.

"Best Books of the Year." *School Library Journal*. Last modified November 29, 2012. http://www.slj.com/2012/11/featured/best-books-2012/.

The monthly magazine issues an annual best-books list. Booklists were collected for the years 2000 through 2012.

"The Best Children's Books of the Year, 2010–2012." Children's Book Committee, Bank Street College, New York, NY. Accessed July 23, 2013. http://bankstreet.edu/center-childrens-literature/childrens-book-committee/best-books-year/past-editions/.

The committee is comprised of writers, illustrators, editors, librarians, teachers, and parents who together recommend the best books for children.

"Best Fiction for Young Adults." Young Adult Library Services Association, American Library Association. Accessed July 24, 2013. http://www.ala.org/yalsa/bfya.

Each year YALSA recommends a best-of-the-best list of fiction books for readers aged 12–18. Booklists were collected for the years 2011 through 2013.

"Better Kid Care Project Reading Aloud Book List." National Network for Child Care. Last modified February 1996. http://www.nncc.org/Literacy/better.read.list.html.

The NNCC unites the expertise of many of the nation's leading universities to bring resources to children.

Book Sense Best Children's Books: 240 Favorites for All Ages Recommended by Independent Booksellers. New York: Newmarket Press, 2005.

The national booksellers organization compiled separate lists for different age groups.

"Booklist Editors' Choice: Books for Youth." American Library Association. Accessed April 6, 2013. http://www.ala.org/awardsgrants/booklist-editors-choice-books-youth.

Each year editors of the book-review magazine select outstanding titles that mix popular appeal with literary excellence. Booklists were collected for the years 1996 through 2012.

"California Reading List." California Department of Education. Accessed September 10, 2010. http://www.cde.ca.gov/ta/tg/sr/readinglist.asp.

The state agency recommends age-appropriate reading lists for students in kindergarten through grade 12.

Carter, Betty, Sally Estes, and Linda Waddle. *Best Books for Young Adults*. Chicago: American Library Association, 2000.
The core of the book is 25 bibliographies of exceptional books.

"CCBC Choices." Cooperative Children's Book Center, School of Education, University of Wisconsin, Madison. Accessed July 25, 2013. http://www.education.wisc.edu/ccbc/books/choices.asp.
The center is a research library for school and public librarians, teachers, early childhood care providers, university students, and others interested in children's and young adult literature. Booklists were collected for the years 2004 through 2013.

"Children's Choices Reading Lists." International Reading Association. Accessed July 25, 2013. http://www.reading.org/resources/booklists/childrenschoices.aspx.
The association surveys thousands of U.S. schoolchildren each year regarding their favorite books. Booklists were collected for the years 1998 through 2013.

"Children's Classics: A Booklist for Parents." *Horn Book* magazine. Accessed April 17, 2013. http://archive.hbook.com/pdf/childrensclassics.pdf.
This is a list of both classic and recent titles.

"Children's Notable Lists." Association for Library Service to Children, American Library Association. Accessed April 1, 2013. http://www.ala.org/alsc/awardsgrants/notalists.
Each year the ALSC complies best-of-the-best lists of children's books. Booklists were collected for the years 1995 through 2013.

Eccleshare, Julia. *1001 Children's Books You Must Read before You Grow Up*. New York: Universe, 2009.
This reference is a compendium of the best 20th-century children's literature.

"Favorite Books for Pre-Readers." Scholastic.com. Accessed April 18, 2013. http://www.scholastic.com/parents/resources/book-list/favorites-classics/favorite-books-pre-readers.
The publishing company surveyed early childhood experts to create this list of favorite books.

Greengrass, Linda. *Best Books to Read Aloud with Children of All Ages*. New York: Bank Street College of Education, 2012.
The Children's Book Committee of the Bank Street College of Education selects and annotates the best-of-the-best books for children.

"Kidsreads Classic Picture Books." Kidsreads.com. Accessed April 17, 2013. http://www.kidsreads.com.asp1-14.dfw1-2.websitetestlink.com/lists/pic-classic.asp.
Kidsreads is a website for children and parents to find information about the best books for young people.

Lipson, Eden Ross. *The New York Times Parent's Guide to the Best Books for Children*. New York: Three Rivers Press, 2000.
This is an annotated compendium of the best 1,001 books for kids.

Northup, Mary. *Picture Books for Children: Fiction, Folktales, and Poetry*. New York: American Library Association, 2012.
This is an annotated list of best books for the classroom, library, or home.

"Notable Children's Books." *New York Times*. Accessed July 25, 2013. http://www .nytimes.com/2012/12/02/books/review/notable-childrens-books-of-2012.html?_r=0.
The children's book editor of the *New York Times Book Review* makes yearly recommendations. Last modified December 23, 2012. Booklists were collected for the years 2004 through 2012.

"Notable Children's Books in the English Language Arts." Children's Literature Assembly of the National Council of Teachers of English. Accessed July 25, 2013. http:// www.childrensliteratureassembly.org/notables.html.
A national committee compiles annual lists of recommended books that demonstrate appeal and excellence in the use of language. Booklists were collected for the years 1997 through 2013.

"NoveList K–8 Plus." EBSCO Information Services. Accessed July 25, 2013. http://www .ebscohost.com/novelist/our-products/novelist-k8.
This is an online database for libraries with titles chosen to support the school curriculum.

Pearl, Nancy. *Book Crush: For Kids and Teens; Recommended Reading for Every Mood, Moment, and Interest*. Seattle, WA: Sasquatch Books, 2007.
Nancy Pearl is one of America's best-known librarians.

"Preschool Summer Reading List." Education.com. Last modified May 10, 2012. http:// www.education.com/magazine/article/preschool-summer-reading-list/.
Research teams recommend books that tell good stories and teach kids how to constructively express themselves and how to generate conversation. Booklists were collected for the years 2009 through 2012.

"Publishers Weekly Best Books." Accessed March 18, 2013. http://www.publishers weekly.com:8080/pw/best-books/2012/childrens-fiction#book/book-1.
The trade news and book review magazine makes yearly best-book selections. Booklists were collected for the years 2009 through 2012.

"Read Aloud America 2013 Reading List." Last modified January 2013. http://www .readaloudamerica.org/booklist.htm.
Read Aloud America is a nonprofit organization that promotes literacy and the love of reading.

Silvey, Anita. *100 Best Books for Children: A Parent's Guide to Making the Right Choices for Your Young Reader, Toddler to Preteen*. Boston: Mariner Books, 2004.
This is an annotated list of classic children's books published between 1902 and 2002.

Sullivan, Joanna. *The Children's Literature Lover's Book of Lists*. San Francisco, CA: Jossey-Bass (2003).

Organized by grade level, theme, and content areas, the book is a catalog of quality literature for preschoolers through grade six.

"Teachers' Choices Reading Lists." International Reading Association. Accessed July 25, 2013. http://www.reading.org/resources/booklists/teacherschoices.aspx.
Each year the association reports the most noteworthy trade books for children and adolescents. Booklists were collected for the years 1998 through 2013.

"Teachers' Top 100 Books for Children." National Education Association. Accessed April 17, 2013. http://www.nea.org/grants/teachers-top-100-books-for-children.html.
Based on a survey of union members, this booklist is intended as a guide for parents and teachers.

"Teenreads.com 2013 Ultimate Teen Reading List." Teenreads.com. Accessed July 26, 2013. http://www.teenreads.com/sites/default/files/2013%20Ultimate%20List.pdf.
This website recommends books based on reader input and staff selections.

"Top 100 Children's Books of All-Time." Children's Book Guide. Accessed March 24, 2013. http://childrensbooksguide.com/top-100.
This website provides excellent book descriptions and categorizations.

"Top 100 Picture Books." *School Library Journal.* Accessed April 8, 2013. http://www.slj .com/wp-content/uploads/2012/08/SLJ_Fuse8_Top100_Picture.pdf.
The readers of the journal voted on what they felt were the best children's novels of all time.

"Top 100 Teen Books." National Public Radio. Last modified August 7, 2012. http:// www.npr.org/2012/08/07/157847723/top-100-teen-books.
NPR did a readers' survey in the summer of 2012 asking for the best young-adult fiction ever written.

Wilson, Elizabeth. *Books Children Love: A Guide to the Best Children's Literature.* Westchester, IL: Crossway Books, 1987.
This best-book guide selected books that embody literary quality and a traditional worldview.

"Young Adults' Choices Reading Lists." International Reading Association. Accessed July 26, 2013. http://www.reading.org/Resources/Booklists/YoungAdultsChoices.aspx.
Under the sponsorship of the IRA, each year thousands of U.S. teenagers select their favorite titles. Booklists were collected for the years 1998 through 2013.

Library and School Reading Lists—Preschool through Young Adult

"100 Best Picture Books." Stockton–San Joaquin County Public Library, Stockton, CA. Accessed April 17, 2013. http://www.ssjcpl.org/books/kids/reading/pictureBooks .html.

"100 Books for Children." St. Paul Public Library, St. Paul, MN. Accessed September 10, 2010. http://www.sppl.org/sites/default/files/rcl/images/100-books-for-children.pdf.

"Best Books for Toddlers and Preschoolers." Cumberland County Library System, Carlisle, PA. Last modified May 19, 2009. http://pa-cumberlandcountylibraries.civicplus.com/index.aspx?NID=493.

Bird, Elizabeth. "Announcing the 100 Titles for Reading and Sharing: Children's Books 2011." New York Public Library, New York, NY. Last modified December 30, 2011. http://www.nypl.org/blog/2011/12/30/100-titles-reading-and-sharing-childrens-books-2011.

"Book Lists." Queens Library, New York, NY. Accessed June 30, 2013. http://www.queenslibrary.org/kids/books-stories/kids-booklist.

"Books by Grade Level." Berkeley Public Library, Berkeley, CA. Accessed April 16, 2013. http://www.berkeleypubliclibrary.org/children/good-books/other-booklists/.

"Books for Preschoolers." Allen County Public Library, Fort Wayne, IN. Last modified September 26, 2012. http://www.acpl.lib.in.us/children/preschoolbooks.html.

"Classics for Teens." Logan Library, Logan, UT. Last modified January 2011. http://library.loganutah.org/books/YA/Classics.cfm.

"Classics for Teens." Yorba Linda Public Library, Yorba Linda, CA. Accessed April 17, 2013. http://www.ylpl.lib.ca.us/ya/ya_classics.php.

"Classics for Young Adults." Wheaton Public Library, Wheaton, IL. Accessed September 10, 2010. http://www.wheatonlibrary.org/pdf/TBib_Classics.pdf.

"College Bound Reading List." Arrowhead Library System, Janesville, WI. Accessed September 10, 2010. http://als.lib.wi.us/Collegebound.html.

"Elementary Reading Lists." Parkway School District, Chesterfield, MO. Accessed July 27, 2013. http://www.pkwy.k12.mo.us/panda/subjectlinks/elemSRL2013.pdf.

"Good Books & Media." Worthington Libraries, Worthington, OH. Accessed May 1, 2013. http://www.worthingtonlibraries.org/kids/books-media.

"Good Reading Lists." Pasadena Public Library, Pasadena, CA. Accessed August 30, 2010. http://cityofpasadena.net/library/kids/books_and_more/.

"Graded Booklists." Salt Lake City Public Library, Salt Lake City, UT. Accessed June 15, 2013. http://classic.slcpl.org/details.jsp?parent_id=265&page_id=271.

"Kids Booklists." San José Public Library, San Jose, CA. Accessed June 14, 2012. http://www.sjpl.org/booklistmenu.

"Little Kids Booklists." Carnegie Library of Pittsburgh, Pittsburgh, PA. Accessed July 24, 2013. http://www.carnegielibrary.org/kids/books/littlekids.cfm.

Milligan, Mary G. "A List of Recommended Books Preschool through Middle School." St. Luke's Episcopal School, Newman Library, San Antonio, TX. Accessed April 15, 2013. https://webapps.pcrsoft.com/ApplicationFiles/Clue/CustomResources/StLukes/2012Recommend-read-List.pdf.

"New York Public Library's 100 Picture Books Everyone Should Know." Ann Arbor District Library, Ann Arbor, MI. Last modified June 5, 2013. http://www.aadl.org/user/lists/26610. (The New York Public Library created this list in 2005, but no longer maintains it on its website.)

"Pre-K–Kindergarten Summer Reading List." Chicago Public Schools, Chicago, IL. Accessed September 10, 2010. http://www.cps.edu/Documents/SummerReading/SummerReadingList.pdf.

"Recommended Reading Lists." Houston Area Independent Schools Library Network, Houston, TX. Last modified March 26, 2013. http://www.haisln.org/recommendedreadinglists.html.

"Suggested Reading." Monmouth County Library, Manalapan, NJ. Accessed July 24, 2013. http://www.monmouthcountylib.org/index.php/books-and-reading.

"Summer Book List." Boston Public Schools, Boston, MA. Accessed July 10, 2012. http://www.bostonpublicschools.org/files/booklist_12_k-2.pdf.

"Summer Reading List—Grade 12 and AP Literature." Boston Latin Academy, Boston, MA. Accessed July 26, 2013. http://latinacademy.org/wp-content/uploads/2013/06/2013Grade12.pdf.

"Summer Reading Lists." Fresno County Public Library, Fresno, CA. Accessed July 25, 2013. http://www.fresnokids.org/p/summer-reading.html.

"Summer Reading Lists." Grandview Preparatory School, Boca Raton, FL. Accessed July 27, 2013. http://www.grandviewprep.net/pdfs/SummerReadingLists2013.pdf.

"Teen Booklists." Plymouth District Library, Plymouth, MI. Accessed July 20, 2013. http://plymouthlibrary.org/index.php/teen/teen-booklists.

"Top 20 Teen Novels." Seattle Public Library, Seattle, WA. Accessed May 1, 2013. http://www.spl.org/audiences/teens/teen-books-and-more/books-for-teens. (Librarians compiled lists for the best novels of the 20th and 21st centuries.)

Book Awards—Adult

"Bram Stoker Awards." Horror Writer's Association. Accessed April 14, 2013. http://www.horror.org/stokerwinnom.htm.

Each year the association presents awards for superior achievement. Award information was collected for the years 1988 through 2011.

"Edgar Awards." The Mystery Writers of America. Accessed May 14, 2013. http://www.theedgars.com/index.html.

The organization presents annual awards for excellence in crime and mystery writing. Award information was collected for the years 1946 through 2013.

"Hugo Awards." World Science Fiction Society. Accessed April 14, 2013. http://www.thehugoawards.org/hugo-history/.

Voted on by thousands of members of the annual World Science Fiction Convention, the yearly Hugo Awards are science fiction's most prestigious prize. Award information was collected for the years 1946 through 2012.

"Los Angeles Times Book Prize for Fiction." *Los Angeles Times*. Accessed April 14, 2013. http://events.latimes.com/bookprizes/.

The annual prize is awarded for literary excellence and to recognize enduring aesthetic and cultural values. Award information was collected for the years 1980 through 2012.

"Man Booker Prize." Booker Prize Foundation. Accessed July 25, 2013. http://www
.themanbookerprize.com/timeline.
The Booker Prize is the United Kingdom's top literary prize and one of the most watched book awards in the English-speaking world. Award information was collected for the years 1969 through 2013.

"National Book Awards." National Book Foundation. Accessed April 14, 2013. http://
www.nationalbook.org/nba2013.html#.UfUOZY7R38s.
The foundation presents annual awards to recognize the best American literature and to enhance the cultural value of good writing. Award information was collected for the years 1950 through 2012.

"National Book Critics Circle Award." National Book Critics Circle. Accessed April 16, 2013. http://bookcritics.org/awards.
The NBCC is an organization of more than 600 book critics, authors, literary bloggers, book publishing personnel, and student members who annually honor the highest-quality writing published in English. Award information was collected for the years 1975 through 2012.

"Nebula Award." Science Fiction and Fantasy Writers of America. Accessed April 14, 2013. http://www.sfwa.org/nebula-awards/.
The annual awards recognize excellence in science fiction and fantasy writing published in the United States. Award information was collected for the years 1966 through 2012.

"PEN/Faulkner Award for Fiction." PEN/Faulkner Foundation. Accessed April 16, 2013. http://www.penfaulkner.org/award-for-fiction/past-award-winners-finalists/.
The award is given out each year to the best American work of fiction. Award information was collected for the years 1981 through 2013.

"Pulitzer Prize Award for Fiction." Columbia University. Accessed April 16, 2013. http://www.pulitzer.org/bycat/Fiction.
Called the Pulitzer Prize for the Novel from 1918 to 1947, the annual award recognizes the most distinguished fiction published in book form by an American author dealing with American life. Award information was collected for the years 1918 through 2013.

"Scotiabank Giller Prize." Accessed April 16, 2013. http://www.scotiabank.com/giller
prize/0,,5821,00.html.
Canada's most distinguished literary award is given each year to a Canadian author for the most exemplary novel or short-story collection published in English. Award information was collected for the years 1994 through 2012.

"Thriller Awards." International Thriller Writers. Accessed July 25, 2013. http://www
.thebigthrill.org.

The organization bestows annual awards for excellence in the thriller genre. Award information was collected for the years 2006 through 2013.

"Women's Prize for Fiction." Women's Prize for Fiction Board. Accessed July 5, 2013. http://www.womensprizeforfiction.co.uk.

Previously called the Orange Prize for Fiction from 1996 to 2012, the award celebrates women's writing from throughout the world and is given for the best novel of the year written by a woman in the English language. Award information was collected for the years 1996 through 2013.

Best-Book Lists—Adult

"100-Best Novels." Modern Library. Accessed March 2, 2013. http://www.modern library.com/top-100/100-best-novels/.

This influential list was intended to establish the best English-language novels of the 20th century.

"100 Greatest Novels of All Time." *Guardian*, London, England. Accessed April 15, 2013. http://www.guardian.co.uk/books/2003/oct/12/features.fiction.

The newspaper gathers the opinions of experts to create the definitive list of fiction reading.

"100 Notable Books." *New York Times*. Accessed November 27, 2012. http://www .nytimes.com/2012/12/02/books/review/100-notable-books-of-2012.html?page wanted=all.

America's newspaper of record provides its long list of the year's outstanding books. Booklists were collected for the years 1981 through 2012.

"100 Novels Everyone Should Read." *Daily Telegraph*, London, England. Last modified January 16, 2009. http://www.telegraph.co.uk/culture/books/4248401/100-novels -everyone-should-read.html.

The newspaper published its essential fiction library.

"Best Books." *New York Times*. Last modified November 30, 2012. http://www.nytimes .com/2012/12/09/books/review/10-best-books-of-2012.html?_r=0.

The editors of the *New York Times Book Review* select the year's 10 best books. Booklists were collected for the years 1981 through 2012.

"Best Fiction." *Kirkus Reviews*. Accessed April 19, 2013. https://www.kirkusreviews .com/lists/best-fiction-2012/.

Each year the magazine editors separate titles of merit from the masses of books that are published. Booklists were collected for the years 2009 through 2012.

"The Best in the West/TOP 100 FICTION," *San Francisco Chronicle*. Last modified November 21, 1999. http://www.sfgate.com/books/article/The-Best-in-the-West -TOP-100-FICTION-2895432.php.

The newspaper polled its readers to identify the best 20th-century fiction involving the western United States.

"Books That Shaped America." Library of Congress. Accessed April 16, 2013. http:// www.loc.gov/bookfest/books-that-shaped-america/.
The world's largest repository of knowledge and information identified 88 influential books as part of its multiyear Celebration of the Book exhibition.

Boxall, Peter, ed. *1001 Books You Must Read before You Die.* New York: Universe, 2010.
This large collection is arranged chronologically and sorted by century.

Damien, Peter. "Book Riot's Best Books of 2012." Book Riot. Last modified December 5, 2012. http://bookriot.com/2012/12/05/book-riots-best-books-of-2012/?utm_ source=feedburner&utm_medium=feed&utm_campaign=Feed%3A+bookriot%2FW lRy+%28BOOK+RIOT%29.
Book Riot is a website devoted to the discussion of interesting books.

Editors of Book-of-the-Month Club. *The Well-Stocked Bookcase: 72 Enduring Novels by Americans Published between 1926 and 1998.* New York: Book-of-the-Month Club, 1998.
The editorial board selected novels that changed how Americans think about themselves.

Ezard, John. "Hype Fails to Sway the Patrons of Hay." *Guardian.* Last modified June 5, 2004. http://www.theguardian.com/uk/2004/jun/05/guardianhayfestival2004 .orangeprizeforfiction2004.
The Orange Prize attendees to the UK's Guardian Hay Festival of Literature and the Arts selected the top essential reads by contemporary authors.

Grossman, Lev. "Top 10 Fiction Books." *Time.* Last modified December 4, 2012. http:// entertainment.time.com/2012/12/04/top-10-arts-lists/slide/all/.
Grossman surveys the best fiction of 2012.

Grossman, Lev, and Richard Lacayo. "All-TIME 100 Novel." *Time.* Last modified January 6, 2010. http://entertainment.time.com/2005/10/16/all-time-100-novels/.
The magazine's critics chose the best English-language fiction from the magazine's founding in 1923 through 2005.

"Harvard Book Store Top 100 Books." Accessed March 29, 2013. http://www.harvard .com/shelves/top100/?/recommended/top100.html.
The bookseller's staff came up with a list of books that they said moved them and changed the way they thought about the world, and that they would happily read over and over again.

"Hungry Mind Review's 100 Best 20th-Century American Books." Accessed April 10, 2013. http://www.english.upenn.edu/~traister/hungrymind100.html.
The now-defunct book review magazine developed this booklist as an alternative to the well-known Modern Library's 100 Best Novels.

"The New Classics: The 100 Best Reads from 1983 to 2008." *Entertainment Weekly.*
Last modified June 17, 2008. http://www.ew.com/ew/article/0,,20207349,00
.html. The magazine compiled this list to celebrate 25 years of achievement.

Nichols, Mark, ed. *Book Sense Best Books: 125 Favorite Books Recommended by Independent Booksellers.* New York: New Market Press, 2004.
The American Booksellers Association voted on the titles it most enjoyed selling.

"Notable Books for Adults." Reference and User Services Association, American Library
Association. Accessed July 28, 2013. http://www.ala.org/rusa/awards/notablebooks.
Each year the ALA Notable Books Council recommends to the nation's adult readers a list of very good, readable, and important books. Booklists were collected for the
years 1998 through 2013.

"Our Editors Select the Best Books of 2012." HuffingtonPost.com. Last modified November 30, 2012. http://www.huffingtonpost.com/2012/10/16/best-books
-2012_n_1952748.html.
This year the book editors said they favored lesser-known risk takers to famous
writers.

Pearl, Nancy. *Book Lust: Recommended Reading for Every Mood, Moment, and Reason.*
Seattle, WA: Sasquatch Books, 2003.
This is a popular guide to good reading by a well-known librarian and book critic.

———. *More Book Lust: Recommended Reading for Every Mood, Moment, and Reason.*
Seattle, WA: Sasquatch Books, 2005.
This is the companion volume to *Book Lust* with new reading lists.

"Radcliffe's 100 Best Novels List." Accessed March 2, 2013. http://www.modernlibrary
.com/top-100/radcliffes-rival-100-best-novels-list/.
As an alternative to the Modern Library's famous list, on July 21, 1998, the Radcliffe Publishing Course compiled and released its own list of the century's top-100
English-language novels.

Shriver, Lionel. *The Book Club Bible: The Definitive Guide That Every Book Club Member
Needs.* London: Michael O'Mara, 2008.
A range of English literature experts recommend 100 books.

"The Slate Book Review Top 10 of 2012." Slate.com. Last modified November 30,
2012.
The book review recognizes the 10 most crucial books of the year. http://www
.slate.com/articles/arts/books/2012/11/best_books_of_2012_gone_girl_beautiful_
forevers_bring_up_the_bodies_wild.html.

Temple, Emily. "*The 50 Books Everyone Needs to Read, 1963–2013.*" Flavorwire.com.
Last modified June 18, 2013. http://flavorwire.com/398812/the-50-books-everyone
-needs-to-read-1963-2013.
Temple chose a single must-read book from each of the last 50 years.

"Waterstone's Top 100 Books of the Century." Accessed April 16, 2013. http://home
.comcast.net/%7Eantaylor1/waterstones100.html.
    The European bookstore chain based its list on the results of a poll of 25,000 readers.

Wittmann, Lucas. "Salman Rushdie's Memoir & Other Favorite Books of 2012."
    Daily Beast. Last modified December 6, 2012. http://www.thedailybeast.com/
    articles/2012/12/06/lucas-wittman-salman-rushdie-s-memoir-other-favorite-books
    -of-2012.html.
    The *Newsweek/Daily Beast* books editor selects the books that most impressed him.

Zane, Peder. *The Top Ten: Writers Pick Their Favorite Books.* New York: W. W. Norton,
    2007.
    One hundred twenty-five top writers were asked to pick their favorite books.

Library and School Reading Lists—Adult

"100 Most Influential Books of the Century." Boston Public Library, Boston, MA. Last
    modified May 2000. http://www.bpl.org/research/adultbooklists/influential.htm.
"Best of 2012: Fiction." Los Angeles Public Library, Los Angeles, CA. Last modified
    April 5, 2013. http://www.lapl.org/collections-resources/lapl-reads/book-lists/best
    -2012-fiction.
"Beyond Bestsellers: The Best of the New." Madison Public Library, Madison, WI.
    Accessed April 14, 2013. http://www.madisonpubliclibrary.org/booklists/beyond
    -bestsellers. Booklists were collected for the years 2011 and 2012.
"Landmarks of Modern Literature." New York Public Library, New York, NY. Ac-
    cessed April 14, 2013. http://www.nypl.org/voices/print-publications/books-of-the
    -century#landmarks.
"The Reading List." St. John's College, Annapolis, MD. Accessed July 30, 2013. http://
    www.stjohnscollege.edu/academic/readlist.shtml.

Additional Reading (Chapter 7)

Atwood, Margaret. *Cat's Eye.* New York: Doubleday, 1988.
———. *The Edible Woman.* Toronto: McClelland & Stewart, 1969.
———. *MaddAddam.* New York: Random House, 2013.
———. *Oryx and Crake.* New York: Nan A. Talese, 2003.
———. *The Robber Bride.* New York: Nan A. Talese/Doubleday, 1993.
———. *The Year of the Flood.* New York: Nan A. Talese/Doubleday, 2009.
Avi. *Crispin: At the Edge of the World.* New York: Hyperion Books for Children, 2006.
———. *Crispin: The End of Time.* New York: Balzer & Bray, 2010.
———. *The Fighting Ground.* New York: Lippincott, 1984.
Cleary, Beverly. *My Own Two Feet.* New York: Morrow Junior Books, 1995.

———. *Petey's Bedtime Story*. New York: Morrow Junior Books, 1993.

———. *Ramona and Her Mother*. New York: Morrow, 1979.

———. *Ramona's World*. New York: Morrow Junior Books, 1999.

Dahl, Roald. *Danny, the Champion of the World*. New York: Knopf, 1975.

———. *Fantastic Mr. Fox*. New York: Knopf, 1970.

———. *The Witches*. New York: Farrar, Straus, Giroux, 1983.

Doctorow, E. L. *The Book of Daniel*. New York: Random House, 1971.

———. *Homer & Langley*. New York: Random House, 2009.

———. *The Waterworks*. New York: Random House, 1994.

———. *Welcome to Hard Times*. New York: Random House, 1960.

———. *World's Fair*. New York: Random House, 1985.

Ehlert, Lois. *Cuckoo/Cucú: A Mexican Folktale/Un cuento folklórico mexicano*. San Diego, CA: Harcourt Brace, 1997.

———. *Eating the Alphabet: Fruits and Vegetables from A to Z*. San Diego, CA: Harcourt Brace Jovanovich, 1989.

———. *Growing Vegetable Soup*. San Diego, CA: Harcourt Brace Jovanovich, 1987.

———. *Planting a Rainbow*. San Diego, CA: Harcourt Brace Jovanovich, 1988.

———. *Snowballs*. San Diego, CA: Harcourt Brace, 1995.

———. *Waiting for Wings*. San Diego, CA: Harcourt, 2000.

Hamilton, Virginia. *Bruh Rabbit and the Tar Baby Girl*. New York: Blue Sky Press, 2003.

———. *Time Pieces: The Book of Times*. New York: Blue Sky Press, 2001.

———. *Wee Winnie Witch's Skinny: An Original African American Scare Tale*. New York: Blue Sky Press, 2004.

Henkes, Kevin. *Junonia*. New York: Greenwillow Books, 2011.

———. *Lilly's Big Day*. New York: Greenwillow Books, 2006.

———. *Little White Rabbit*. New York: Greenwillow Books, 2011.

———. *Olive's Ocean*. New York: Greenwillow Books, 2005.

———. *Penny and Her Song*. New York: Greenwillow Books, 2012.

———. *The Year of Billy Miller*. New York: HarperCollins Children's Books, 2013.

Lowry, Lois. *Autumn Street*. Boston: Houghton Mifflin, 1980.

———. *The Birthday Ball*. Boston: Houghton Mifflin Books for Children, 2010.

———. *Bless This Mouse*. Boston: Houghton Mifflin Books for Children, 2011.

———. *Like the Willow Tree*. New York: Scholastic, 2011.

———. *Messenger*. Boston: Houghton Mifflin, 2004.

———. *Rabble Starkey*. Boston: Houghton Mifflin, 1987.

———. *A Summer to Die*. Boston: Houghton Mifflin, 1977.

Martin, Bill, Jr. *Panda Bear, Panda Bear, What Do You See?* New York: Henry Holt, 2003.

———. *Polar Bear, Polar Bear, What Do You Hear?* New York: Henry Holt, 1991.

Martin, Bill, Jr., and Michael Sampson. *Chicka Chicka 1, 2, 3!* New York: Simon & Schuster Books for Young Readers, 2004.

———. *The Little Squeegy Bug*. Delray Beach, FL: Winslow Press, 2001.

McCloskey, Robert. *Centerburg Tales: More Adventures of Homer Price*. New York: Scholastic, 1951.

———. *Dow, Deep-Water Man.* New York: Viking Press, 1963.

———. *Lentil.* New York: Viking Press, 1940.

———. *One Morning in Maine.* New York: Viking Press, 1952.

Myers, Walter Dean. *The Cruisers.* New York: Scholastic Press, 2011.

———. *Malcolm X: By Any Means Necessary.* New York: Scholastic, 1994.

———. *Somewhere in the Darkness.* New York: Scholastic, 1993.

———. *A Star Is Born.* New York: Scholastic, 2012.

———. *We Were Heroes: The Journal of Scott Pendleton Collins, a World War II Soldier.* New York: Scholastic Paperbacks, 2012.

Paterson, Katherine. *Bread and Roses, Too.* New York: Clarion Books, 2006.

———. *The Day of the Pelican.* New York: Clarion Books, 2009.

———. *The Master Puppeteer.* New York: Crowell, 1975.

———. *The Same Stuff as Stars.* New York: Clarion Books, 2002.

Pinkney, Jerry. *Puss in Boots.* New York: Dial Books for Young Readers, 2012.

———. *Twinkle, Twinkle Little Star.* New York: Little, Brown, 2011.

Roth, Philip. *The Anatomy Lesson.* New York: Farrar, Straus & Giroux, 1984.

———. *The Counterlife.* New York: Farrar, Straus & Giroux, 1987.

———. *The Ghost Writer.* New York: Farrar, Straus & Giroux, 1980.

———. *Goodbye Columbus.* New York: Houghton Mifflin, 1960.

———. *My Life as a Man.* New York: Holt, Rinehart & Winston, 1975.

———. *Nemeses.* New York: Houghton Mifflin Harcourt, 2010.

———. *Operation Shylock.* London: Cape, 1993.

———. *Patrimony.* New York: Simon & Schuster, 1992.

———. *The Professor of Desire.* New York: Farrar, Straus & Giroux, 1978.

———. *Sabbath's Theater.* Boston: Houghton Mifflin, 1995.

Rowling, J. K. *The Casual Vacancy.* New York: Little, Brown, 2012.

———. [Robert Galbraith, pseud.]. *The Cuckoo's Calling.* New York: Mulholland Books, 2013.

Sendak, Maurice. *Bumble-Ardy.* New York: HarperCollins, 2011.

———. *My Brother's Book.* New York: HarperCollins, 2013.

Seuss, Dr. *Bartholomew and the Oobleck.* New York: Random House, 1949.

———. *Fox in Socks.* New York: Beginner Books, 1965.

———. *McElligot's Pool.* New York: Random House, 1947.

———. *Mr. Brown Can Moo! Can You?* New York: Random House, 1970.

———. *Oh, the Places You'll Go!* New York: Random House, 1990.

———. *One Fish, Two Fish, Red Fish, Blue Fish.* New York: Beginner Books, 1960.

———. *Yertle the Turtle and Other Stories.* New York: Random House, 1958.

Steig, William. *The Amazing Bone.* New York: Farrar, Straus, Giroux, 1976.

———. *Made for Each Other.* New York: Joanna Cotler Books, 2000.

———. *Shrek!* New York: Farrar, Straus, Giroux, 1990.

———. *When Everybody Wore a Hat.* New York: Joanna Cotler Books, 2003.

———. *Wizzil.* New York: Farrar Straus Giroux, 2000.

Steig, William, illus. *A Gift from Zeus.* By Jeanne Steig. New York: Joanna Cotler Books, 2001.

Tolkien, J. R. R. *The Silmarillion*. Boston: Houghton Mifflin, 1977.

Twain, Mark. *A Connecticut Yankee in King Arthur's Court*. New York: Charles L. Webster & Co., 1889.

———. *The Mysterious Stranger*. New York: Harper & Brothers, 1916.

———. *Personal Recollections of Joan of Arc*. New York: Harper & Brothers, 1896.

———. *Pudd'nhead Wilson*. New York: Charles L. Webster & Co., 1894.

Updike, John. *The Centaur*. New York: Knopf, 1963.

———. *Couples*. New York: Knopf, 1968.

———. *John Updike: The Collected Stories*. New York: Library of America, 2013.

———. *Terrorist*. New York: Knopf, 2006.

———. *The Witches of Eastwick*. New York: Knopf, 1984.

Wiesner, David. *Art & Max*. Boston: Clarion Books, 2010.

———. *Free Fall*. New York: Lothrop, Lee & Shepard Books, 1988.

———. *Hurricane*. Boston: Clarion Books, 1990.

———. *June 29, 1999*. New York: Clarion Books, 1992.

———. *Mr. Wuffles!* New York: Houghton Mifflin Harcourt, 2013.

———. *The Three Pigs*. New York: Clarion Books, 2001.

Wiesner, David, illus. *Night of the Gargoyles*. By Eve Bunting. New York: Clarion Books, 1994.

Wiesner, David, and Kim Kahng. *The Loathsome Dragon*. Boston: Clarion Books, 2005.

Willems, Mo. *Are You Ready to Play Outside?* New York: Hyperion Books for Children, 2008.

———. *I Broke My Trunk*. New York: Hyperion Books for Children, 2011.

———. *I'm a Frog*. New York: Disney-Hyperion, 2013.

———. *The Pigeon Needs a Bath!* New York: Disney-Hyperion, 2014.

———. *There Is a Bird on Your Head*. New York: Hyperion, 2007.

———. *We Are in a Book!* New York: Hyperion, 2010.

———. *You Can Never Find a Rickshaw When It Monsoons: The World on One Cartoon a Day*. New York: Hyperion Paperbacks, 2006.

Wood, Audrey. *The Birthday Queen*. Illus. Don Wood. New York: Blue Sky Press, 2013.

———. *Heckedy Peg*. San Diego: Harcourt Brace Jovanovich, 1987.

———. *Piggies*. San Diego: Harcourt Brace Jovanovich, 1991.

Yolen, Jane. *The Emily Sonnets: The Life of Emily Dickinson*. Mankato, MN: Creative Editions, 2012.

———. *The Emperor and the Kite*. Cleveland: World Publishing Company, 1967.

———. *The Hostage Prince*. New York: Viking, 2013.

———. *Wee Rhymes*. New York: Simon & Schuster Books for Young Readers, 2013.

Yolen, Jane, Remy Charlip, and Demetra Maraslis. *The Seeing Stick*. New York: Thomas Y. Crowell Company, 1977.

Zelinsky, Paul O., illus. *Earwig and the Witch*. By Diana Wynne. New York: Greenwillow Books, 2012.

———. *Hansel and Gretel*. Retold by Rika Lesser. New York: Dodd, Mead & Company, 1984.

———. *Knick-Knack Paddywhack!* New York: Dutton Children's Books, 2002.

———. *The Lion and the Stoat.* By Pliny the Elder. New York: Greenwillow Books, 1984.

———. *The Maid and the Mouse and the Odd-Shaped House.* New York: Dodd, Mead, 1981.

———. *Rumpelstiltskin.* By the Brothers Grimm. New York: E. P. Dutton, 1986.

———. *The Wheels on the Bus.* New York: Dutton's Children's Books, 1990.

———. *Z Is for Moose.* By Kelly L. Bingham. New York: Greenwillow Books, 2012.